THREE THOUSAND YEARS

The contributors to this book are distinguished experts. Professor C. P. Fitzgerald has spent a lifetime studying the country; he is Emeritus Professor at the Australian National University in Canberra and is particularly well known as the author of *China: A Short Cultural History*. Dr Michael Freeberne lectures at the School of Oriental and African Studies of London University. Brian Hook, formerly a senior official in the Hong Kong government, is now attached to the Department of Chinese Studies at the University of Leeds. Louis Heren, Deputy Editor and Foreign Editor of *The Times*, is a journalist with a long and distinguished record; David Bonavia is now resident correspondent in Peking for *The Times*.

CHINA'S THREE THOUSAND YEARS

THE STORY OF A GREAT CIVILISATION

Louis Heren
C. P. Fitzgerald
Michael Freeberne
Brian Hook
David Bonavia

Times Newspapers Limited

First published in Great Britain in 1973 by
Times Newspapers Limited
Printing House Square
London EC4P 4DE
© Times Newspapers Limited 1973
© in Part Five: David Bonavia 1973
ISBN 0 7230 0108 1
Designed by Jeanette Collins
Printed and bound in Great Britain by
Cox & Wyman Ltd
London, Fakenham and Reading

Contents

Illustrations

Colour plates
(between pages 128 and 129)
A pottery bowl from the fourth or third millenium
A tripod pottery jug
The funèral suit of Tou Wan
A celadon tripod vessel
Bronze galloping horse
Bronze horse and carriage group
Traditional opera in Peking
The Temple of the Ancestors, Canton
Harvesting a fodder crop
The avenue to Tien An Men, Peking
The entrance to the former Imperial Palaces

Monochrome
(between pages 64 and 65)
A stone rubbing of Confucius
Lao-Tze, the founder of Taoism
The magnetic compass
Diagrams illustrating acupuncture treatment
Paper being made with bamboo leaves
The manufacture of silk during the seventeenth century
A woodcut demonstrating rice planting
Man leading a camel by Yang Yin
An illustration in a novel of the Ming period
A painting of Hsi Wang-Mu by Wo-Wei (1458–1508)
Traditional Chinese opera (Hangchow)
A group of mandarins
A military mandarin on horseback
A high-class opium house in about 1890
The Japanese attack on Port Arthur in 1894
A study of two Manchu ladies
A group of strolling players

vi

P'u-yi, the last Manchu emperor, at the age of three
Provincial viceroys arriving under escort at Shanghai
A Cabinet meeting in 1913
Peking at the turn of the century
Physic Street, Canton in the early 1920s
The wearing of pigtails was imposed on the Chinese by the Manchus. After the fall
of the dynasty in 1911 the habit gradually died out
A 'down with foreigners' demonstration in Shanghai

(between pages 192 and 193)
The emperor P'u-yi with Chiang Kai-shek in 1935
Soldiers under instruction at Yenan
A suspected communist being searched by an armed picket in Shanghai
Japanese outrages in Nanking
The communist People's Liberation Army on duty at the Great Wall
Villagers during the appalling famine of 1943
Peasants in a communist 'base area'
An attack by the PLA on Chinchow in 1946
PLA soldiers arriving in Nanking
Mao Tse-tung in 1946
Queues outside a bank in Shanghai in 1948
Chairman Mao with Marshal Bulganin and Nikita Khrushchev
A mass meeting of Red Guards in 1967 during the Cultural Revolution
President Nixon in China in February 1972
A shop on the Gao Kan commune near Anshan
Lunchtime at a kindergarten in Shanghai
Children at a school in Canton
A worker's bedroom at Wuhsi
Making embroidery in a commune workshop
Commune brigade leaders in Kiangsu
The new physics wing of Peking University
The Yangtze river bridge in Wuhan
Students helping to build a road

Acknowledgements

The publishers would like to thank all
those who have helped in the
production of this book, particularly
Richard Harris, Louis Heren and
Jeanette Collins of *The Times*,
Penelope Brown for the picture
research, Duncan Mil for preparing
the maps and John Gurnett for
compiling the index. Acknowledgement
is also due to the Percival David
Foundation for permission to use their
Chronology, and to the following
photographers and copyright owners
of illustrative material used in the
book: Black Star, David Bonavia,
Camera Press, J. Allan Cash,
Christina Gascoigne, John Hillelson,
the Mansell Collection, John Massey
Stewart, Don McCullin, Paul Popper,
Radio Times Hulton, Sundication
International, the Victoria and Albert
Museum, Derek Witty.

Chronology of dynasties and periods

NEOLITHIC PERIOD		? to 1765 or 1522 BC
SHANG	*Traditional chronology*	1766–1122
	Revised chronology	1523–1028
WESTERN CHOU	*Traditional chronology*	1122–772
	Revised chronology	1028–772
EASTERN CHOU		771–256
Spring and Autumn era		722–481
Warring States era		480–221
CH'IN		221–206
WESTERN (FORMER) HAN		206–AD 25
EASTERN (LATER) HAN		AD 25–220
THE SIX DYNASTIES		221–581
The Three Kingdoms		221–280
Western and Eastern China		265–419
PERIOD OF NORTHERN AND SOUTHERN DYNASTIES		386–581
North		
Northern Wei		386–535
Eastern Wei		534–550
Western Wei		535–557
Northern Ch'i		550–577
Northern Chou		557–581
South		
(Liu) Sung		420–478
Southern Ch'i		479–502
Liang		502–556
Ch'ên		557–581

SUI			581–618
T'ANG			618–906
THE FIVE DYNASTIES			907–960
LIAO			907–1125
SUNG			960–1279
Northern Sung			960–1127
Southern Sung			1128–1279
CHIN (Ju-chên or Golden Tartars)			1115–1234
YÜAN (Mongols)			1260–1368
MING			1368–1644
Hung-wu	1368–1398	Hung-chih	1488–1505
Chien-wên	1399–1402	Chêng-tê	1506–1521
Yung-lo	1402–1424	Chia-ching	1522–1566
Hsüan-tê	1426–1435	Lung-ch'ing	1567–1572
Chêng-t'ung	1436–1449	Wan-li	1573–1619
Ching-t'ai	1450–1457	T'ai-ch'ang	1620
T'ien-shun	1457–1464	T'ien-ch'i	1621–1627
Ch'êng-hua	1465–1487	Ch'ung-chêng	1628–1644
CH'ING			1644–1912
Shun-chih	1644–1661	Tao-kuang	1822–1851
K'ang-hsi	1662–1722	Hsien-fêng	1851–1862
Yung-cheng	1723–1735	T'ung-chih	1862–1875
Ch'ien-lung	1736–1795	Kuang-hsü	1875–1908
Chia-ch'ing	1796–1821	Hsüan-t'ung	1908–1912
REPUBLIC			1912

x

China

U.S.S.R

Mongolia

Heilungkiang

Harbin

Kirin

Changchun

Tienshan Mts

Altai Mts

Inner Mongolia

Fu-shun
Shenyang

Sinkiang Uighur Autonomous Region

Urumchi

Liaoning

Sea of
Japan

Huhehot

PEKING

Luta

Korea

Kansu

Tientsin

Pohai Sea

Altyn Mts

Yinchuan

Hopei

Kunlun Mts

Tai-yuan

Yenan

Shansi

Shantung

Tsingtao

Tsinghai

Sining

Lanchow

Shensi

Yellow R.

Yellow Sea

Karakoram Mts

Sian

Chengchow

Kiangsu

Tibetan Autonomous Region

Szechuan

Chinling Mts

Honan

Anhwei

Nanking

Nepal

Himalayas

Lhasa

Hupeh

Hofei

Shanghai

Hangchow

Bhutan

Wuhan

Chekiang

Chengtu

Chungking

Yangtze R.

Nanchang

East China Sea

Bangladesh

Kiangsi

Fukien

Kweiyang

Hunan

Foochow

India

Kunming

Kweichow

Kwangtung

Taiwan

Yunnan

Kwangsi Chuang

Canton

Nanning

Hong Kong (Br)

Burma

Vietnam

Macao (Port)

Pacific Ocean

Chankiang

Laos

Hainan

Bay of Bengal

South China Sea

Andaman Sea

Indian Ocean

──────── China's international frontiers

‐ ‐ ‐ ‐ ‐ Provincial boundaries

Population Density

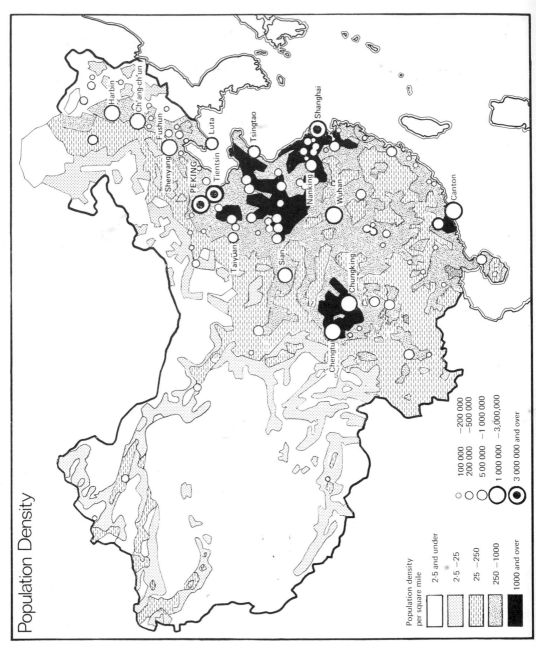

Population density
per square mile

	2·5 and under
	2·5 —25
	25 —250
	250 —1000
	1000 and over

100 000 —200 000
200 000 —500 000
500 000 —1 000 000
1 000 000 —3,000,000
3 000 000 and over

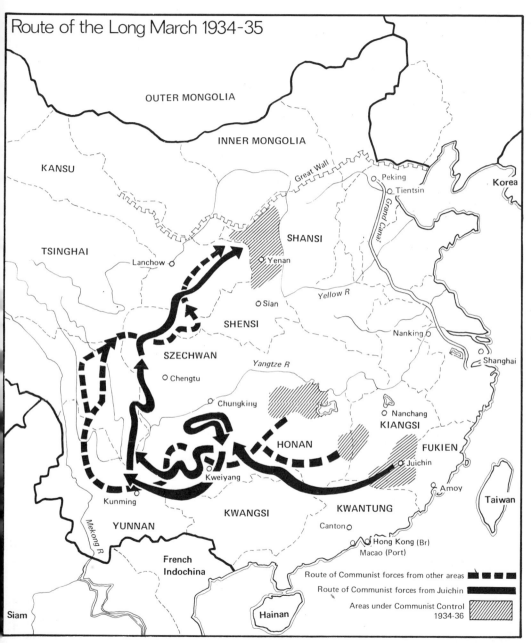

Route of the Long March 1934-35

OUTER MONGOLIA

INNER MONGOLIA

KANSU

Great Wall

Peking
Tientsin

Korea

TSINGHAI

SHANSI

Lanchow

Yenan

Grand Canal

Sian

Yellow R

SHENSI

Nanking

SZECHWAN

Yangtze R

Shanghai

Chengtu

Chungking

Nanchang

KIANGSI

HONAN

FUKIEN

Kweiyang

Juichin

Kunming

KWANGSI

KWANTUNG

Amoy

Taiwan

YUNNAN

Canton

Mekong R

French
Indochina

Hong Kong (Br)
Macao (Port)

Route of Communist forces from other areas

Route of Communist forces from Juichin

Areas under Communist Control
1934-36

Siam

Hainan

xiii

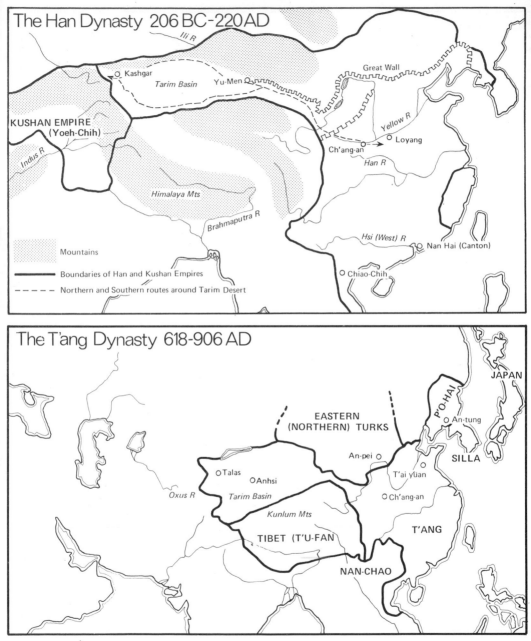

The Han Dynasty 206 BC-220 AD

Ili R

Kashgar ○

Tarim Basin

Yu-Men ○

Great Wall

**KUSHAN EMPIRE
(Yoeh-Chih)**

Yellow R

Ch'ang-an ○ → ○ Loyang

Indus R

Han R

Himalaya Mts

Brahmaputra R

Hsi (West) R

○ Nan Hai (Canton)

Mountains

——— Boundaries of Han and Kushan Empires

– – – Northern and Southern routes around Tarim Desert

○ Chiao-Chih

The T'ang Dynasty 618-906 AD

JAPAN

**EASTERN
(NORTHERN) TURKS**

P'O-HAI

An-tung ○

An-pei ○

SILLA

○ Talas

○ Anhsi

T'ai yüan ○

Oxus R

Tarim Basin

○ Ch'ang-an

Kunlum Mts

TIBET (T'U-FAN

T'ANG

NAN-CHAO

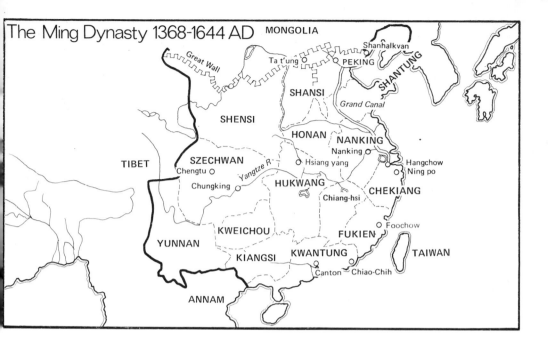

The Ming Dynasty 1368-1644 AD

The map on page xi shows the principal
political features of China today:
the international boundaries (note especially
the large number of China's neighbours),
the provinces and the principal cities.
China is roughly the same size as the
United States (covering some 3·6 million
square miles); its population is more than
three times that of the USA while only
11 per cent of its landmass is cultivated.
The map on page xii indicates the density
and distribution of the country's
population.
The route of the Long March, the most
remarkable episode of the Civil War, is also
shown (page xiii).
On this and the facing page
a comparison of the extent of Chinese
territory during three of the most
significant dynastic periods can be made.

Introduction

One of the most important events of the post-war years was the decision of Chairman Mao to end the isolation of China. One could argue that the decision finally marked the end of the post-war period. Certainly it followed upon a series of developments largely intended to dispose of the unfinished business of the second world war. Why, when and where this process began is still not entirely clear, but some time in the 'sixties the Soviet Union concluded that China posed more of a threat to its national security than did the United States and the European allies, and in effect decided to secure its rear in the west. The conclusion may have been erroneous, but it led to negotiations with West Germany, the European Security Conference and talks between the Warsaw Pact countries and Nato on mutual and balanced force reductions. There were other reasons for this *détente* diplomacy with the West, including Russian crop failures and the need to import western technology as well as food. The high cost of nuclear weapons, especially anti-ballistic weapons, also persuaded them to begin strategic arms limitation talks with the Americans.

Viewed from Peking, these developments looked very disturbing, especially after the Cultural Revolution, which strained and weakened the economy and administration. In spite of American protestations, the two super powers must have looked as if they were ganging up on China. Being a shrewd people, the Chinese pondered the possible consequences and concluded that they too needed friends in the outside world. They also needed to import food and technology, and one must assume that they wanted to take their rightful place in the world. The age of the Middle Kingdom had long since passed, but a people nurtured and strengthened by an ancient civilisation must have resented the consequences of isolation. With the obvious exceptions of the Soviet Union and Taiwan, most countries welcomed the decision. Apprehensive or otherwise, they agreed that the world would be a safer place with China in it. With extraordinary rapidity, Chinese ping-pong diplomacy led to membership of the United Nations, President Nixon's visit to China, and the exchange of missions between Washington and Peking.

The interest aroused remains boundless, but outside a small circle of scholars little is known about the country, and even scholars have little or no personal experience of China today. The general reader is more ignorant because in the lifetime of most China was rarely united and at peace with itself until 1949 when the so-called bamboo curtain quickly descended. The western world is filled with people who knew nothing about China except the warlords and the Shanghai Club. The recent voyages of rediscovery made by the fortunate few in recent years have produced only tentative reports. Positive or otherwise, they amount to little more than impressions.

For me, when I returned to China in 1972, the first impression was of silence and emptiness. The anticipated teeming millions did not teem. They came silently on rubber-soled shoes or unlighted bicycles, and the honking of occasional lorries and cars only enhanced the pervading silence. Shanghai had an emptiness of its own, although statistics prove beyond doubt that the old treaty port has become the world's largest city. The old European quarter looked abandoned. The taipans had gone, leaving behind only two British bank managers.

How different from India. There the restless press of humanity had been a physical affront on my first visit. In Shanghai, on the rim of the most densely populated country in the world, the silence and apparent emptiness were soothing. The difference was between a Hindu religious picture, all writhing limbs and bold assertion, and a Chinese water-colour.

The Chinese silence had a special quality difficult to define. Western-ers are so accustomed to noise – even refrigerators hum in the so-called still of the night – that the absence of such sounds suggested a special quality of Chinese life. I thought that it had something to do with Chinese frugality. It reinforced another impression: that Chinese poverty had also assumed an aesthetic quality. The Chinese wore their patched cottons with easy pride. Even when they were enjoying them-selves, they had a quiet dignity which Europeans have rarely possessed. It was immensely attractive. If one had to be poor, then be poor the Chinese way.

These impressions were not entirely correct. Certainly Chinese life has these very attractive aesthetic qualities, but there are more earthy explanations. The silence of China is the silence of the pre-industrial world, where the only non-human sound to be heard is that of the hoe or plough. Nuclear devices had been exploded and more steel plants built. Rural electrification is spreading steadily. New factories and workshops can be seen in many places, but the countryside still has the timelessness of those old watercolours. Poised between the old and the new, China is in a kind of limbo.

This sense of limbo was my most lasting and, I am sure, my truest impression. It was confirmed in Peking. Who governed more than 750 million Chinese, and how did they do it? I asked such questions repeatedly, but apart from vague references to democratic centralism heard no persuasive answers. How China had been governed since the Cultural Revolution remained a mystery. There was no party or state constitution, only an acting head of state, the politburo and central committee were under strength, and many ministries did not have ministers. All the evidence suggested that the country was well governed. I did not see any undernourished people anywhere. China must be the only country without beggars. For all the revolutionary committees, which were supposed to run the country, clearly government was in the hands of the bureaucrats, ironically enough those against whom the Cultural Revolution was launched. Even the army's role was diminishing, if one could judge from the small number of army men on the committees. The promise of more Cultural Revolutions, indeed of revolution without end, seemed to make the questions irrelevant. They were not, of course, but as the countryside seemed poised between the agrarian past and the promised future so Peking was in another and larger limbo, poised between Mao – and whom?

When I asked Mr Chou En-lai about the political future, the Prime Minister spoke confidently of a collective leadership, and of a hundred thousand well-trained cadres unknown to the West but quite capable of taking over. I am willing to believe that many such men exist, but succession more often than not has exposed an essential weakness of socialist countries. Government does not pass in any orderly fashion from one political party to another because there can only be one unified party. Personal or factional rivalry has led to bloodshed. The compromise of collective leadership has rarely been successful, with the often-forgotten example of North Vietnam. The Chinese may be able to make collective leadership work, although the cult of Mao indicates that they need an ideological godhead. Certainly they seem to be more attuned to such a leadership than the more anarchical Slavs. They are not individuals in the western sense. They have always seen themselves as members of a society, with responsibilities to it. This has its weaknesses, but it explains how China survived the Cultural Revolution and promises that it will survive the present limbo.

19

Some doubts remain, of course. The struggle between the two lines of true Marxism–Leninism and revisionism has yet to be resolved. What these labels really mean is anybody's guess. The words are familiar, but I suspect that for most Chinese they are as indecipherable as Chairman Mao's calligraphy. What they do mean is that China will surely remain in limbo for many years to come, until these differences are resolved and ideological purity achieved. They could be difficult years for China, and for the world. They will certainly be hard to understand. Hence this book.

Louis Heren

Part One

Chinese civilisation

1 Philosophy and religion

The outstanding characteristic of Chinese culture is the commitment to the humanist outlook: the duty of man towards his fellow men comes before his duty to serve deities. Confucius was to make this explicit in his answer to a pupil who asked how he should serve the gods. 'You do not yet know how to serve mankind,' the Master replied. 'When you know this, then you may consider how to serve the gods.'

In their ways of thinking the ancient Chinese, as far back as we can discover, clearly held the same priorities. The most ancient evidence of religious rites in China is the inscriptions on bones and tortoise shells which are records of the questions put to an oracle, and of the answers that were received. The oracle was the spirit of a deceased king, the father or an ancestor of the ruling monarch. It was supposed that the ancestral spirits took an active interest in the fate of their living descendants; they could be appealed to by prayer to intercede in averting calamity or restoring prosperity. Their virtue was a protective inheritance which shielded the living generation from danger and misfortune. The pre-eminence of the spirits of the dead over the deities in all that concerned mankind was accepted without question.

The gods were of a more vague character. The ancient Chinese did not represent them in anthropomorphic shape, but by symbols made of jade, a sacred substance. The gods presided over the natural world – the four points of the compass, the mountains and rivers, the rain and the weather. The supreme being, the head of an hierarchical order, was Shang Ti, or T'ien. The latter word means 'the sky', and also 'day'. T'ien ch'i – 'the breath of heaven' – is the weather. Shang Ti, a term which centuries later the Christian missionaries used to express the word God, is of doubtful etymology. Some scholars think that it meant, in very early times, 'supreme ancestor', possibly the founder of the royal house, and thus the chief ancestral spirit. T'ien, the sky god, seems to have become the more common term for the supreme deity in the later period of antiquity, the Chou dynasty. It has been conjectured that his cult was introduced by the Chou rulers, but the paucity of early texts makes this uncertain. What is clear from the few authentic very early texts is that the ancestral spirit of the deceased king was seen as most powerful, able to avert death and to accept, or decline, the offer of a substitute victim for the sick monarch.

T'ien, the arbiter of the weather, sent the rain or withheld it, thus deciding the prosperity or distress of an agricultural society living in a climate with marked seasonal variations between wet and dry conditions. From very early times the king acted as the chief priest of two cults, whose temples stood to east and west of the south gate of his palace; the temple of the royal ancestors to the east, the temple of heaven to the west. Rites and intercessions at the ancestral temple secured the continuation and power of the royal house; others, at the altar of heaven, assured the clemency of the weather and the fertility of the crops. The ancestors were personally linked to the living rulers; but the gods were impersonal – forces rather than beings. Their intervention was directed to correcting imbalances in the natural order rather than to answering the prayers of men or protecting them from disaster. Man was the centre of a universe whose physical characteristics were determined by forces beyond his control, and not necessarily interested in his fate.

In later times, particularly with the creation of a central united empire under the Han dynasty (202 BC to AD 220), T'ien acquired more direct interest in human welfare. It was held that the moral and physical orders were connected, or even formed a unity. The calamities of bad seasons were caused by the misconduct of the rulers of mankind, that is, by the emperor himself. Virtue was rewarded with good seasons and the absence of natural calamities; vice would cause the physical world to react in an alarming, even a catastrophic manner. This was a good doctrine to teach responsibility to an otherwise untrammelled autocrat. It coincided with another doctrine, also of great antiquity: the theory of the Yin and the Yang. The Yang is the positive force in nature: male, heat, the sun, land, dry. Yin is the negative aspect: female, cool, shade, the moon, the sea. The two forces are not in conflict but in continuous harmonious interchange and interaction, symbolised by the circle equally divided by a curving line, so that the two parts represent a constant balanced flux. Yin and Yang are not deities, and have no personality; they are the operation of nature, linked with the operation of the moral order. Misconduct upsets the harmony. Too much Yang will bring drought and fire, and too much Yin causes floods and unseasonable rain. Man must always adjust to nature, but he is himself a major force in nature, and his conduct affects the natural order of seasons and weather.

The idea that the virtue or vice of men was linked with the working of nature was one that undoubtedly came later than the earliest age of Chinese antiquity. The emphasis on moral conduct – as opposed to the simple performance of rites which, if correctly performed, ensures success, but if negligently carried out brings disaster – was the great contribution of the teaching of Confucius. Using the feudal terminology of his age he described the *chun tzu*, the aristocrat, as a moral being who based his life on the performance of moral duties and guided his conduct on ethical principles. The worship of gods was secondary. The 'lesser man' was self-seeking, ambitious for his own advancement and thus lacking in true loyalty to his prince, greedy for gain and heedless of moral duty. Confucius invented, for China, the concept of ethic, but he did not link it with any supernatural sanction. He and his followers, both immediate and later ones, constructed a system of reciprocal relations as the model for human society. The prince must govern with benevolence, mercy and sincerity; the ministers serve him with loyalty, honesty, and in accordance with moral imperatives. Fathers must treat their children with love and give them protection and upbringing; children owe their parents filial piety, obedience and respect, and the duty of supporting them in old age. Children were also responsible for carrying on the male line of the family so that the ancestors would never lack descendants to maintain their tombs, sacrifice to their spirits and keep a record of their lives and virtues. Women must be treated with respect and kindness, but must obey their fathers and elder brothers, and then their husbands. Once a girl was married she ceased to belong to her family of birth and became a member of the family into which she had married. The family was the main base of society; duty to the family ranked as high as, and almost in conflict with, duty to the prince. The monarch was the head of the human family, and his subjects were his children; this rationalisation sought to resolve the conflict. The hierarchy of age was essential. Elder brothers could command their younger siblings; only the eldest son was the heir to his father's throne or position. His eldest son, in turn, was preferred over his uncles. Manners were regulated to ascertain who was senior, and to ensure that the proper respect was shown. A first question between chance acquaintances was 'What is your honourable age?', and the answer determined the standing of the two parties.

Confucianism thus built a new moral interpretation of the world upon the oldest and soundest foundation, the family system. It could be fitted to the political system, thus ensuring that monarchy, as an apotheosis of paternalism, should be the only conceivable form of government. The government must, however, be restrained and guided by ethical teaching and exercised in conformity with high moral principles.

The Chinese gave consideration and some allegiance to other doctrines, but Confucianism, rooted in the foundations of their society, always held first place. The essence of that teaching is the central importance in the universe of man.

The chief alternative doctrine which has at all times, in varying forms, attracted the thinking of the Chinese people, is generally known as Taoism. Tao means 'the Way'; but, as its first exponent says in the beginning of his treatise: 'The Way which can be expressed is not the true Way.' The Way must be learned, not by teaching but by experience; it must be followed, not by precept but by instinct. The follower of the Way seeks no worldly success or power; ideally he retreats to the seclusion of remote mountains where he can commune with nature and learn its secret. He sees the utility of objects in their negative qualities: it is the empty space which makes a bowl useful, the hole in the centre of the wheel, without which it is of no value. Only by emptying the soul and making it available to the influence of Tao, the Way, is the body given any meaning. Outward appearances are deceptive and may be delusive. Chuang Tzu, a famous Taoist, illustrates this thought in his 'butterfly dream'. He dreamt he was a butterfly, flitting about from flower to flower. Is he, now awake, a man who dreamed that he was a butterfly; or a butterfly dreaming that he is a man?

Taoism derives from a famous book, *Tao Te Ching*, the 'Classic of the Way and its Power'. For centuries this was believed to be the work of a certain Lao Tzu (which simply means 'Old Master') who was thought to be an older contemporary of Confucius. It has now been shown that the book was written many years later, dating from the third century BC, and that Lao Tzu is a pseudonym, used by a philosopher who cannot be identified. It is strongly anti-Confucian in tone, as are many later Taoist works, and would seem to be a polemic directed against the Confucian school. The ideal it sets up is certainly almost the contrary of the Confucian model, expressly condemning as useless all the deep commitment to social aims and involvement which is the heart of Confucian teaching. In its original philosophic aspect Taoism appealed to those who saw little hope in a decaying feudal society in which violence and guile were replacing the ancient ordered loyalties. Confucius sought to build a new moral order to buttress the ancient society; Taoism denied its value and claimed that all such effort was fruitless. *Wu Wei*, 'non-acting', was Taoism's injunction to the inquirer.

24

'By non-ácting all is regulated.' If things are allowed to develop in accordance with the Way, they will inevitably arrive at true equilibrium. The idea of the Yin and the Yang is present in this thought; a self-correcting mechanism which will constantly adjust and restore an even balance.

Perhaps, in reaction to the profound conflict between these two interpretations of the universe and man's role in it, there arose other rival doctrines. Mo Ti taught that the need of mankind was universal love; war was never justified, for it arose from hatred; all men were truly brothers, let them treat each other as brothers of the same kin and there would be an end to strife, injustice, cruelty and crime. Influential in his time, not long after the death of Confucius (480 BC), Mohism failed to survive the violent end of the old feudal world and the Ch'in proscription of the philosophic books. Its texts are scant and corrupt, but from references to his teaching in the works of Confucian and other contemporaries, it is clear that he was much admired, and his following for a time very influential. His chief objection to the Confucian doctrine was its emphasis on the family and its solidarity, which Mo Ti saw as an obstacle to the wider universal love which he sought to promote.

The School of the Law, which for a time was to inspire the state which unified China and created the First Empire (255 BC), was not a philosophy so much as a social programme, and one of extreme rigid harshness. The law, enacted by the king, must be supreme, taking precedence over any doctrine and every moral principle. All must obey it, on pain of cruel punishments. No distinction between noble and serf, not even in favour of princes of the blood, was admitted in respect of the law. With this instrument any king could rule secure; he did not need to be wise or virtuous, only powerful. No rival or alternative teaching was permitted, and all books dealing with such systems were banned. So were the arts. Music and painting, poetry and history served no useful purpose; they distracted men from their sole duty, which was to fight for the king or till his fields. War and agriculture – to feed the soldiers – were the only permissible or desirable activities, the aggrandisement of the state of Ch'in the only legitimate objective – and the overriding purpose of life.

These ideas did not in fact originate with men of Ch'in, a rather backward western mountain state, but in the minds of exiles, aristocratic fugitives from the court feuds of the eastern, more civilised, kingdoms, who put their talents, and perhaps sought their revenge, in the service of the harsh kings of semi-barbarous Ch'in.

They certainly succeeded in building a state dedicated to war and aggression. In the long struggle of the Warring States, ruthless and faithless Ch'in was the ultimate victor, and then imposed an inhuman society upon the united empire which the victory had created. It did not last; what may have been acceptable for a few generations in a remote warlike kingdom was repudiated in a vast revolt by the mass of the Chinese people. But although Ch'in perished, and with it the School of the Law, it left its mark. Derided and condemned from that day to this, the law of Ch'in gave China a tendency to impose harsh punishments for crime; and also left law itself with a bad name, associated with crime, cruelty and inhumanity. There was never in later China any civil law; only criminal codes, which did reflect some of the harsh character of the law of Ch'in. Civil disputes of all kinds were left outside the scope of government for regulation by arbitration by family elders, village leaders or merchant guilds. The later dynasties of China shied away from the law and its evil reputation, lest they be smeared with the memory of the terrible law of Ch'in.

The last phase of the pre-Buddhist period of Chinese civilisation was the Han dynasty (202 BC to AD 220), during which Confucianism became the orthodox doctrine of the Chinese state. It incorporated some aspects of other teaching, the Yin and Yang theory, and elaborated the doctrine of moral responsibility and its alleged relation to the physical world. It also became the repository for the most ancient literature and traditions of the Chinese world, thus perpetuating many very old rites and preserving the vestiges of the beliefs of long past. History, the great literary activity of this age, was inspired by Confucian ideas and written to carry the message of Confucian morality. Fortunately, the reverence for antiquity which Confucianism taught served to preserve pieces of early literature which do not by any means support all the assumptions of Confucian interpretation of ancient legend and myth. Han scholarship was indefatigable in hunting out and restoring long-lost texts; some of these reconstructions would not be supported today but the Han scholars faithfully preserved what they found and transmitted it to posterity.

In the Han period, Taoism also developed new characteristics. In the original teaching the Taoist sages had used analogies, perhaps as literary devices, to drive home their doctrine. The man who had merged his personality in the Way became superior to mortal distresses; he was an 'immortal', above and aloof from the normal human condition. In later Taoism this was taken literally. Immortals, men who had left society to identify with Tao in the remote mountains, did indeed live, if not for ever, at least to immense ages. Their profound studies of the Way taught them the secrets of nature, how to brew the drug of immortality, and how to turn base metal into gold. These magical beliefs, in part drawing strength from cults native to the eastern coast, a region by this time fully incorporated into the empire, were the origin of the pseudo-science of alchemy, which reached the Roman world some two centuries later and thus passed into the culture of the West.

The Immortals were indifferent to time. A woodcutter, wandering into the high peaks of a remote mountain, came upon two old gentlemen playing the game of Wei Ch'i – a kind of chess. Absorbed, he stood and watched until the game ended, then made his way home to his village. When he reached the valley, he could not recognise familiar woods and fields; no one in his village knew him, and he could not find his house or family. Centuries had passed while he watched the Immortals playing Wei Ch'i.

Mystical and magical Taoism developed along these lines, offering vain hopes of immortality and wealth, but incidentally making important discoveries which more mundane men were to put to varying uses: the making of gunpowder, and the magnetic needle from which the maritime compass derived. Taoism thus constituted a kind of unofficial opposition to scholarly Confucianism, and became more identified with the populace than with the educated gentry. Taoist sects, with some new magical credo, were to be the inspiration for many of the major peasant revolts in Chinese history. The roots of these beliefs went far back into classical times, when they can be identified with Shamanist cults conducted by the 'Wu' – wizards drawn from the common people by reason of some personality peculiarity.

About the beginning of the first century AD China, now in contact with both India and Persia by the 'silk road' across Central Asia, acquired knowledge of Buddhism. Indian missionary monks travelled east and preached the new religion. This had probably been going on for at least half a century before it was officially recognised by the Imperial court – the reigning emperor having a dream which he identified as a vision of Buddha. True to Chinese prejudice and settled outlook, a new doctrine could not spread as the consequence of the teaching of alien instructors: it had to arise from some spontaneous initiative of the Emperor himself. But the recognition of Buddhism implies that it was already a serious factor in social life which the government could not ignore.

Nevertheless, the spread of the new religion was slow. There are very few references to Buddhist monasteries in Han literature, and the laborious work of translating the Sanskrit texts into Chinese occupied the time of Indian monks and Chinese converts for more than two centuries. The Chinese had hitherto no acquaintance with any written language other than their own. The principles of Sanskrit grammar and the system of writing could not have been more different from those of the Chinese language, and the long Sanskrit words were almost unpronounceable in Chinese. Inevitably something of the real flavour of the original doctrine was lost, and more than a little of Chinese outlook and belief crept in. Certain similarities between the new mystical Taoism and the doctrines of Buddhism were obvious, and these exerted their influence on both religions. When Buddhism gradually became an accepted and important aspect of contemporary culture it aroused in Confucian scholars a hostility which never abated, though it did not take violent form. There were no harsh persecutions and very few, if any, real martyrdoms; though the Confucians, when in the ascendant, would compel Buddhist monks to marry Buddhist nuns, since they objected to celibacy as contrary to nature, inimical to the cult of ancestral worship, and thus harmful to society. Taoism was also a rival, but one which competed in the same field, and for the same objectives, more than Confucianism, which found the Buddhist ideal repugnant.

Buddhism was already an old religion when it reached China, perhaps upwards of four hundred years since the life of Gautama. In India it was already in decline with the revival of orthodox Hinduism, but it was flourishing in the Central Asian region, in what is now Afghanistan, and had penetrated Ceylon and the western islands of Indonesia. Chinese monks in search of precious relics and authentic texts of the Sanskrit Sutras travelled across Central Asia, braved the terrors of the Hindu Kush, and sought for enlightenment in the cities of India and the monasteries of the Afghan mountains. They also travelled, or returned by sea from the south Indian coast, to Sumatra and then to south China. Thus Buddhism soon contributed much to the Chinese knowledge of the outside world. These pilgrimages have become in later times the stuff of romantic semi-religious tales and novels. Here, too, the association of Buddhism with popular culture is very evident.

There was also, of course, the scholarly side to Chinese Buddhism. The main doctrinal division between Mahayana and Theravada (Hinayana) Buddhism had occurred before the religion reached China, which was converted by Mahayanist teaching. But the knowledge of the alternative was not ignored. There was, for a time, a Theravada school in China, but it did not persist, and finally died out. Other varying interpretations thrived, and among them the teaching of Ch'an (Japanese Zen) which, with a somewhat suspect Taoist character, decried book learning, stressed contemplation and believed in the sudden personal revelation of truth. Formal instruction was deemed almost useless – a very Taoist point of view.

The Buddhist conversion of China has been likened to the Christian conversion of the Roman world; but there are very significant differences. Buddhism was known, and always recognised, as an alien creed coming from India. It did not derive from the teaching of any subject of the Chinese emperor. The conversion was never total; Taoism held its own, and Confucianism, as the ethic of the scholar, the doctrine of the teacher and the orthodoxy of the government, was never really challenged. Buddhism is not a social religion. It preaches enlightenment through learning, contemplation and withdrawal from everyday life. It did not rally the mass of the people in communal services, nor was it concerned with the pomps and responsibilities of political power. Such things are 'illusion'; concern with them hinders the enlightenment and postpones the attainment of Buddhahood. Consequently the Confucians retained control of the organs of government and the system of education.

To some degree this development stressed the division between the culture of scholars and gentry and that of the people, which is today seen by communist historians as one of the fundamental contradictions of the old Chinese society. This aspect had, in the long course of centuries, a further effect. To the educated Confucian, especially after the work of the Sung (AD 960–1279) philosophers had reshaped Confucian doctrine on modern lines and had almost wholly excluded any aspect of deism from their system, all supernatural belief became unsophisticated superstition, suitable for the uneducated but not worthy of the scholarly gentleman. Buddhism never lacked some educated support, but it was minority support, and was itself infected with the more secular attitude of the educated majority of Confucian-trained scholars.

For many centuries, particularly in the period following the fall of the Han empire (fourth to sixth centuries AD), Buddhism was a real force. Famous monasteries were founded, and the influence of the new religion on art was profound. The Tatar courts in north China were strongholds of Buddhism, and yet it was not strong enough to oust Chinese as the language of administration and literature nor to substitute the Sanskrit script (which might have been more suitable for the Tatar languages) for written Chinese. Sanskrit remained a sacred script, only being used for religious texts. Many rulers, both Chinese and Tatar, were devout Buddhists; the Liang Emperor Wu three times renounced his throne to become a monk, allowing himself to be ransomed for secular authority by payment of enormous compensation to the Buddhist church. The third time proved too much for his subjects, who preferred to dethrone him. Under such rulers Buddhism enjoyed great favour and, as the story of Liang Wu Ti shows, tended to abuse it by gathering great wealth, which was contrary to the teaching of the religion.

The human temptation to turn power into money was one to which the old Chinese society was always prone, and it infected the Buddhist clergy, who for the most part did not come from the higher social classes. The social consequences were a decline in Buddhist support and the fervour of the faithful. The disappearance of Buddhism in India, and the Islamic conquest and conversion of Afghanistan, Central Asia and Indonesia ended the age of Chinese pilgrimage. Henceforth the foreign Buddhist lands were relatively small and had never been centres of Buddhist learning and pilgrimage. Burma, Ceylon, Thailand and Cambodia followed the Theravada form of Buddhism, while China, and those to whom she passed on the faith – Japan, Korea and Vietnam – were Mahayana. Consequently, foreign contact and inspiration waned away. Mongolia and Tibet had adopted the Lamaist form of Buddhism, heavily affected by the pre-Buddhist Shamanism of those peoples, and it was a form which never held great appeal for the Chinese, only flourishing in so far as it was supported for political reasons by the patronage of the throne. If these were the underlying reasons for the decline of Buddhism in the last five or six centuries, it still remained an important characteristic of popular culture, although often fused in practice among the peasantry with the cults of Taoist divinities.

It is often ignored that China also has a Muslim population now of about fourteen million. Higher estimates used to be accepted, but the lower figure seems to be better authenticated by recent census returns. In origin the Chinese Muslims were foreigners. In the middle of the eighth century AD the important Tatar tribe of the Uighurs were converted to Islam, and at the same period played a major role in Chinese affairs as mercenary soldiers. In the seventh and eighth centuries Arab traders, who came in large numbers to the south China ports, brought Islam with them. The two oldest mosques in China are respectively at Canton and at Sian, the former Ch'angan, capital of the T'ang empire, in which the Uighurs were employed. A common name for Muslims is Hui Tzu, which is said to be derived from the name Uighur.

In the twelfth century AD the Mongol conquerors brought into China large numbers of Muslim soldiers whom they stationed as garrisons, especially in the south-west and north-west. They settled and married locally, and their descendants, while keeping their religion, lost any alien language and became, in all other respects, Chinese. The Muslims also followed the practice of buying the young children of starving refugees in times of famine or war, and bringing them up as Muslims.

30

In this way their numbers grew, and they moved into all parts of the Chinese empire. There is no province without them, but the main concentrations are still in the north-west and south-west. For the most part Chinese Confucian historians have ignored the Muslims. Their settlement is unnoticed, their story unrecorded. They set up in Sian a monument purporting to record the story of their coming into China; unfortunately it can be shown to be a sixteenth-century fake, modelled on the genuine Nestorian tablet in the same city, which dates from the eighth century.

Socially the Chinese Muslims, living rather to themselves, have concentrated on certain trades and occupations, some of which are clearly linked with their origins. They are largely dominant in the camel caravan trade in the north and west, prominent in the mule caravan trade of the western mountain provinces. They may well have inherited these occupations from their first forbears. They are also dominant in the restaurant business in many parts of China, and are the preferred butchers for all classes and creeds. This is because Islam prescribes certain ways of killing and preparing meat which are better guarantees of cleanliness than those used by non-Muslim butchers. (Pork, of course, remains the monopoly of the latter group.) Muslims also specialise in the curio and art trade. The reason would seem to be that as they themselves abhor graven images and are forbidden to make pictures or other representations of the human figure, they have no religious scruples in stealing, buying or otherwise disposing of Buddhist pictures and sculpture, which are valued by the infidel public. As the Chinese proverb puts it: 'The maker of clay images does not believe in Buddha.'

The only other religion of foreign origin which has entered to some degree into the Chinese culture is Christianity, and not only in modern times. A consequence of the restoration of the unified empire by the T'ang dynasty in AD 618 was the renewed and strengthened contact between China and both western Asia and eastern Europe. Chinese authority reached to the north-eastern frontiers of the Persian empire, with which contact was close and friendly. Chinese envoys, or travellers whose experiences and knowledge were later incorporated in the dynastic history, reached Constantinople and described it. From these relations the Nestorian Christians, heretics from Byzantine orthodoxy but strong in Syria and the Middle East, sent missions to China, and in the reign of the great T'ai Tsung (who died in AD 649) such a mission was received by the Emperor and given permission to dwell and teach in China. All this the Nestorians recorded on a monument which they erected in the capital to commemorate the restoration of their principal churches after a devastating rebellion. It dates from the middle of the eighth century, and is still well preserved. It claims to have brought to China the 'pure truth religion' from a land which is specifically identified as the Roman Empire, i.e. in this case Syria. The Nestorian tablet rejoices in the success and esteem which Christianity has enjoyed in China, and does not fail to note the patronage of princes and princesses, and also of the major political figure of the age, Kuo Tzu-yi, commander-in-chief of the Imperial Army and saviour of the dynasty. It is not claimed that any of these mighty people were actually converts, but the tablet does testify to their contribution towards the restoration expenses.

It is known from other, less explicit, monuments and relics of the Nestorian Church that it did indeed flourish for nearly three centuries in the T'ang empire. Its fall and total disappearance after that time are still unexplained. The Confucian historians never mention Nestorianism, nor admit that it was patronised by the Court in the mid-eighth century. In late T'ang times a severe persecution of Buddhism occurred, directed more at the wealth than at the doctrine of the monks. It is thought that the Nestorians may have been included in this proscription, lost their wealth and their churches and were without the resources or strength to recover, as the Buddhists did, in the troubled era which followed shortly afterwards. Early in the eleventh century visiting Nestorians found the churches in ruins and the faithful dispersed or disappeared.

Five hundred years later, when the first Catholic missionaries came to teach in China, the memory of the Nestorian Church in China, if it had ever been present, had wholly faded from the consciousness of European peoples. When they discovered the melancholy evidence of the decline and disappearance of a once flourishing Christian community they found consolation in the view that this was in fact no augury for their own mission but due to the fact that Nestorianism was, after all, not true doctrine but heresy. Catholic missionaries from Ricci, who reached Peking in 1610, in the last decades of the Ming dynasty, were accepted by the Chinese authorities because of their skill in mathematics and technology. They corrected errors in the Chinese calendar and could cast better cannon. They were learned men, and so were able to make contact with the Chinese scholar class, especially as the missionaries made successful and arduous efforts to acquire classical Chinese education. The idea of conversion from the top, the hope of a Chinese Constantine, inspired their activity. In order to minimise opposition they permitted the use of certain Chinese customs such as discharging fire crackers at religious ceremonies – including the Mass – which were later to be condemned by the Church. These Jesuit missionaries also tolerated veneration of ancestors, claiming that this custom was not truly a pagan rite, but in line with the Christian commandment to 'honour thy father and thy mother'.

A late pretender to the Ming throne, when he had lost four-fifths of China, seemed to offer the hope of a Chinese Constantine. His mother was a convert, and there were others in the Imperial family. But this youth was soon to be driven from his shaky throne to be betrayed and put to death by the victorious Manchu (Ch'ing) dynasty. The vain hope of Portuguese mercenary assistance rather than religious conviction seems to have inspired this approach to conversion. The Jesuit missionaries had at the same time won the good graces of the new Emperor, K'ang Hsi of the Manchu dynasty, whom they served as mathematicians and technological experts. They also made converts among the educated class and the Manchu rank and file, men perhaps less deeply committed to Chinese custom and religion, since they were aliens who had not many generations earlier been Shamanist pagans. The Rites Controversy, arising from the jealousy of other Catholic orders for Jesuit predominance, and their criticisms of the practices which the Jesuits tolerated, brought a sudden disastrous change to the status of the Catholic missions. When Emperor K'ang Hsi learned that a foreign, in his view barbarian, potentate, the Pope, was assuming the right to give orders on religious matters in the Chinese empire, he was highly indignant. He expelled all missionaries, save a very few who were retained to carry on mathematical studies but were prohibited from preaching or teaching their faith.

That those who remained did nevertheless succeed, under K'ang Hsi and his two successors, in maintaining a more or less clandestine mission, and gaining converts, is certain. Yet by the end of the eighteenth century, after two hundred years of endeavour, the results were small. There were one or two major centres of missionary activity, like the Siccawei monastery near Shanghai, and conversion among the Manchu commoners in Peking, and in some villages in the north. The mass of the Chinese people remained untouched, indeed ignorant of the very existence of Christian missions. After 1842, when the Chinese government was compelled by defeat in war to admit missionaries of all Christian faiths with equal privileges, including that of residence in any place and the right to acquire property, both Catholic and newly arrived Protestant missions multiplied. They operated in every part of the empire, and in almost all cities. Their presence was never welcomed by the Chinese people, and was as far as possible opposed by the educated class and the officials. There were frequent sanguinary riots.

Some progress was made until towards the early twentieth century, when it was estimated that the Christian community totalled about four million, more or less equally divided between Catholic and Protestant sects. The population of the empire was at that time probably under-estimated as 400 million. The Chinese, except in sophisticated educated circles, believed the two forms of Christianity to be quite distinct religions – the 'Jesus doctrine' (Protestant) and the 'Lord of heaven doctrine' (Catholic). The ordinary people in rural China, moreover, believed that these two religions were the national faiths of England and France respectively – the only two foreign nations of which they were conscious – and that the missionaries were the paid emissaries of these two governments.

Under the double handicap of foreign tuition and leadership and a teaching which ran counter to many long-established Chinese beliefs and practices, it is hardly surprising that Christianity did not make a major impact, and what was achieved was largely due to the educational effort in founding and running schools where English or French could be learned. The later missionaries, like their first Jesuit predecessors, were valued by the Chinese for their skills and their knowledge of secular learning; the prime objective of their mission, religious conversion, was not appreciated.

By the nineteenth century the 'three religions of China', as they were called – Confucianism, Buddhism and Taoism – were all in decline. The ethical teaching of Confucianism, not truly religious and overtly anti-deist, had become the rather conventional mode of the upper scholar gentry class, without a social message or forward-looking attitude. The two popular religions, Buddhism and Taoism, had become in the minds of the people a synthesised polytheism making no distinctions between Boddhisatvas and Taoist gods. The majority of its fervent followers were women. Islam was the peculiar characteristic of a group whose non-Chinese origin was never forgotten. Christianity was a small minority faith, with some appeal to intellectuals and to those who for one reason or another were discontented with the existing society and aspired to see a regeneration of the Chinese nation. The Chinese people as a whole were not strongly motivated by any religious belief and it no longer played a prominent part in their culture. 'Three ways to one goal' was the common saying, but the goal was not so much salvation as the harmonious life on earth, the humanist ideal which had inspired Chinese religious thought from the earliest times.

2 The art of China

The ancient art of China is known only through archaeology. There are no major ruined cities in China, very few buildings over one thousand years old, and the archaeological sites of long-vanished towns are found deeply buried in alluvial soil. The Chinese culture did not arise and flourish on the edge of a desert, and consequently there are no ancient monuments preserved by dry air in a wilderness. The Chinese built both their early and their later cities near great rivers in a plain subject to vast floods; they built in brick, rarely using stone, which is not plentiful in the regions of their early civilisation. Their buildings were of relatively light construction using timber and tiled roofs, with brick walls filling the back and side walls, timber doors and windows enclosing the front. This type of construction, graceful and harmonious, superbly proportioned in surviving examples, is not very durable. It is easily destroyed by fire and flood.

The most important remains of early Chinese civilisation are the tombs of the dead, in which many superb examples of their art and craftsmanship were buried. If it were not for the fact that these objects had often been used by the living, or represented what the spirit of the deceased hoped to use in his after-life, there would be no assurance that the mortuary art of China truly reflected the taste and customs of its time.

There is as yet only an imperfect knowledge of the periods of antique Chinese art. Until very modern times the tombs were found by skilled tomb robbers, who marketed their treasures in cities where the prospects were good, only supplying very vague or wholly misleading information about their provenance. The archaeologists who, in the early 1930s, first excavated the site of an ancient city, the Shang capital at Anyang, were guided to the site by the reputation which this spot had long held for being the source of bronze vessels, of obvious high antiquity, which had been collected by connoisseurs for several centuries. It is possible to distinguish, not always with certainty, between works of the Shang period (which ended in 1025 BC) and the succeeding Chou period. But there are clearly other categories which still remain vague. The style of the south, and of other regions, may well have differed; but only very shaky identifications of such regional styles can yet be made, and these are often based on examples whose exact location at discovery is not known. Evidence from a collation of sites verified by archaeology suggests very strongly that the art of bronze vessels arose in central China, the Shang kingdom in Honan, and radiated outwards to the south, west and east.

Shang tombs, including those of the kings found at Anyang, were not furnished with sculpture or with murals, unless these have wholly decayed. Bronze vessels of very great beauty and decoration, bronze weapons, also often decorated, and some carving in low relief on bone and stone were the principal finds. There are also pottery vessels decorated in the manner of the bronzes, but these are not plentiful; nor is it certain that they are contemporary with the bronze examples. Shang bronzes have some short inscriptions, which can be deciphered; they usually consist of a dedication of the precious vessel with an injunction to sons and descendants to preserve it for ever. In early Chou times – the tenth century BC – there are vessels with longer inscriptions which record the investiture of a feudal lord by the king, and it would seem that the bronze itself is the authenticating document. It is established that bronze vessels of several different types were used for the preparation and presentation of food and wine (rice wine) at ceremonies and sacrifices for the dead ancestors. It is possible that the tombs themselves were used as chapels for these ceremonies, being closed when not in use.

The early Chinese had attained very great skill in the casting of bronzes, often of massive dimensions. It has been proved that they did not use the *cire perdu* (lost wax) method known in the West and in western Asia, but cast the larger bronzes in fitted moulds of baked clay. The pieces were then joined together under heat, and all traces of the join filed and polished away until it it is now only possible to detect these joins with a microscope.

The handling of a large quantity of molten metal, in at least one extant example weighing three-quarters of a ton, presents very real problems, which were successfully overcome. Fragments of clay moulds have been found which confirm that this method of casting was the one employed in China. No evidence of alien influence, in either the shapes, the decorative motifs or the method of casting, exists. Shang and Chou bronzes appear to have grown from a native tradition, possibly first

36

exemplified in pottery. It is also probable, on the negative evidence of no alien influence, that the discovery of the art of smelting and casting was made in China, possibly as an unforeseen result of firing clay which had metal ore content in the high-temperature kilns which the Chinese had devised, using the slopes of hillsides to increase draught.

The art which reached a point of perfection in Shang and early Chou times did not pass away. In later Chou times styles changed, and a new, freer, less formal decoration came into fashion, with inlay of silver and gold. The motifs of the most ancient decoration, in so far as they can be understood, relate to religious symbols: the dragon, god of the rain, and the *tao t'ieh* masque, which some scholars see as a frontal view of a dragon's head, although other explanations have been advanced. In the style of the Warring States, later Chou, the new free decoration is often secular: the hunt and battle scenes, as well as mythological figures, are depicted. It thus seems to reflect the taste of a more warlike, secular-minded aristocracy that that of the austere dedication of the earlier age.

Jade was a sacred substance to the ancient Chinese. It was used only for religious purposes, and some early references to its misuse for secular luxury make the point plain. A dissolute king was blamed for making chopsticks of ivory – an unheard-of luxury. 'And soon he will make a wine cup of jade,' concluded the critic, suggesting that sacrilege would be added to extravagance. Antique jades are not of the same material as the more modern jade which has been used for several centuries past. The ancient jade was found on the surface, not mined, and seems to have come from the semi-desert borders of north-west China. Consequently it was rare, and its sporadic occurrence on the ground surface suggested that it had fallen from heaven. It was usually employed to represent the symbols by which the major deities were known. The circular disc pierced by a round hole in the centre was the symbol of T'ien, the sky god, with the sun in the centre of the heavens. The other symbols are not so self-evident. The *kuei*, like a broad-bladed knife, has a shape which suggests that it might derive from a neolithic stone implement, perhaps used in sacrifice. The tube-like pieces, some-times squared on the outside, are the symbol for the earth. The connection is not apparent, unless the suggestion that in remote times these pieces formed a scabbard or case for a phallic symbol, and thus came to stand for earth and its fertility, is accepted. The early and authentic prayer of the Duke of Chou, brother of the founder of the Chou king-dom, when interceding with the ancestors for the recovery from sickness of his nephew, the second king of Chou, mentions ceremonial action with the 'round and square jades' which may be a reference to the sym-bols of heaven and of earth. Jade plaques representing a tiger are interpreted as the deity presiding over the west; western China is mountain country, and therefore the home and refuge of tigers. Later, small jades in the form of the cicada were placed upon the tongue and sometimes other parts of the body of a deceased person. The cicada is an emblem of spring, and thus of rebirth: its purpose on corpses was to assist the dead to cross to the after-life. The idea that jade was a preservative of life, proof against decay (which in itself it is) was the inspiration for much mortuary use of jade long after the period of high antiquity. The recently discovered jade suits of the Han princes are a magnificent example of this belief. Jade has continued in high esteem both for its beauty and undoubtedly for the surviving sentiments of happiness, good luck and preservation which cling to it from remote antiquity.

The Han period, a stable age of consolidated empire following the constant strife of the Warring States, created a new society, which in turn expressed its taste in new art forms. Bronze vessels were still made and used but they were no longer the masterpieces nor the chief contribution of the times. As with the earlier period, no Han temples, palaces or other monuments survive, only tombs. These are very numerous and their exploration has yielded a wide range of art forms and objects. The Han gentry, for only the tombs of the better off remain as evidence, were decorated with scenes intended to recall the pleasures and interests of the deceased when living. Bas-reliefs were a new form, sometimes carved in stone but often incised on bricks. The style is free and active, the scenes chosen from historical events, mythology, the hunt, domestic festivities and scenes of everyday life. The gentry ride forth in elegant light chariots drawn by high-stepping, fiery horses; sometimes their names and ranks are indicated in inscriptions. Such dramatic historical events as the attempt to assassinate the Ch'in First Emperor in his hall of audience, are also valuable confirmation of written history. A fierce battle is fought on a bridge, while peaceful fishermen in the river near by pursue their calling unconcerned; mythological figures of the legendary rulers of the Golden Age are, interestingly, represented in quasi-human form, with dragon tails.

Much of this decorative art is concerned with hunting, feasting and musical entertainments. The Han gentry would seem to have had hedonistic tastes. Representations of grave scholars discussing learned texts are not a common feature. In addition to bas-reliefs there are some scarce examples of mural painting, preserved where climatic conditions were favourable. The motifs are similar to those of the bas-reliefs, but they do not have a close relationship to later classical Chinese painting. Landscape is not shown; the human element is dominant, the scenes often showing men watching dancing girls or listening to musicians.

In Han times it was no longer felt that jade could be used only for strictly religious purposes. Horse heads and other small animal statues in jade are among the finest examples of their art. Bronze could also be used, as in the celebrated *Flying Horse of Kansu.*

The Han society was much concerned with horses. The use of cavalry had spread in the Warring States period, and it was now the main arm of the Imperial Army, especially in the constant wars with the northern nomadic peoples beyond the Great Wall. Expeditions, both diplomatic and military, were sent to western central Asia to obtain breeding stock of the famous horses of the region, larger, stronger and faster than the small Mongolian pony which was the horse of China. Communications across the vast extent of the new empire also required a relay system of mounted couriers carrying imperial orders and transmitting reports. The horse, hardly represented in early art, became a prominent theme in the Han period.

Han tombs have been found containing very beautiful, finely worked ornaments in gold and silver; lacquer, which has been found in southern Chinese tombs of the Warring States period, was much more common in Han times, as was fine pottery, which was sometimes glazed, though not yet true porcelain. An interesting aspect of this Han art is that many of the tombs which have yielded the finest treasures are situated on what was then the frontier of the empire: in North Korea, southern Manchuria, and near the desert frontier with central Asia. These distant provincial officials and army officers cannot have had the resources, the standing or the arrogance to compete in furnishing their tombs with the princes of the imperial family or with great ministers, and least of all with His Majesty. But owing to the destruction of the Han capitals and the plundering of imperial tombs – still identifiable – in past ages, there is almost nothing which can be associated with the art and taste of the capital and court. Archaeology may fill part of the gap, as with the Liu tombs and their jade suits, but it must be assumed that what is known from the tombs of minor gentry and officers is only an inadequate sketch of the full flower of Han art.

The Han period is also the earliest from which there are examples of another funerary art, that of grave figures. These were made of baked clay and painted. They represented servants, soldiers, women attendants, grooms and others attending on animals from horses to camels, which are also found. They were intended to serve as magical prototypes which would have spiritual reality for the deceased in the next life where he could enjoy the same standard of luxury, attention and pleasure as he had known on earth.

This custom continued for many centuries, becoming ever more elaborate and detailed. Han examples sometimes show very interesting characteristics of semi-abstract art – dancing figures from which an arm, not needed for the design, is omitted. Han figures also have a more spiritual, magical quality, expressing the idea of potent spells and transformation. In many later examples this quality is absent; the figures are faithful to living models, without the suggestion of magical powers. This art receives no notice in Chinese historical writing, indeed it is not considered an 'art' at all. It was only employed for funerary use, and no corresponding sculpture for the living existed. It tells more about the actual religion of the Han people than can be gleaned from the formal records of Confucian scholars. With this exception, sculpture in the round was not an art practised in China in the pre-Buddhist period. There exists one exception, a funerary monument to a famous Han general which stood at his tomb. It is not a graceful work, but heavy, if powerful. Whether it is unique because all others have been destroyed, or whether it was an example of an individual's taste, cannot be known.

It is also characteristic of Han art, the first period in which the human form is frequently the subject, that the body is never shown nude. Han figures are always fully robed. This is a characteristic of Chinese art which has endured. In early Buddhist sculpture, much under Indian influence, the figures are shown with naked torso or limbs, but secular Chinese art did not respond to this style. Male and female continued to be shown in flowing robes, as they have been until modern times. When this convention was not observed, it is understood that the intention is pornographic.

The period between the fall of the Han empire and the rise of the Sung dynasty, some seven centuries (AD 221 to 960), constitutes the Chinese equivalent of the Middle Ages of the West, although in some aspects the end of that period would be better placed in the ninth century AD in the second half of the T'ang dynasty. It was a society controlled by an aristocratic class but not one with true feudal powers. The great families who dominated the mostly short-lived dynasties derived power from the command of armies, and the ability to raise them, rather than from fixed territorial fiefs. Throughout this age, art was dominated by Buddhist inspiration, marking a sharp transition from the last phase of antique Chinese art, the Han empire. Buddhism and its rival, the later Taoism, appealed to cultivated men in an age of strife and instability. The scholar who withdrew to the mountains, to a monastery or as a Taoist hermit, was a new kind of artist, no longer the anonymous carver of bas-reliefs or painter of murals, but very often also a poet, who sought inspiration from nature in the Taoist tradition, or painted the Buddhist recluse – the Rishi – in settings which owed much to the same tradition as the Taoist. In this period we begin to know the names of famous painters. There are even descriptions of their work, canons of artistic criticism – everything, in fact, but the pictures themselves. Some very very few pictures are considered authentic productions of the sixth and following centuries, but the Chinese practice of making exact and accurate copies of the works of former masters, often very soon after the originals were painted, makes identification of such copies or originals very difficult, especially when both are centuries old.

From those that survive, and from later copies, it is possible to appreciate the new style to some degree. Man is no longer the centre of the subject; human figures, sages in meditation, scholars wandering in wild scenery, are present, but always almost insignificant in the wild grandeur of nature about them. The majority of these pictures are inspired by religious or philosophic thinking, and the hedonism of Han decorative art is no more to be seen. This tradition continued under the restored central empire of the T'ang, to develop into the classical painting of the Sung period. It was certainly not the only style in fashion during the Chinese Middle Ages. Mostly of T'ang date, the paintings in the cave temples of Tun Huang on the north-west frontier of China, exhibit another style, which more clearly derives from the art of the Han. Secular scenes are common: there are horsemen and warriors and domestic occasions, as well as a large representation of religious subjects with what appear to be portrait studies of important people, sometimes in the guise of Buddhist monks. That portraits were painted in T'ang times is proved by tomb discoveries, in which lively and almost impressionistic pictures of the deceased or his family have been found, works in a free style markedly unlike the formal painting of the time. There are also traditional copies, as is alleged, of portraits of some of the T'ang emperors.

Pictorial art was therefore affected but not entirely dominated by the Buddhist influence. Some aspects of the secular art of the T'ang period seem to have inspired the much later Persian and Mogul schools; contact with Persia and with India was close in T'ang times, so the transfer of motifs and style is not impossible.

Sculpture in China, with the exception of the tomb figures in baked clay, is essentially a Buddhist art. In cave temples near Tatung in northern China, a city which was one of the capitals of the Wei dynasty, a Tatar régime, in the fifth century AD, there are well-preserved sculptures of this period, and at a somewhat later site, Lung Men, near the old capital at Loyang, there are extensive caves with sculpture from the Wei dynasty through to the middle T'ang period. In the early examples the style is quite unlike the antique art of Han bas-reliefs. It has obvious Indian connections, and also echoes of the hellenistic art of north-west India. Some of this work shows hardly any Chinese motifs, and it has been conjectured that it was not in fact the production of Chinese artists. It is entirely devoted to religious subjects. The Buddha is shown seated, standing or reclining, surrounded by his disciples, all in Indian-style robes. The artists did not concentrate attention on the human form so much as on the head and face, to which they gave expression of aloof spiritual calm, compassion and tranquillity. These are representations of men who have attained divinity.

At Lung Men, which dates more from the T'ang than from the Wei dynasties, a subtle change appears, which is more evident the later the date of the work. Chinese characteristics are now present, and increase. In the Yunkang caves near Tatung there are hardly any Chinese inscriptions. At Lung Men they are frequent. The figures of the Apsaras – angels – and of the Boddhisatvas become much more human, the treatment of the body and limbs more naturalistic, and the beauty of the faces also more secular. As this tendency increased a T'ang scholar is on record as having criticised it in a trenchant phrase: 'Sculptors now make Boddhisatvas look like dancing girls; so every dancing girl thinks she is a Boddhisatva.' At Lung Men one can see that the criticism has force. At the same site, near the capital, which during part of this period was the seat of the famous, and strongly Buddhist, Empress Wu, much of the sculpture is of colossal proportions; great standing or seated Buddhas, carved from the rock and guarded by the fierce warriors – portrayed in contemporary armour – who traditionally attend the Buddha. Other sites, in both northern and southern China, show similar work, proving that a constant style was in use in all parts of the empire.

The T'ang was the last age of this style of sculpture in stone or rock carving. In later times the statues of the Buddhist pantheon were more often either cast in iron or carved in wood. Rock sculpture did not wholly disappear, but it ceased to be executed on the scale of Lung Men, and became infrequent. There had also, probably under Buddhist inspiration, grown up a style of more secular sculpture of which the surviving examples are found almost exclusively at the approaches to imperial tombs. The lions which guard the entrance to the now-vanished Liang tombs near Nanking are magnificent specimens of this art, and perhaps the earliest examples, dating from the sixth century AD. The lion is, in China, a Buddhist symbolic beast, and in later times was often used in sculpture to flank the entrances of palaces and temples.

The approach to the tomb of the T'ang emperor T'ai Tsung was flanked by life-size bas-reliefs of his six war chargers, killed in battle. These unique masterpieces of animal sculpture are almost the only ones which can be ascribed to a known artist. They are recorded as having been carved from the designs of Yen Li-pen, a scholar official and a well-known artist of the time (AD 649). The art of sculpture was in later times largely confined, outside Buddhist and Taoist temples, to this purpose. The approaches to the tombs of imperial persons and great officials – and sometimes lesser ones also – were decorated with such works, but few of the later examples have the quality of the Liang lions or the horses of T'ang T'ai Tsung.

The making of clay grave figures for burial with the dead was an unacknowledged art which in T'ang times reached its highest point. The variety and the grace of these figures is astonishing since, as far as can be known, they were not the work of any well-known artist. Apart from their merit as works of art, the grave figures provide a social documentation of T'ang and pre-T'ang society which no surviving text can match. There are sets of figures showing a polo match – and the players are girls. Horsemen in armour of the sixth century AD are shown with their horses also armoured, a development not known in Europe until more than six centuries later. The first evidence of the use of the stirrup, apparently a Chinese invention, comes from a stele dated AD 301; a century later the armed horsemen are all equipped with stirrups. It is also clear that the T'ang ruling classes employed scores of foreign servants in a wide variety of duties. Camel men and grooms are shown plainly as central Asians, with prominent noses. There were dancers from India; and Negroes, presumably from the east coast of Africa – which was known, at least by hearsay, to the Chinese of that age. Some obviously European types, famous in China as jugglers and acrobats, have been tentatively identified as subjects of Byzantium. There is little to tell who these people were – slaves, paid servants, or independent entertainers. They must have been both numerous and fashionable.

The art of making grave figures seems to have declined after the T'ang period. More stereotyped forms, soon to be made in porcelain rather than clay and with stylised, less varied decoration, replaced the hand-painted, individual and flexible style of the T'ang, where varying fashions in dress from age to age are faithfully represented. In still later times the custom was replaced by burning paper effigies at the funeral of the deceased. Since there is some literary evidence which indicates that the custom originated in high antiquity as a more civilised and humane substitute for human sacrifice at the funeral of a monarch or other grandee, the use of tomb figures in their varying forms, and their ultimate transformation into paper effigies, must be one of the longest-living funerary customs in any part of the world. The Shang kings were certainly interred with an extensive entourage of human sacrifice.

The middle period of the T'ang dynasty, the eighth century AD, was the age when the old aristocratic society gradually gave way to a new bureaucratic, gentry-dominated social system. The recruitment of officials by public examination instead of recommendation by patrons was inaugurated by the Emperor T'ai Tsung, and 150 years later it had virtually replaced the old aristrocracy. In the Sung period, AD 960–1279, the bureaucratic absolute monarchy was firmly established. If the word 'modern' seems out of place, Chinese society from that time on must be named 'late'.

Early in the tenth century the Chinese, who had been experimenting with printing for some hundred years, made the art sufficiently useful to print the texts of the Classical Books, the standard dynastic histories, and a wide variety of other works. Manuscript copies went out of use, and very few old manuscripts now survive. Some printed editions of Sung date are extant, and very many more that were reprinted from them in later centuries. One consequence of this was a great spread of learning, an extensive growth of the literate class, and therefore a new and critical attitude to established doctrines. The enlarged educated class adopted the refined art standards which had been élite in T'ang times, and as it was essentially a scholar's art, it was concentrated on painting, rather than on sculpture.

The Sung landscape painters (although they did not confine their work to this one field) were inspired by an outlook rather different from those of T'ang and earlier periods, so far as we can judge these. Much Sung work has survived, and still more authentic copies. The age of the Sung was preoccupied with a new and more sophisticated interpretation of the ancient classical literature and Confucian doctrine. On the one hand it was a reaction against the long supremacy of Buddhism and Taoism, though on the other it borrowed the manners of that art for a new purpose. The landscape painters show man in a universe dominated by wild nature, but adapting himself to it and making it the symbol of the human virtues. The pine tree clinging to a sheer cliff is a symbol for the upright scholar holding out for truth and justice against blind forces of oppression and destruction. The very exaggerated ruggedness of the landscape stands for the perils of earthly life; the scholar, calm and contemplative in this awesome environment, writes a poem, or studies a book in a rustic shelter, asserting the supremacy of the Confucian humanist outlook. Man must harmonise with nature, but he must not be dominated by it, nor indulge in superstitious interpretations. It was now accepted that the good Confucian should

44

also retreat, from time to time, or at retirement, to some peaceful and beautiful place where he could contemplate and engage in literary pursuits without the hurly-burly of daily political life. Almost all the great Sung painters were also prominent officials, and very often philosophic writers as well.

No one can question the supreme achievements of the Sung painters. Unfortunately, they were to be taken as models in subsequent ages and thus influenced all subsequent art, to some extent sapping its originality. The fact that their art was so clearly the product of a highly cultivated society tended to throw discredit on any art form with which they had not been directly associated. Painting was the art for the scholar gentleman; sculpture was not, nor were the fine works of craftsman-ship, jewellery, bronzes, even porcelain, admitted to the studio of the scholar. Or rather, they were there to be admired, but not to be emulated.

Porcelain has for so long been associated with the Chinese that the word 'China' has come to mean both the country and the ware. Yet it was many centuries before true porcelain was made. The progress towards this achievement was by slow stages. In remote antiquity it can be shown that the Chinese used kilns for their pottery which gene-rated very high temperatures. In Han times, if not somewhat earlier, the first application of glaze to pottery was made, and painting of the surface of pots had an earlier origin. It is in T'ang times that the first true porcelain was made. It was exclusively white, and to judge by sur-viving pieces and sherds, no large pieces were yet made. The wealthy T'ang Chinese still preferred silver for their luxurious feasts. By the early Sung period, during the tenth and eleventh centuries AD, the manufacture of porcelain had greatly extended; there were centres each with a special type in northern and southern China, and many of these pieces are still in existence. The Sung court took up the development of the new art and commissioned 'Kuan' ware, i.e. official or imperial orders, which produced the first use of colour, the celebrated Sung monochrome porcelain of these centuries. The names of some at least of the inventors and producers of these superlative pieces have been preserved, but it is not at all clear to what social stratum they belonged. In this age the imperial kilns at Ching Te Chen, in Kiangsi province, were set up near the town significantly called Kaolin (High Wood), a name which has passed into most languages as the term for China clay, whether in porcelain or in medical use. The vast deposit of very pure clay of this kind has sustained the industry from the tenth century to the present time.

The new art soon became a major industry, in demand from a wealthy society of widely educated people, and used in cheaper forms by the populace also, who appreciated its superior qualities over earthenware. An export trade developed, with Asia, both east and west, and with the east coast of Africa. A handful of pieces even reached Europe, to be treasured by princes and mounted in gold or silver. Porcelain was still further developed in the succeeding dynasties. The first 'blue and white' appears in the Yüan or Mongol period (1279–1368), and may be a consequence of a new facility in obtaining the colour ingredient which the Chinese called 'Mohammedan Blue'. 'Blue and white' was fully used in the Ming period, when polychrome wares were also produced. The reigns of the Ming emperors, known to all collectors by the reign styles of those rulers – Ch'eng Hua, Cheng Te, Chia Ching and Wan Li – cover the period when Chinese porcelain was most creative and artistic in its inspiration. Actual potting perfection was not achieved until the following period, the Ch'ing, or Manchu dynasty, in the second half of the seventeenth and eighteenth centuries. Here, too, the reign styles K'ang Hsi, Yung Cheng and Ch'ien Lung are as well known to all connoisseurs as the political fortunes of the monarchs they designate. It became the custom in that age to produce exact copies of the famous Ming vessels, including the reign mark, and reign marks in themselves can consequently be misleading. A beautiful vase marked Hsüan Te, which is a Ming reign title, can be a reproduction of the Yung Cheng period, three hundred years later. It is often detected by the fact that the technical excellence of the potting is superior in the reproduction to that of the original.

Reign marks were only put upon pieces produced by the imperial pottery at Ching Te Chen. There were also many private kilns, each with their distinctive mark, and often producing wares of very high quality. The industry was very large and worked also for a wide and expanding export market, which had begun with the countries of south-east Asia but spread to India, Persia, Turkey and Europe. Among the curiosities of the last market was the demand in the eighteenth century for armorial China; noble families sent designs of their arms to agents in China, who commissioned the production of whole dinner sets with the arms as decoration. The Chinese makers could not interpret the words used in mottoes, and sometimes inadvertently incorporated instructions, unwisely written on the design, as being a part of it. 'A dozen of these' may appear beneath the arms of a duke.

In a short survey it is necessary to treat the development of the major arts in the period when they first attained supremacy, but while Chinese culture did unfold gradually, each age adding a new aspect, it is also true that no art wholly declined – all were continued. If architecture is associated primarily with the Ming and Ch'ing periods, it is because very little of earlier times remains in existence. Descriptions of palaces and temples from the earlier ages remain, but they are not always detailed enough to judge whether the existing splendid buildings of the Ming period are advances upon, or only reproductions of, their predecessors. A very few, not more than four or five, pagodas and as many temples still remain from later T'ang and Sung times. The differences in style which they exhibit are not substantial, and surviving pictures also show a considerable conformity to existing buildings. It would seem that the yellow, green and blue tiles which are one of the beautiful features of Ming and later palace and temple buildings may not have been known at earlier times, and could be a consequence of the development of porcelain. Very few coloured tiles have been recovered from the known sites of T'ang palaces, whereas if the roofs of these great buildings had been covered with them (yellow for the imperial residence), there should be hundreds of broken fragments on the sites. In general design, dimensions and most features of decoration, such as the painted roof beams, it is unlikely that there has been a great change from the early examples. The Ming palace buildings, and those at the Ming tombs, are superbly proportioned; whether their predecessors had this quality it is not possible to decide. The scientific examination and excavation of earlier palace sites, known for centuries in such cities as Ch'angan and Loyang, has only recently begun.

Painting, the scholar's art, flourished throughout the later dynasties; critics have sometimes suggested that it represents a decline from Sung achievement, but this may well be a subjective assessment. There is inevitably much more Ming and Ch'ing painting extant, the best and the lesser alike. From the Sung we have probably only a relatively small selection of the best, the most carefully preserved and treasured work. Ming and later artists also frequently copied Sung masters; the originals are often lost, and without their work we would know even less of early Chinese painting. There were artists of great originality and power in the later dynasties, and styles were by no means uniform reproductions of the Sung schools.

The antiquity of Chinese works of art can give rise to a certain unreality in judgement. Very few cultures in the world can still display pictures painted more than 1000 years ago, or even of five centuries past. But the Ming came to power in the late fourteenth century; Ming painting is extant in large quantities, and none of it is less than three hundred years old.

3   Literature and learning

The Chinese language is unique. No other has an unbroken continuity in the form of script from the earliest records until the present day. The ideographic script was devised in China; it shows no characteristics of alien origin, and when the first known inscriptions, the oracle bones, were written it is obvious that the use of writing was already developed to the point of ideographic rather than mere pictorial record. The script of the Shang oracle bones can be learned by anyone literate in Chinese in a very short time; it is more ornate, more elaborate, than the later standard form, but many of the ideographs are so similar to the later forms that there is no difficulty in reading them. Chinese scholars who first examined the oracle bones, and short bronze inscriptions of similar date – about the thirteenth or fourteenth centuries BC – were able to decipher them with hardly more difficulty than a European would find with an early manuscript of the Middle Ages. Only one aspect is baffling. There are place and personal names in these inscriptions which have no modern counterparts or, if they have, in forms so changed that they cannot be positively identified with the early forms. Since Chinese script is divorced from the pronunciation of sound, an ideogram of which the sound is unknown and cannot be deduced from context, as with a place name, remains an enigma. Such names occur with some frequency in these inscriptions. The king goes hunting at some place, and asks the oracle (his ancestor) whether he will get a good bag; he makes war upon some enemy, named, and asks whether he will win a victory. We do not know where he hunted, nor upon whom he made war, nor can we guess the sound of these names.

The ideographic script is constructed upon the same principle as the Arabic numerals: a symbol, such as '5', can be pronounced in many ways by different peoples; its meaning is constant. All Chinese ideographs are of this character. Meaning is fixed, sound may vary according to place, period or dialect. This has two very significant consequences: the literature of the most remote past is easily intelligible, and the content of literature is equally intelligible to all readers of the Chinese script, no matter how they pronounce the words. The result has been to bind Chinese civilisation with a continuing link with antiquity, and also to consolidate and unify the literary culture of the whole Chinese world.

In the long course of centuries some changes in the form of the script occurred. Chinese scholars distinguish the 'Great Seal' style, the most ancient, from the later 'Lesser Seal', which was used in the Chou period and the Warring States, and then the new, more simplified, style which was introduced with the unified empire in the late third century BC and remained in use until modern times. Quite recently, the present government has introduced a number of still more simple forms for ideographs of very common use when these were of complex structure. The forms are not truly new; they were used by clerks as a kind of shorthand, and to some degree by the Japanese, too, but in China they were not printed until the recent reform.

The ancient Chinese did not write on clay tablets, which endure, but on bamboo slips, incised with a sharp stylus. The oracle bones are also incised in this way. The invention of ink and paper at about the end of the third century BC was the main reason why the old styles went out of common use and became reserves for inscriptions on stone and on seals. Ink enabled the writer to use more flowing forms, and gave birth to the highly esteemed art of calligraphy, which in China ranks with painting.

Bamboo slips are perishable, except in exceptionally favourable circumstances. Consequently, the oldest Chinese literature – apart from bronze and bone inscriptions – is only known through copies made throughout history. Only one or two texts written on bamboo slips have been recovered in modern times from excavated tombs. They are of classical works, and exhibit practically no textual differences from the extant versions, although pre-dating any other existing text of the same book by about a thousand years. Apart from a few stone stele inscriptions giving the texts of the classical books, made in the seventh to ninth centuries AD, there are no ancient manuscripts, and all early Chinese literature is, like the later, extant in printed editions, the earliest dating from the Sung period, in the eleventh century AD.

The most ancient literature was preserved by the Confucian school; and after the proscription of such books by the Ch'in First Emperor in the last decade of the third century BC it was reconstructed, from hidden examples and the memories of old men, in the succeeding Han dynasty. For this reason most of what has survived was the literature which the

Confucian school valued; the writings of their opponents and rivals of the other 'Hundred Schools' (a term not to be taken literally) are more fragmentary. Fortunately, the Confucians were very historically minded and preserved much which was not necessarily in true accord with their own teaching, simply because it was ancient and authentic. From these sources there exist some documents of the early Chou period (1025–722 BC), collected in the *Book of History*. There are also the Odes, poetry of about the same or slightly later dates, which modern scholarship regards as a kind of court poetry imitating rustic themes, and possibly deriving from songs. Confucian scholars in the past attributed these and other collections to Confucius himself, which accounts for the veneration and preservation they received. His own teaching is preserved in the book called *The Analects*, which seems to have been assembled by his immediate disciples and remains the most authentic text of the early philosophy.

The concept of authorship in the modern sense was not present in antiquity. A book was made, perhaps by more than one hand, embodying a doctrine or a collection of documents, and also the annals of the feudal courts, the work of the archivists whom they employed. Attribution of personal authorship was a later convention, a kind of authentication of the work. Style varied; the annals are laconic, factual and without comment or explanatory passages. Other early historical record is much more detailed and revealing, and in early times these works, the most famous being the *Tso Ch'uan*, were considered to be commentaries upon the annals. This view no longer prevails. The classical literature of all schools, not only the Confucian, is defined as all that has survived from the pre-Ch'in period. It has always had in China an esteem derived from its supposed authorship or connection with Confucius, its antiquity and its style. It became, and for two thousand years remained, the foundation of all education, playing the same role in Chinese culture as a combination of Greek classical literature and the Christian Bible has had in our own.

In addition to undertaking the great work of restoration of the early literature, the Han scholars devoted their labours above all to history. The name of Ssu-ma Ch'ien, a Han scholar of the first century AD, is honoured as the founder of the later tradition of Chinese historiography. He held a position at the court of the Emperor Wu (140–87 BC) which gave him access to the imperial library in which were preserved a range of sources unobtainable elsewhere. His work, the *Shih Chi*, was meant to be a complete history of the Chinese world from the earliest times down to his own lifetime. His method was compilation: all documents are quoted in full, sometimes in differing versions. The reader is left to make his own judgement on their validity. In the later sections he did indeed draw on his own knowledge and experience, and as he did not love his master these chapters contain some very important critical comments upon the policies of Emperor Wu. The great contribution of his work is that it assembled all the traditional and legendary material then current, it included as far as was possible the full annals of the feudal states, and it set a standard of accuracy, objectivity and comparative criticism which has no equal in the ancient literature of any other culture.

The example of Ssu-ma Ch'ien was followed in the first century AD by Pan Ku, who wrote the *History of the Western Han*, the period from 202 BC to AD 9. Unlike Ssu-ma's work this is confined to the single period of one dynasty, a model which has since been followed until the present day. The arrangement of the work has also been copied ever since. There are annals, which are a bare record of imperial decrees, movements, promotions, dismissals and other events at court, very accurately dated to day, month and year. In Ssu-ma Ch'ien's work the dating before the Chou period is speculative and until the end of the eight century BC cannot be considered accurate. The Han *History* also has an extensive section of biographies, covering the lives of all persons of importance in many different spheres of life, though not that of the Emperor himself. These biographies are the flesh upon the bare bones of the annals. They fill in the full story, but they are not dated – for dates one must go to the annals. Moreover, each subject is treated individually; events in which several people were concerned must be collated from their own biographies to obtain a complete record. Other sections of the work contain monographs dealing with a variety of subjects, like taxation, administration, water control, astronomy and other matters of concern to the government. Subjects outside that range are not included. Consequently there is very little except indirect evidence on popular religion and many other social developments. Tables of pedigrees and ranks provide valuable reference material, and there are short notices of all the foreign countries and peoples with which the Han empire had made official contact. It is from these sections that the earliest history of south-east Asia is known, and the record and evidence of Chinese contact with the Roman Empire and the western countries of Asia.

The model of the *History* was carefully followed in every succeeding age; all dynasties, however brief, have their official dynastic history. In later times the task was given to a group of scholars who had access to the archives of the late régime, or sometimes, in times of rapid change, to those of more than one fallen dynasty which had not yet been published. It was the firm custom never to publish the history of the reigning dynasty, even when it had been in power for more than two centuries. The assumption that none would endure for ever, and that their story could wait until political pressure would not be present to distort it, was accepted and respected. It is a remarkable testimony to the true power of the scholar bureaucracy that no monarch, however autocratic and high-handed in other matters, dared to demand falsification of his record, or even the right to see what had been said about him. It is recorded that the great T'ang T'ai Tsung made such a request; it was refused, and the high official concerned added: 'Moreover, even the fact that you asked for this and I refused, will inevitably be recorded.' And it was.

In these respects, in truth, accuracy, continuity and orderly arrangement (if not the kind of arrangement which moderns find most convenient), the Chinese historical record is unique in the world. But it had its defects and its assumptions. The defects were firstly, that nothing which Confucian scholar historians did not deem worthy of record was included; and this omission covers a very wide range of what interests the modern scholar. Secondly, it was written with a purpose, to justify the orthodox morality, to exhibit the benefit which came from conforming with it, and the disasters which followed from immoral, incorrect or merely neglectful behaviour. History was a mirror (the simile is frequently used) in which the ruler could see his predecessors and make comparison with his own conduct. Nothing, therefore, must be concealed, distorted, slurred over or omitted. Virtue is displayed, and also vice as a warning. Catastrophe is linked with conduct, if bad; plenty and peace arise from justice, benevolence, sincerity and loyalty, the Confucian virtues. This imports a prejudice: capable rulers who did not conform, or were in other respects out of step, are given but grudging acknowledgement of success, and their failures stressed as the consequence of their errors. There also arose a theory of the 'dynastic cycle', which propounded the view that all dynasties would rise, flourish, decline and fall, for very much the same reasons and with much the same sequence of events, all due to the gradually waning virtue of the monarchs. It is a theory which does not stand the test of the events which the dynastic histories themselves record, but it was swallowed by the early western historians of China, and often still appears to linger in the popular understanding.

There was no period in which the writing of history failed, no dark age where the record can only be eked out by inscriptions and coins. In the course of time, especially from the T'ang period onwards, non-official histories were published, and also a new presentation of the orthodox historical texts, grouped in subjects or with a continuous record covering many years, which incorporated the annals and the biographical information in one narrative. These are the basis of almost all translations and presentations of Chinese history in foreign languages. But the sheer mass of Chinese historical record is so huge that no comprehensive translation of more than small portions of it has yet been accomplished.

The T'ang period is as much associated with poetry as the Han with history, although there was poetry from long before T'ang and some historical record much earlier than Han. After the classical Odes, the late period of the Warring States and also the Han empire produced some poetry which has continued to be read and very greatly admired. The period following the Han empire, when Buddhism and later Taoism had great influence, saw the development of a new style of nature poetry of great beauty, sophistication and technical skill, which can be linked with the better-known poetry of the T'ang dynasty. Most of the very famous names belong to this age, and to the first two hundred years of it, from AD 600 to 800. Li Po, T'u Fu, Meng Hao-jan, and many others were contemporaries, and P'o Chu-yi was of the next generation. These are the Chinese poets best known outside China (as well as within it) and whose works have been translated by sensitive scholars such as the late Arthur Waley.

The characteristics of Chinese poetry, written in an ideographic script in which the components of the ideograph are a factor in the reader's appreciation as much as the sound and the meaning, are very hard to render. Certain qualities of their poetry and some of its lacks can be more readily appreciated. The Chinese short four-line poem in which 'the sound stops but the meaning goes on' is a form which has no very close parallel elsewhere. The evocation of a complex idea in very few words, whose meaning is also related to the shape of the ideographs chosen and to literary illusions which assume a wide knowledge of Chinese literature, is none the less harmonious and moving to readers lacking some of these qualifications.

Chinese poetry has no, or rather possibly only one, epic. There are no religious epics such as those which are the foundation of the culture of many other nations. The Chinese preferred fictionalised history. Po Chu-yi's poem on the death of the concubine Yang Kuei Fei, sacrificed to mutinous soldiers by her lover, the Emperor Hsüan Tsung (Ming Huang) is of epic type, and is one of the best known poems in the Chinese language. The poet was a near contemporary with the subject of the poem. Poetry was thus not under the restriction from which history suffered, of being forbidden to deal with the contemporary world and people of fame and power, as well as with the sorrows and joys of ordinary men. Most Chinese poets chose such themes: parting of old friends and reunions after many years; nostalgia for the far-off home; nature and its power and grandeur. The theme of parting was natural to a class of men, mainly in official service, who were frequently sent on long journeys to distant places and thus separated from the friends with whom they had lived and studied perhaps since childhood. Love poetry, in the Chinese marriage system, had less scope. Men were not parted from their wives in the ordinary course of duty: they took them with them. Love outside marriage was a taboo subject. The devotion of a wife to her husband, and his treatment of her, was a theme used in poems about men of fame and power, as with the Emperor T'ang Hsüan Tsung, or the hero of the end of the Ch'in dynasty, Hsiang Yu.

It was common for Chinese poets to be scholars and officials and, at least in earlier times, there were very few who did not fit these categories, for to be a poet it was necessary to be literate, and the ideographic script is not mastered except by comparatively long study. Only the well-to-do could afford the expense of education; accordingly, only from this class could literate poets emerge. Poetic gifts which could not be expressed in the ideographic script were unrecorded. Chinese poetry, like painting – and for the same reasons – was thus a scholar's art, catering to the taste and expressing the outlook of the talented élite. As great poets are not confined by any social convention, so also in China there is a poetry of protest, or compassionate power, which transcends the limitations that education and background had imposed. Such a poet is T'u Fu, and the fact that he can be, and is, republished with approval by the present régime in China testifies to his universality.

There was a tendency, characteristic of the old Chinese culture, always to look back to past models and golden ages: the classical age for philosophy, the Han for history, the T'ang for poetry. In later ages there were many famous poets, but the styles and models of the T'ang continued to dominate. It seems almost as if later dynasties found some inner compulsion to seek a new outlet for creative genius, while still honouring and continuing the received tradition. The contribution of the Sung period is of this character. In this age, the empire being re-unified after the fall of the T'ang, the Sung turned to a reinterpretation of the Confucian philosophy. Confucian studies had long been conventional. No writer had challenged the Han scholars, no revaluation of the old tradition had been made. In the Sung period these questions were taken up by a succession of philosophic writers who were frequently high officials as well, and mingled their political and philosophic theories in a way which seemed wholly compatible to the thinking of the time.

The Sung philosophers found a real problem. Traditional Confucian doctrine did not pronounce upon the ultimate questions of the nature of the cosmos, the personality or impersonality of the supreme being, or whether in fact there was such a being, or the basic character of man, on which early texts put forth more than one view. Buddhism, with its Indian metaphysical background, offered answers, and Confucianism had no clear message in reply. This the Sung scholars set out to rectify. In the mental climate of their time they did not seek to formulate new doctrines as such; they claimed, instead, to be restoring the real meaning of ancient teaching, overlaid by neglect, and to give proper recognition to the doctrines embodied in some early books which, they argued, had been misinterpreted or ignored. It might seem an astonishing proposition, that in the very shrine of orthodoxy such misconceptions could prevail for so long. But not in eleventh-century China; truth had once been expounded, by the Sage himself; in an examination of his words and those of the disciples he had inspired that truth could now be rediscovered.

The debate continued for the best part of two centuries. It was finally synthesised and the new doctrine (or restored doctrine) established by the last and most famous of the Sung philosophers, Ch'u Hsi, who died in the year 1200. It turned upon the nature of the Supreme Ultimate, T'ai Ch'i, which Ch'u Hsi finally settled by declaring that 'there is no man in heaven judging sin'. T'ien and Shang Ti, the ancient sky deities, were now reshaped as a moral force, linked with the physical universe in a continuum which could not be separated. The relationship between heaven and its manifestations, and between man and his moral or immoral behaviour, was no longer seen as in some way a system of reward and punishment but as an automatic reaction, without conscious intervention by any supreme being. There was no such being, only an all-pervasive moral force, which reacted – like the Yin and the Yang – to imbalance in man or in nature. Deism having been abolished, and belief in supernatural beings decried as unsophisticated and rustic, the Sung philosophers had to deal with the nature of man.

The original classical texts had put forward diverse views, in so far as they met this problem at all. Mencius held that the original nature of man was good: evil conduct came about from a failure to cultivate that nature and a neglect of proper education. Hsün Tzu, a slightly later Confucian whose views were seen with some sympathy by the harsh schoolmen of the Law of Ch'in, held that the nature of man was bad, and that only law and the threat of severe punishment could prevent it manifesting itself in bad conduct and criminal activity. Another school of Sung philosophers claimed to find ancient textual authority for the view called, picturesquely, the 'whirling water' theory. At birth the nature of man was neither good nor bad, but like water whirling in a confined rocky gorge it found the outlet which was most convenient, and took its course accordingly. Education and moral training was thus essential to direct it to the proper channel.

Ch'u Hsi decided that as Confucius had never overtly subscribed to the view that the nature of man was bad or even undetermined, he had by the implication of much of his teaching held the view that it was good, but too often neglected and ill-trained. He illustrated this doctrine, as was the Chinese custom, by simple analogies. The nature of man at birth was like a bright mirror, ready to reflect good teaching; neglected, it became covered with dust, lost its capacity to reflect, and turned dull and useless. Education, proper moral training, would keep the mirror bright and, the nature of man being innately good, all that was needed was to prevent the encroachment of evil habits.

These were the doctrines which were to become orthodox Confucian teaching for the succeeding ages. The sources of these theories were frequently rather obscure passages in early literature which no one had hitherto examined very closely; but they were there, in the classical books, and now they were given a meaning which had been ignored too long. It is at least clear that the new interpretation was satisfactory to the thinking of the educated class, for it was never seriously disputed in later times. Confucian Chinese scholars, which meant, by training, the whole educated class, henceforth did not formally believe in a deity in heaven, and framed their thinking on the view that the nature of man was inherently good. These two doctrines were obviously a very serious obstacle to any acceptance of religions such as Christianity, which teaches their opposite.

It is known that in the Sung period another intellectual activity, unrelated to Confucian studies, was stirring in circles perhaps more inspired by later Taoist magic than by classical learning. In this period the Taoists, who had perfected the compass and understood the properties of the magnetic needle, passed on their invention to the mariners; gunpowder, also, issuing from Taoist alchemy, was used in war (as opposed to its early use to 'drive out devils') in the early twelfth century. It seems that at first a simple form of grenade was used to scare the horses of the enemy Tatar cavalry. Before long, primitive cannon were in use at sieges. Mathematics made important advances in Sung times, or rather the evidence for such advance dates from this period, largely, perhaps, because after the invention and use of printing in the tenth century, books multiplied and more have survived. Technical proficiency in the manufacture of fine porcelain, silk weaving and other crafts developed along with the use of water power in mills. Experiments were made with paddle boats, but the only motive power was still human muscle. Economic theories for equalising taxation, controlling the grain supply to cities and relieving peasant indebtedness were advanced, tried out, contested and modified. In a wide variety of activities the Sung period showed a sophisticated approach which is in sharp contrast to the standards of other societies of the same epoch. Scholars and historians have speculated on what this might have led to had not the Sung society been overwhelmed by ferocious, and far less civilised, enemies.

The event which cut short the development of Sung culture was the Mongol conquest of China. The Tatar Ch'in dynasty had been in possession of north China for a hundred years, but contemporaries agree that this imposition of an alien dynasty had not made a very deleterious impression on the society of the northern provinces. Ch'u Hsi, for example, was as much appreciated in the northern empire as in the southern Sung, where indeed the ruling monarch did not share his ideas. The Mongols were different. Their proficiency and their range in warfare far exceeded that of any previous nomadic eruption. They conquered most of Asia and penetrated deeply into Europe. Their tactics of terror, which included the total massacre of the inhabitants of any city which made the least resistance, and a similar depopulation of rural areas, made their conquest a long series of devastations which were only slightly modified in the later stages.

When Kublai reigned supreme and unchallenged over all China and a great part of Asia he had to organise and govern this vast empire, and he adopted the policy of employing the different subject peoples in countries other than their own. Chinese officials served the Great Khan in the Middle East; Arabs, Persians and central Asians were installed as governors and officials in China. The Chinese scholar class for the first time found itself unemployed, or at any rate under-employed. In this era of subjection they seem to have found a new literary outlet. Confucian studies were not of interest to their rulers, and the great questions were regarded as settled. The Mongol period in China, short as it was (1206–1368), is celebrated for the rise and growth of Chinese drama. There is evidence of court drama as far back as the T'ang era, and the famous Emperor Ming Huang is still the patron of actors, but from what can be known of this early form it consisted of short one-act or one-scene plays, and of elaborate pageants with dancing and mime.

It seems apparent that some new and powerful influence affected the Chinese scholars who interested themselves in drama in the Mongol age. Their work is always wholly concerned with Chinese themes, historical, mythical or domestic, but the new art, with its elaborate costumes, stage, orchestra (on the stage) and division into scenes does suggest a relationship with drama in other parts of the world. If so, the links are hard to trace. Chinese historians do not record such things, and other writers do not seem to have been aware of Chinese drama (Marco Polo never mentions it), perhaps because as they did not understand Chinese they never attended plays. It is known that the opening of the trade routes across Asia as a consequence of the Mongol conquest brought a great interchange of merchants and travellers from all over Asia and far beyond, including Europe and north Africa. It seems possible that travelling companies from the Near East may have accompanied the caravans or armies which moved to and fro, and that Chinese writers drew inspiration from watching such performances.

It is evident that drama attracted men of real ability and literary skill. The new art won swift popular support, and also enjoyed the patronage of the educated and of the court, certainly after Chinese rule was restored by the Ming. The evolution of the varying forms of Chinese drama, the Peking Opera, other types of operatic performance known in different provinces, and also the shorter, frequently comic scenes interposed in the sung part of the piece, has been the subject of much research in modern times. It is not well documented, and little was to be gathered from the official histories. Even the names of the best Yüan (Mongol) period dramatists, if known, are isolated facts; little is known of their background or their lives. Supported by, and very popular with, both the educated and the populace, Chinese drama was one of the few arts fully shared by both classes in the nation, and was also, when it could be seen, welcomed in the countryside. Temples in villages and small towns would often have a roofed stage, with the audience left in the open. When a fair was held, throngs would listen to a travelling company performing one of the favourite operas – or several in succession.

Emperors did not find it beneath their dignity to attend and to patronise. Ch'ien Lung, always anxious to avoid any covert criticism of his dynasty and its alien origin (the Manchus), prescribed the costumes which could be shown on the stage; these were modelled on Ming styles, sufficiently different from the Manchu attire to leave no possibility of satire upon his officers and their rule. The Empress Dowager Tz'u Hsi, in the last age of the monarchy, was an ardent patron of the theatre and Chinese opera, although the performances she attended were enacted in her private theatres within the palace. A late flower of Chinese culture, drama is by no means the least.

The novel, like drama, was a later development in Chinese literature. There are no Han novels to match their Roman or Greek contemporaries and it would seem that in China the novel is unknown before Ming times. Short stories are older, but it was the prompt book of the storyteller, whose work was an oral tradition founded or assisted by a précis book, which gave birth to the Chinese novel. Using this material, men of letters began to record the whole story in detail, with the dialogue which the storyteller had used, but still retaining some conventions of the original source which reveal its origin. The early Chinese novels begin each chapter with the invocation: 'Honoured reader, you will recall how . . .' this or that event of the previous instalment; and end: 'Honoured reader, if you wish to know what next happened to so-and-so, please listen to the explanation in the next instalment.' After which one can imagine the hat being passed round for contributions. The stories were traditional, historical, mythological and perhaps, later, domestic; the last of these types often drawn from one chapter of a well-known historical novel and expanded into a full-length story.

The earliest of the classical novels is the *Romance of the Three Kingdoms*, a saga of the heroes of that age (AD 221–265) written from the standpoint of one who advocated the legitimate dynasty and unification of the empire. It was in fact written in the early Ming, when these ideas were held very strongly. This is perhaps the best of the historical novels, although it had several worthy imitators which followed the same pattern. Historical figures are the protagonists, but their lives, as known, are embellished with fictional episodes, characteristics and adventures. The story follows the main historical facts – one consequence being that as the novel is known to millions, whereas the historical texts are the preserve of scholars, the fictional version has largely displaced the historical story in the public mind.

One or two generations later the public mood had changed. The Shui Hu Ch'uan *Chronicle of the Waters and Lakes* is a tale of the Robin Hood type, in many episodes, which relates how worthy and honest men of all classes of society were driven by oppressive officials to seek refuge in the wilds and become outlaws. They form a band which holds an inaccessible mountain stronghold, from which they sally forth to deliver the oppressed, rescue the innocent victims of the officials and invariably, by cunning stratagems, defeat the feckless and cowardly forces of the government. The episodes which describe how the victim of official corruption or oppression lived, suffered and escaped are convincing accounts of social life, shown with individual treatment of very diverse characters. The novel is clearly subversive in tone and content, and was banned by the imperial government under both the Ming and the Ch'ing dynasties. It was none the less universally read and admired.

From one chapter of this work a later author constructed another novel, on the domestic theme of the lives of a rich young wastrel and his wives. *Chin P'ing Mei* (a title compounded of parts of the names of the three heroines) is frankly erotic, and was banned on that account, with no more effect. Modern taste would hardly find very much to surprise or to shock, and in general the novel is well constructed, and being solely concerned with the lives of the characters, not with political or historical themes, gives a vivid if somewhat exaggerated account of life in the late Ming period.

This theme was taken up, in more decorous style, by the greatest of the Chinese classical novels, *The Dream in the Red Chamber – Hung Lou Meng* – the story of a great family in the early Ch'ing (the seventeenth century) and its decline. It is supposed to be in part autobiographical, and certainly draws from the personal experience of the author. The interesting aspect of this book, apart from its fine literary quality, is that the hero and heroines are children and adolescents, and the theme is the constraint upon the young to obey their parents, marry as the elders wish, and suffer the frustrations of forbidden love and unwelcome careers. It is the first Chinese protest against the conventions of the old society, representing the parental generation as hidebound, harsh, insensitive and basically incompetent. These attitudes were no more pleasing to authority than those of earlier works, but their objections were equally fruitless.

The theme of myth and legend was also exploited in famous novels. The pilgrimage of the T'ang monk Hsüan Tsang to India to find sacred texts has been published in English under the title *Monkey*, translated by the late Arthur Waley. It tells of the adventures of the pilgrim and his companions, one of whom is the wilful, mischievous Monkey. Like Bunyan's *Pilgrim's Progress*, it is a religious work developing the idea of gradual enlightenment, but enlivened by excitement and adventure and with a large measure of supernatural events. Monkey is made to wear a tight iron helmet to control his impulses; at last the pilgrim tells him he may take it off, but by then Monkey no longer feels it, and had forgotten that he wore it.

All these novels became the subjects of plays and were very popular. They were known to all educated and many less well-educated people. They had many imitators, of varying quality. Yet the authors remain obscure figures, writing under pseudonyms, and have only been identified, sometimes tentatively, in recent years. Novels were not 'literature'. Men of learning should neither write nor read them. But if the identifications of modern scholars are correct, the *Romance of the Three Kingdoms* was written by a retired Grand Counsellor, and the others by men of reputation and high education.

This last active and innovating phase of the old literature has had an important influence on modern culture. The language of the novels is the colloquial of the educated people of their time, not the classical language of all other literature. It was thus there to provide a model for the reformers of the early twentieth century who wished to bring in a new colloquial style in literature, partly to promote popular education. The novels were rescued from official obloquy and became honoured classics; the subversive content of many was a further point in their favour during a revolutionary age. No longer do men of eminence and learning pretend never to have read them; Mao Tse-tung has acknowledged that they were his favourite books as a youth, and the proper social interpretation of the *Dream of the Red Chamber* has been a matter for political dispute among the intellectuals of the People's Republic. The assessment which should be made, and the value accorded to the old culture in all its forms, remains a matter of keen interest, debate and changing emphasis in modern China. There is not a repudiation of the past so much as a need to reinterpret it.

Part Two

The land and its people

1 Nature and the natural environment

Legend has it that the origins of a written language – the very foundation of Chinese culture date from the third millennium BC, when a dragon horse emerged from the depths of the Huang Ho bearing strange symbols on its back, and that adaptations of these markings were eventually shaped into characters. Certainly the earliest pictographs were simply drawings of objects, often natural phenomena. This response to nature reflects a basic force in the Chinese psyche. It has even been suggested that, as it was vitally necessary to control China's great river systems to prevent flooding and to provide irrigation, the art of writing developed in order to meet the administrative requirements of river control. The contrasting landscapes of China – majestic river valleys and vaporous hills in the east, and high-climbing mountains and raging torrents in the west – provided artists and poets with a 'cosmic inspiration; a feeling of affinity between the human spirit and the energies of the elements'. Also, both Confucianism and Taoism were greatly influenced by the natural world. Man's ideal was to live in harmony and tranquillity with nature; should the natural order be upset, disasters such as floods, droughts or earthquakes might occur, and dynasties topple.

In this predominantly agricultural society, nature influenced the ordering of everyday life, whether of emperor or of peasant. From the ninth century onwards construction work was influenced by the concept of *feng-shui* (literally 'wind and water'); houses, palaces, temples, roads, canals, bridges, mines, and even graves, were all sited and planned according to the *forms* of mountains, plains, rocks, water and vegetation. In the nineteenth and twentieth centuries, this principle hampered the building of railways and factories.

Up to the nineteenth century the Chinese empire evolved largely in isolation, and at the height of the Ch'ing dynasty was seemingly all-powerful, self-sufficient, resplendent. Towering mountain ranges, high, hostile plateaux and vast, blistering deserts constitute a formidable physical wall to the south, west and north which, though breached intermittently by nomadic raiders from the northern steppes, and by occasional explorers and traders, largely protected China from outside influences; while to the east the oceans were comparatively little exploited. Yet it was mainly along the eastern littoral that the impact of the western powers was felt, especially after 1840.

Although the dominant aspects of the country's physical and human geography remain apparently immutable constants in the Chinese equation, a marked discontinuity in the philosophical and practical approach to nature has occurred since 1949. Instead of living in peace with the physical world through meticulous husbanding of resources, an all-out, uncompromising and lasting war is to be waged against the environment; man is the superior force and will surely transform and conquer nature, strengthened in the knowledge that the harder the battle, the greater will be the victory. This stern ideology is epitomised in a Chinese fable which Mao Tse-tung retells in *The Foolish Old Man Who Removed the Mountains*. 'The Foolish Old Man's house faced south and beyond his doorway stood the two great peaks, Taihang and Wangwu, obstructing the way. He called his sons, and hoe in hand they began to dig up these mountains with great determination. Another greybeard known as the Wise Old Man, saw them and said derisively, "How silly of you to do this! It is quite impossible for you four to dig up these two huge mountains." The Foolish Old Man replied, "When I die, my sons will carry on; when they die, there will be my grandsons, and then their sons and grandsons, and so on to infinity. High as they are, the mountains cannot grow any higher and every bit we dig, they will be that much lower. Why can't we clear them away!" Having refuted the Wise Old Man's wrong view, he went on digging every day, unshaken in his conviction. God was moved by this, and he sent down two angels, who carried the mountains away on their backs.'

The Chinese refer to their own land as the Middle Kingdom, which draws attention to their traditional view of the world, with China at the centre, surrounded by concentric rings of states or zones, where Chinese influence diminished in more or less direct relation to the distance from the Chinese capital, yet whose rulers most fittingly owed tribute to the emperor, even if this was not always forthcoming. Indeed, the same basic order persists: China stands at the centre, while all other nations are, by definition, peripheral, and therefore inferior.

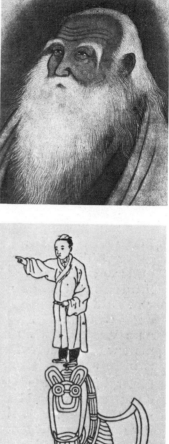

Above: A stone rubbing representation
of the philosopher Confucius.

Top: Lao-Tze, about whom
nothing certain is known, is
regarded as the founder of Taoism.
Above: The magnetic compass,
invented by the Chinese and first
used in the third century A.D.

Right, top to bottom: Taken
from a treatise written over
500 years ago, these diagrams
illustrate the correct application for
acupuncture treatment.
Papermaking is an ancient
Chinese skill; in this eighteenth-
century illustration the paper is
being made with bamboo leaves.
Preparation of the warp in the
manufacture of silk during the
seventeenth century.
Below: A woodcut from a
seventeenth-century book
demonstrating the process of
rice planting.

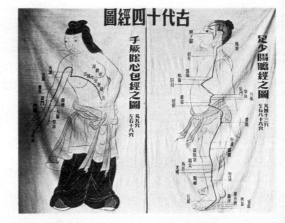

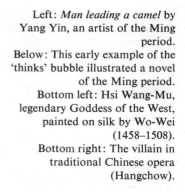

Left: *Man leading a camel* by Yang Yin, an artist of the Ming period.
Below: This early example of the 'thinks' bubble illustrated a novel of the Ming period.
Bottom left: Hsi Wang-Mu, legendary Goddess of the West, painted on silk by Wo-Wei (1458–1508).
Bottom right: The villain in traditional Chinese opera (Hangchow).

Top: The Japanese attack on Port
Arthur in 1894.
Left: A study of two Manchu ladies. Modern
Chinese dress for women has, perhaps
surprisingly, derived from this alien attire.
Above: A group of strolling players with
their performing animals, photographed
early in the present century.

Facing page: A group of mandarins
photographed in about 1875.
A military mandarin on horseback.
A scene in a high-class opium house
in about 1890.

Facing page: P'u-yi, the last
Manchu emperor, succeeded his
father in 1908, when this picture
was taken, at the age of three.

Top right: During the troubled
periods between the beginning of
this century and the Japanese war,
many Chinese – like these
provincial viceroys arriving under
escort at Shanghai – made use of
the security offered by the Treaty
Ports administered by the foreign
powers.

Right: A Cabinet meeting in 1913
during the attempt to set up a
constitutional government under
Sun Yat-sen, seen here presiding
over the meeting.

Below: A view of the central
street in the southern part of
Peking at the turn of the century.

Right: Physic Street, Canton in the early 1920s.
Below: The wearing of pigtails was imposed on the Chinese by the Manchus. After the fall of the dynasty in 1911 the habit gradually died out.

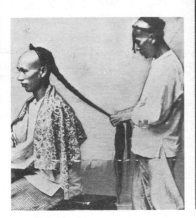

Right: A 'down with foreigners' demonstration in Shanghai in 1927, on the anniversary of the Nanking Road shootings of 1925.

Nodality is closely associated with size, for China is the third largest country in the world, after the Soviet Union and Canada. In fact, with an area of some 3.6 million square miles the People's Republic is much the same size as the United States, and stretches over distances of about two thousand miles from north to south and over three thousand miles east to west. Administratively the vast expanse of territory has always presented problems for the exercise of firm central control. In late Ch'ing times the journey from Peking to Lanchow took 55 days, to both Chengtu and Canton 90 days, and to Kunming, 110 days; by the 1940s these travelling times had been reduced to 7, 10, 3 and 10 days respectively. It used to take three months to travel by yak from Yaan in Szechuan to Lhasa in Tibet, and the road was only passable for three months in the year; the highway journey now takes two weeks. Currently, in terms of economic development, for example, distance is critical in the siting of industry. But, perhaps more important, geopolitically while the People's Republic consistently argues that it wants nothing of super-power status – believing that this would compromise its ambitions to lead the developing countries – its size nevertheless inevitably overshadows the remainder of Asia. In fact, especially since joining the United Nations in 1971, and despite the fact that it shares many characteristics of other developing countries (for instance resource base deficiencies and vulnerability to demographic pressures) China does rank as a great nation, and in future no meaningful 'world' decisions may be taken without its approval.

Spatial problems are also inherent in the extraordinary length of China's international boundary, some 20,000 kilometres (12,427 miles) long. This is shared with twelve other countries (Afghanistan, Bhutan, Burma, India, Laos, Mongolia, Nepal, North Korea, North Vietnam, Pakistan, Sikkim and the Soviet Union). Several frontiers are disputed and border issues continue to cloud Sino–Indian and Sino–Soviet relations. Furthermore, China claims that its territorial waters stretch as far south as latitude 4°N. These seas include over five thousand islands, ranging from provincial-scale Hainan and Taiwan to tiny, pin-prick rocks such as the Tiaoyutais (off north-east Taiwan), which have a significance out of all proportion to their size because it is reported that China's continental shelf possesses a huge off-shore oil potential. This partly explains why China supports Latin American claims for a 200-mile limit on territorial waters.

But what of the *quality* of the Chinese realm? On the one hand there is the view that because the country is so large it must be correspondingly rich. 'This Countrie May bee said to excell in these particulars: Antiquity, largenesse, Ritchenesse, healthynesse, Plentiffullnesse' (*The*

65

Travels of Peter Mundy in Europe and Asia 1608–1667) is a sentiment corroborated by a westerner in 1966: 'the riches of the Chinese earth are very great', and by Chinese reference to 'superior natural conditions'. On the other hand, their resource base is only incompletely known, even to the Chinese. Yet what have been appreciated for many years are the very real hardships imposed by the physical background and explosive demographic situation. Indeed, there is a tacit recognition of the natural limitations in the contemporary fight against nature. Some of these problems are highlighted in the review of relief, land forms, climate, soils, vegetation, flora and fauna and minerals below.

Relief and land forms

Generally high in the west and comparatively low in the east, the relief is arranged 'like a three-section staircase'. The Tsinghai–Tibet plateau in the west forms the highest land mass in the world, and is mostly over 4000 metres in height. To the north and east lies a great arc of plateaux and basins, comprising the second flight of steps, where the land drops away to between 2000 and 1000 metres above sea level. Much of the land in the third and lowest flight (other than the mountains in the south-east and a number of transverse ranges), is located in the most densely populated and economically most significant parts of China: the middle and lower reaches of the Yangtze, the North China Plain and the north-east plain, and lies below 500 metres in height.

It has been calculated that throughout almost ninety per cent of China the terrain limits or completely excludes human endeavours. About one-third of the country is mountainous, for example. The Himalayas include Mount Everest (called Jolmo Lungma by the Chinese), at 8882 metres the world's highest mountain. Another east–west range, the Chinling mountains, forms a natural divide between the temperate north and the subtropical south, while ranges running from north-east to south-west, especially the Greater Khingan and Taihang mountains, stand in the way of the south-east monsoon, forming a second divide between the moist east and the arid west.

Plateaux account for over a quarter of China's surface area. The largest are the Tsinghai–Tibet, Inner Mongolian, Loess and Yunnan–Kweichow plateaux. The limestone hills of Yunnan, Kweichow and Kwangsi, and the yellow earth of the loess compose some of the most distinctive Chinese landscapes. Covering 400,000 square kilometres and averaging over 1000 metres in height the Loess plateau is bounded by the Great Wall in the north, the Chinling range in the south, the

Taihang mountains in the east and the Wuhsiao mountains in the west. Loess is a loose, loamy soil, yellowish in colour, carried by the wind from the highland deserts of Inner Mongolia over hundreds of thousands of years, and laid down in deposits of between 50 and 100 metres in thickness. Sparse vegetation and the heavy concentration of summer rains has resulted in devastating soil erosion over the centuries, leaving a landscape 'scarred and disfigured', distorted by deep gullies and precipitous cliffs. It is no accident that the nationally famous model village of Tachai is located in these badlands (see pages 100–101).

Totally different environments are found in China's great interior basins, which together occupy twenty per cent of the country. On the one hand, there is the very densely peopled, immensely fertile, well-watered rice-bowl of the Red Basin of Szechuan – so called because of the colour of the soil, although the jade hues of the terraced rice fields, which lace the countryside with an intricate cobweb, are as characteristic; on the other hand, the Tarim basin of Sinkiang has China's largest (320,000 square kilometres) desert at its heart, the Taklamakan.* The Tarim is one of the world's biggest inland-drainage basins. Water comes mainly from the melting snows in the surrounding mountains, and feeds a string of oasis settlements along the fringe of the desert, farms producing wheat, maize, rice, cotton, hemp and fruits. Lopnor (a salt lake) is the main nuclear testing site. A third basin, the Tsaidam in Tsinghai, is earmarked for rapid future economic expansion as, like the Tarim and Dzungarian (also in Sinkiang) basins, it is rich in coal, iron, oil and other non-ferrous metals.

A further ten per cent of China's land area may be classified as hill country, found mainly in Fukien, Chekiang, Kiangsi, Hunan, Shantung and Liaoning.

Finally, the remaining twelve per cent is made up of plains. The three largest, each about 300,000 square kilometres in area, are the North China, the Middle and Lower Yangtze, and the north-east plains, the first-named of which saw the birth and initial flush of Chinese civilisation, and the last the most recent major expansion of Chinese population. But it is perhaps the Yangtze valley which typifies Chinese rural scenery, a landscape criss-crossed by rivers and studded with jewel-like lakes. The delta is known as the 'water country', 'the land of fish and rice', for cheek by jowl between the water courses are paddy fields, mulberry trees, bamboo groves and fish ponds. Ponds are dug and the earth is piled up around them, so that fish may be bred in the pools, while mulberry or fruit trees are planted on the embankments. A

* The name is a Uighur word meaning 'go in and you won't come out'.

67

delicate symbiosis results as pond mud is used to fertilise the embankment crops, while mulberry leaves and silkworm droppings go to feed the fish.

Land use

The above account of the regional diversity of China underlines the tremendous range in the productive capacity of its agricultural areas between, say, the high yields of over 1000 *jin* (a *jin* = 1.1 lb) per *mou* (a *mou* = one-sixth of an acre) in the southerly Pearl River delta and those of pioneer lands in Heilungkiang or Sinkiang. Official Chinese land-use figures indicate much the same sort of problem. Only eleven per cent of China's land is used for agriculture, with an additional twelve per cent classified as reclaimable wasteland. However, while they claim that the cultivated area can be more than doubled, the Chinese rarely draw attention to the high investment cost measured in money and manpower. Roughly ten per cent is forested and about twenty-eight per cent is pastureland. Thus almost forty per cent of the total area of China remains unclassified, and is presumably largely wasteland by virtue of being too high, too dry, too cold or too isolated.

Water resources

China has often been described as land where there is either far too much water, leading to flooding, or alternatively far too little, with resulting droughts. This is due to the climate (see pages 71–74), but is also caused by the unruly character of its rivers. The three best known rivers, flowing west to east across northern, central and southern China respectively, are the Yellow River (Huang Ho), 4845 kilometres in length; the Yangtze, 5800 kilometres long and with a drainage basin covering a fifth of the country, inhabited by at least 250 million people; and the Sikiang, 2100 kilometres long. Of these perhaps the most famous is the Yellow River, or 'China's Sorrow'. Over the last two thousand years the river in its lower reaches has burst its banks 1500 times and there have been 1070 droughts; on twenty-six separate occasions there were major changes in its course – sometimes it entered the sea to the south of the Shantung peninsula, sometimes, as now, to the north. As it cut its way through the friable loess-lands, the river used to carry away a thousand million tons of silt each year, some of which it deposited as it flowed across the North China Plain. Countless lives were lost in the floods, which affected an area of a quarter of a million square kilometres. In an attempt to slow down the Japanese advance in 1938, the

Kuomintang bombed the dyke at Huayuankow, near Chengchow, causing flooding over an area of 54,000 square kilometres in Honan, Anhwei and Kiangsu, in which 890,000 people were drowned and 12.5 million people were left homeless. In an attempt to control the Yellow River permanently, since 1949 five major water conservation centres have been established along the river and its tributaries, and it is claimed that each centre has developed a huge drainage, irrigation and power generation capacity. Afforestation schemes and the construction of thousands of reservoirs help to check erosion and the danger of flood. Since 1949, too, it is claimed that all the 1800 kilometres of dykes along the lower course of the river have been heightened and strengthened, to prove that 'the people are stronger than the river, that the Yellow River can be conquered'.

In the field of flood control it is 'man's will, not heaven' that decides. Two projects, along the Huai and Haiho Rivers, have become more or less symbolic of the struggle against nature, and both schemes have received Mao Tse-tung's personal blessing. Progress in the case of the Haiho work, for example, is said to have made three provinces in the 265,000 square kilometre basin self-sufficient in grain production for the first time in history, so that they no longer need to import grain from regions to the south.

Some current water-control projects involve the restoration and expansion of ancient systems. In western Szechuan, at Kuanhsien (north-west of Chengtu), the turbulent Min River enters an immensely rich agricultural plain. As long ago as 320 BC the river was dredged at this point to counter flooding, and in 250 BC a scheme for more permanent control was begun. An irrigation network was built, consisting of 2000 dykes, ten trunk and 520 branch canals. The dykes were made from sausage-shaped baskets of woven bamboo filled with stones, a technique which is still used over two thousand years later. Because of silting, by 1949 flooding was again causing extensive damage and the irrigated area was reduced from 200,000 to 134,000 hectares. Renovation carried out since then has improved the effectiveness of the Tukiangyen scheme, and by 1971 467,000 hectares could be irrigated.

China's lakes, of course, provide natural reservoirs. In the north and west of the country they are generally salt, and in the south and east mostly freshwater lakes. The latter provide irrigation water, transport and fish-breeding facilities, while 'some are the sites of health and pleasure resorts'. The lakes of the interior, on the other hand, provide raw materials such as salt and alkali for the chemical industry. Altogether there are over 130 lakes, exceeding one hundred square kilometres in area. The Chinese expression 'five lakes and four seas' – which means all corners of the land – refers to Poyang (4000 square kilometres), Tungting, Hungtse, Taihu and Chao lakes, situated north and south of the Yangtze.

An additional source of water is locked up in China's alpine glaciers, which occupy 44,000 square kilometres in the Altai, Tienshan, Kulun, Chilien and Himalayan mountains, and contain a potential source of 2,300,000 million cubic metres of water. Melted summer snow and ice provide almost all the water in the rivers which feed the oases in the Dzungarian, Tarim and Turfan basins and the farmland and pastures in southern Tibet. Chinese scientists are studying how to speed up the melting processes by spreading black powder over the surface of the glaciers.

Apart from irrigation and transport, water is also a source of power, and it is claimed that China ranks high in terms of hydro-electric power potential. Yet the richest hydro-electric power resources, in the Hengtuan mountains, are both isolated and extremely difficult to reach. Similarly nothing has been heard of the progress on the Sanmen Gorge (Yellow River) multi-purpose project for many years. Some sources have suggested that despite erosion control programmes upstream from the dam, silting has seriously hampered the scheme; alternatively, that the electric power generated is used to feed China's nuclear programme, instead of providing irrigation for crops.

There are physical hazards in connection with the breaking-in of new, and the improvement of existing agricultural lands. Irrigation may cause salination and poisoning of the soil, just as deep-ploughing may in its turn lead to the creation of dust-bowls. Use of underground water resources may indeed offer 'the permanent solution to the problem of insufficient water resources above ground', but by digging too many wells in a particular locality the level of the water-table may drop excessively and the wells run dry. A related problem was revealed as long ago as 1921, when it was discovered that like Venice, Shanghai was sinking; by 1965 the worst affected areas had sunk 2.37 metres from the earlier four metres above sea level. Apparently it was only during the 1960s that the reason for the subsidence was confirmed, the phenomenon being most pronounced where textile mills were pumping up large quantities of subterranean water for industrial cooling purposes. Between 1966 and 1971 the Shanghai Hydro-geological Brigade devised a system for continuing to draw off water during the summer months, and recharging the wells, and hence the water-table and land surface, during winter. The surface recharging process involves a complex arrangement by which the starting of pumping operations has to be synchronised and the stopping staggered. Not only has the brigade prevented further subsidence but they have actually made the ground rise 16 millimetres, 'using Chairman Mao's philosophical thinking to guide them'.

Climate

The regional disparities in water resource, with, generally, a surplus in the south and a deficit in the north, are aggravated by the seasonal incidence of rainfall. Located in the south-eastern segment of Eurasia, the world's largest continent, and flanked by the world's largest ocean, the Pacific, China has a climate dominated by a monsoonal régime. Because of the different heat-absorbing capacity of land and water, the land mass warms more quickly in summer than the sea. Air pressure is relatively low over central Asia, therefore, and high over the Pacific during the summer months. Rain-bearing winds blow on-shore pre-dominantly from the south-east but also from the south-west. In winter this fundamental pattern is reversed with dry, off-shore winds, blowing mainly from the north-west. Given the size of the country and the complex nature of the terrain – where, for instance, mountains may protect a region like Szechuan from invasion by cold waves, or may create rain-shadow conditions and deprive an area of rainfall – all kinds of weather is experienced, ranging from cold continental in the extreme north-east to tropical maritime in the far south. This makes it possible to grow a wide variety of crops. At the same time the climate is notoriously fickle and natural calamities are common. However, 'if the people understand the laws of their climate they can make best use of a favour-able climate for production and overcome difficulties caused by an unfavourable one'. (See pages 72–73 for comments on desert and snow control.)

Over most of China the annual rainfall is heavily concentrated into a few, all-too-short summer months. The country may be more or less equally divided into humid and arid areas: humid and semi-humid; semi-arid and arid. Most of the south-eastern part of the country falls within the humid zone, receiving an average rainfall of over 750 mm ($29\frac{1}{2}$ ins); indeed along the coast it often exceeds 2000 mm ($78\frac{3}{4}$ ins), and south of the Yangtze and on the Yunnan–Kweichow plateau preci-pitation is about 1000 mm ($39\frac{3}{8}$ ins). Semi-humid conditions extend over parts of the North China and north-east plains and the south-eastern part of the Tsinghai–Tibet plateau, with averages of 500 mm ($19\frac{3}{4}$ ins), compared with the somewhat higher range along the Yellow River valley itself of from 600 to 800 mm ($23\frac{5}{8}$ to $31\frac{1}{2}$ ins). Average rainfall decreases to 300 mm (11¾ ins) in the semi-arid zone, over most of the remainder of the Tsinghai–Tibet, Loess and Inner Mongolian plateaux. Finally, the arid zone embraces the north-western Tsinghai–Tibet plateau, the western part of Inner Mongolia and Sinkiang, where the rainfall falls below 250 mm (9¾ ins), and where there are extensive deserts. Over the country as a whole more than eighty per cent of the year's rainfall occurs between May and October, while in both the semi-humid and semi-arid zones the heaviest rains fall in July and August.

Deserts blanket over one million square kilometres (out of a total of 9.6 million), running in a northern belt between the Taklamakan and Kurban–Tungut deserts in the west and the Khorchin and Hulubuir 'sandy lands' in the east. And (until recently at any rate) the deserts have been on the march, moving southwards, swallowing up villages and agricultural land. In the past 250 years, for example, the Maowusu desert in southern Inner Mongolia has shifted 60 kilometres. Certain localities have been successful in checking the encroaching deserts by planting shelter belts, providing irrigation and fixing, or even removing, sand dunes. Hengshan county, south-west of Yulin (Shensi), has converted 330,000 *mou* of sand wastes into farmland or woodland. A 1600 kilometre-long sand break is reported as skirting the southern fringe of the Tyngeri desert in Kansu, while in Sinkiang it is claimed that since 1949 the area of cultivated land has been increased two and a half times, mainly as a result of desert reclamation.

Short of water, the deserts overheat during the day, yet freeze at night. Temperatures over the country at large reveal comparatively equable conditions in summer, with July averages of about 28 ° C in the south and more than 20 °C over much of Heilungkiang. The average temperatures in Canton in the south and Harbin in the north differ by as little as 5 °C (41 °F) in summer, compared with 33 °C (91 °F) in winter, when northern temperatures drop dramatically. Just as the south-eastern coast is liable to be ravaged by typhoons in summer, in winter an average of five or six cold waves strike the more northerly regions as cold air accumulates over Asia and 'explodes southward in a howling north wind that causes a sharp drop in temperature', so that 'the north is bound in ice and snow'.

Again nature has flung down a gauntlet, promptly picked up by the Chinese. In Sinkiang's Tienshan mountains, snow often brought road traffic to a halt from October to April. Recent experiments have made it possible to implement a comprehensive plan which has eliminated the danger of snow-blockage on more than half the threatened highway sections; the work places the primary emphasis on prevention, clearance by snow ploughs playing only a secondary role. These preventive methods include the erection of snow-fences and wind-deflection panels, recambering of road surfaces and recontouring of sideslopes.

China is a country which has suffered from innumerable physical disasters throughout recorded time – hence the unenviable name 'land of famine'. Snow, ice, frost, hail, flood, drought, insect and plant pests, earthquakes and typhoons are common experiences. In 1877–8 a drought famine hit the provinces of Shensi, Shansi, Honan and Hopei, which cost between nine and thirteen million lives. The imperial commissioner described the scene in Shansi during the winter of 1877: 'Sometimes my cart had to detour in order to avoid rolling over human skeletons which piled up on the highways. Many of those still alive fell flat on the ground after calling for help . . . all that my eyes could see were those thin and emaciated human figures and all that my ears could hear were the howls of males and screams of females.'

Yet famine has allegedly been banished from the land since 1949: in this respect improved communications and distribution facilities must have been critical. As in India, the behaviour of the summer monsoon is absolutely vital. In 1954, for example, cold air from the north blocked the advance of the monsoon so that the belt of heavy rain lingered over the Yangtze and Huai basins until late July, causing the most serious flooding in a hundred years. In 1959, on the other hand, the monsoon struck with particular force so that the belt of heavy rain moved north faster than normal, resulting in a two-month drought in the Yangtze, and flooding further north. 1959 was the first of 'three bitter years', when 650 million *mou* were affected by calamities. This area, it has been asserted, increased to 900 million *mou*, or half the total cultivated area, in both 1960 and 1961.

Following hard on the heels of the 'Great Leap Forward' in 1958 (see pages 86–87), the Chinese economy ran into serious difficulties. There were agricultural short-falls, and there were grave food shortages in the winter of 1960–1. In fact the natural disasters were exaggerated and exploited as excuses for human errors in planning – man-made disasters. Weather, however, continues as a dialectical spur and the 1971 and 1972 harvests were both reaped in the face of calamities. 'The country suffered the most serious drought in several decades in 1972. Some areas were also hit by waterlogging, frost, windstorms, hail and insects . . . The drought in Hopei was the most serious since 1920. Most of the reservoirs dried up and the water table of the wells sank . . . The dry spell in Shansi was the longest since 1877, with rainfall less than half that of any previous year. Hsiyang County, where the famous Tachai production brigade is located, did not have a saturating rain for 300 days.'

Hence special force attaches to Mao's injunction: *Be prepared against war, be prepared against natural disaster, and do everything for the people.**

Soils

Owing to the action of wind and water, the stripping of vegetation and farming malpractices, the devastation caused by soil erosion presents difficulties in widely separated parts of the country almost serious enough to have given birth to the proverb: 'Once the skin is gone, where can the hair grow?' Yet China is a land where traditionally man has enjoyed a profoundly intimate relationship with the natural environment. 'There is no other peasantry in the world which gives such an impression of absolute genuineness and of belonging so much to the soil . . . Man belongs to the soil, not the soil to man.'

A common misconception persists that the agricultural land is *naturally* very fertile. This is not so; in fact forty per cent of the soils are termed poor – partly because the soils have been overworked and have become exhausted, partly because of erosion and partly because of their chemical composition and physical structure. Admittedly, the black earths (chernozems) of the north-east plain and the soils of the Red Basin of Szechuan are extremely rich. Generally, however, China's agricultural lands are so hungry for fertilisers, whether human† or artificial, that the night soil collector has become a contemporary folk-hero, likely to retain this elevated status until the factories can produce sufficient chemical fertilisers, for at the moment industry supplies less than half the quantity needed. Also, while soil conservation and amelioration programmes have brought undoubted benefit to some parts of the country since 1949,‡ according to a recent Soviet source 'the soils of many regions of China have been subjected to washout' and soil fertility has been 'significantly reduced'.

---

* At the same time the Chinese are not afraid to draw a different conclusion from Russian experience: 'Fairly big natural calamities hit the Soviet Union last year (1972) and agricultural production was affected. But the fundamental reason for the failure in Soviet agriculture lies in the series of revisionist policies pursued by the Soviet revisionist ruling clique.'

† An account of the setting up of a commune in Szechuan in 1958 relates how there was 'an old belief that people would go blind if night soil or cow manure were used to enrich the soil'.

‡ 'The nationwide mass movement to transform China's mountains and rivers is moving another step ahead to rational utilisation of land resources and improvement of soil centred around soil conservation' (*China Reconstructs*, 1972).

Flora and fauna

The destruction of the woodlands and forests of China proper is graphically described in a fourteenth-century source from Shansi: '. . . axes fell like rain, and shouts shook the mountain . . . As a result, the land of fresh, shady scenery began to look like a pasture for cattle and horses.' Cumulatively, centuries of tree felling and fuel scavenging have resulted in the over-concentration of China's timber reserves in the north-eastern parts of the country, with sixty per cent of the forest resources forming a horse-shoe shaped belt in the Greater and Lesser Khinghan mountains and the Changpaishan massif. Thus the main region for commercial timber production is comparatively remote and its climate difficult. At the same time, the transport network has been extended since 1949 and timber is produced the year round, instead of following the former pattern of felling in winter and moving the timber in summer. A hundred new small towns and lumber camps have been established in the Lesser Khinghans alone.

As well as these cold-temperate deciduous pine and temperate deciduous broadleaf forests, south of the Chinling Shan-Huai River line are subtropical evergreen forests and, in the far south, tropical rain-forests. However, while Chinese sources claim that vast areas of natural vegetation remain, there is in fact a serious lack of workable timber, certainly at local level where, for example, boats, pit props and railway sleepers are made of concrete. Nevertheless, throughout China afforestation work carried out by the communes, especially in winter, is of considerable importance, not only in improving the supply of timber but also in checking soil crosion. Similarly, in the lumber areas of the north-east and south-west replanting is undertaken along with felling to meet future demands.

The vast size of China ensures that both the flora and fauna are extremely varied: there are almost 30,000 species of higher plants, 1150 species of birds and 409 species of animals, perhaps the most famous being the giant panda from the bamboo groves of the south-western mountains. Hunting animals and birds for food and pelts provides an important supplementary income to communes in mountainous regions. Animals, such as the horse in Inner Mongolia, the Bactrian camel in Sinkiang and the yak in Tibet, provide transport, while the water buffalo is prized as a draught animal in the rice-growing lands of south China.

Breeding farms have been established for fur-bearing animals such as sable, otter, mink and coypu, as well as deer. Deer antlers are used in traditional Chinese medicine and they are much sought after as an aphrodisiac, particularly by overseas Chinese. In one particular deer farm set up in Heilungkiang as recently as 1968, the deer were kept in enclosures to begin with; because they did not develop properly it was decided to raise them on an open range basis. But the deer were very shy, and easily frightened by people, other animals and strange noises. To overcome the first two problems the deer were bribed with titbits and gradually introduced to other animals. As for noise, the farm workers drove tractors, blew car horns and let off firecrackers near the deer enclosure to acclimatise them.

A number of nature reserves have been opened in order to protect rare species as well as animals and birds which are economically valuable. During the mid-1950s there was a campaign to wipe-out 'the four pests', rats, flies, mosquitoes and sparrows. When an excessive number of caterpillars were discovered, it was decided to reprieve the sparrows and substitute bed-bugs. Latterly, 'protection of insect-eating birds such as titmice, and hanging up nesting boxes for them have been a boon (in) eliminating insect pests'.

Minerals

For strategic reasons information concerning the Chinese mineral base is incomplete. Northern China has long been known to possess rich coal and iron ore deposits. Since the beginning of the Cultural Revolution (1966) many small coal mines have been opened, particularly south of the Yangtze, in regions previously considered to be lacking in coal.

Until recently at least, China's known oil reserves were meagre. Output is about twenty million tons a year – minute when compared with the huge population. Yet China claims self-sufficiency in oil and may soon export a million tons of oil a year to Japan. Also new discoveries, especially of off-shore reserves, may alter the picture radically in the near future.

China has abundant reserves of manganese, tungsten and molybdenum, vast salt fields, moderate quantities of sulphur and comparatively large amounts of tin, fluorite, graphite, magnesite, talc, asbestos and barytes. Copper, zinc, lead and nickel are in short supply, and phosphates need development. Great stress has been laid on the discovery of many new minerals during the Cultural Revolution, and the opening-up of regions like the Tsaidam basin in Tsinghai, but the relative distance of such areas from industrial centres reduces the economic significance of the finds. However, current policies are seeking to decentralise industrial activity in China, and in this context recent discoveries are important at local rather than national level. The point to be emphasised is that China is not so richly endowed with minerals that it will be in a position to join the ranks of the major industrial countries of the world in the immediate future.

2   The structure of population

Just as any assessment of the Chinese model of economic development must consider the physical background and the striking regional contrasts, so is an awareness of the main characteristics of population absolutely fundamental. And, again, like nature, people constitute an ideological issue. Given a population of almost 900 million people, or between twenty and twenty-five per cent of the world's total population, the demographic situation poses immense problems of providing adequate food, clothes, houses, schools and medical facilities. Even more daunting is the reproductive potential of the existing population. The Chinese believe that the great numbers of Chinese represent a productive force of unparalleled might. Mao Tse-tung, in 1958, recognised that the Chinese 'have two remarkable peculiarities, they are, first of all, poor, and secondly, blank'. Here the dialectic emerges once again: '*That may seem like a bad thing, but it is really a good thing.* Poor people want change, want to do things, want revolution. A clean sheet of paper has no blotches, and so the newest and most beautiful words can be written on it, the newest and most beautiful pictures can be painted on it ... The working people ... of China have really begun to rule this land' (italics added).

Ideology apart, with a population of 895 million in 1973,* China is confronted by demographic pressures of potentially frightening proportions. These strains are aggravated by the imbalance of population distribution, with extremely high densities on the more fertile agricultural land in the south-eastern half of the country. Thus while the average population density may be about 250 people per square mile, the *nutritional density* approaches something like ten times this figure, or 2500 per square mile, with substantially higher figures in the high-

* The highest figure in Chinese sources is 830 million in 1971.

yield farming districts. Expressed in another way: ninety per cent of the population is concentrated into fifteen per cent of the surface area of China.

Also relevant in terms of the composition of population are the racial, religious and linguistic patterns; features such as age–sex ratios, and birth, death and natural increase rates.

Six per cent of China's total population, or about fifty-five million people, are not Chinese ethnically, but belong to one or another of fifty-four so-called 'national minority' groups, some distinctive in their religious beliefs, as in the case of Buddhist Tibet or Muslim Sinkiang; some traditionally engaged in alternative economic systems like the Mongols, Kirghiz and Kazakhs who are nomadic pastoralists, or others in the south-west who practise shifting cultivation, and still others who were and are mainly hunters and fishermen. Living mostly in the peripheral parts of the country, these non-Chinese peoples have proved difficult to integrate with present-day Chinese society. Since 1949, there has been constant friction between 'great Han chauvinism' and 'local nationalism', leading to a number of serious anti-Chinese rebellions in both Tibet and Sinkiang.

Besides the various minority languages, there are seven major Chinese dialects, some of which, for example Mandarin and Cantonese, are not mutually intelligible. It was thus necessary to adopt as the national language a modified version of the Peking dialect, although bilingualism persists. A Chinese source indicated last year (1972) that although the dialects remain very strong, 'In performing their functions, organs of self-government of (national minority) autonomous areas employ the spoken and written language or languages commonly used' by the local inhabitants.

While there are several different dialects, there is a common though complex written language. Language reform has involved the simplification of over two thousand characters, which, according to *Red Flag* in 1972, is merely a step towards the ultimate replacement of the ancient characters by the Roman phonetic alphabet. In 1949 ninety-five per cent of the population was unable to read and write. One western source believes that seventy-five per cent of the adult population remains illiterate. A 1973 description of a commune in Hupeh gives some idea of the problem. Less than one per cent of the local population was literate in 1949. Now 4350 people, or nearly half the population, are enroled in seventy-seven regular night schools. 'At nightfall, diligent peasant-students arrive promptly at their well-lit classrooms to learn to read and write, study proletarian politics and science and technology. . . . Schooling equivalent to that of primary school has been provided for

290 people who were illiterate. Another 120 who could read and write a little have reached middle-school level.' What does this convey in terms of day-to-day practical issues? Back in the late 1950s one aspect of the Great Leap Forward was that many people doing accounting work at local level were at best only semi-literate, and statistical chaos ensued. During the cultural revolution the national education system was suspended, initially for a period of six months while new syllabuses were drawn up, but in effect for as long as four years in many regions. The impact upon the literacy programmes in particular and on educational progress in general must have been disastrous.

It is possible to regard Chinese society as polarised by its age structure, for a vital gap has opened up between the miniscule, ageing leadership on the one hand, and the teeming, youthful population at large on the other, as two-thirds of the population is under thirty years old. Part of the logic behind the Cultural Revolution was that the young Red Guards would be worthy heirs to the Chinese revolution, but in fact youth came into conflict mostly with the middle echelons and middle-aged members of the government. A young population then, fertile in a revolutionary sense and certainly fertile in terms of population growth potential.

Generally, the imbalance in the sex-ratio between males and females is not especially important in explaining population growth trends. But the changing role of women in China has wider economic implications. Full sexual equality is probably acknowledged by most young people although while women make major contributions to both agricultural and industrial output, their remuneration is not always equal to a man's. Among older people, however, there is strong resistance to 'women's lib'. Hearing that women wished to go deep-sea fishing, a Liaoning commune fisherman exploded: 'That's like a baby chick trying to eat a soyabean – she'll choke on it!' Nevertheless Chinese women are determined to prove the truth of the folk saying: 'Women hold up half of the heaven.'

Before 1949 birth and death rates were both high. Marked improvements in the health services have lowered death rates from 25 per thousand in 1952 to 15 per thousand in 1970. Meanwhile birth rates have remained comparatively high, falling from 45 to 37 per thousand in the same period, during which the natural increase rose and fell several times, yet grew slightly from 20 to 22 per thousand between 1952 and 1970. In April this year (1973) Chou En-lai stated that China hopes to reduce the growth rate to 15 per thousand by 1980, admitting this objective 'is very difficult'. By 1978 the population will probably exceed 1000 million, to reach 1300 million by 1990.

Birth control

Given this massive growth in the number of Chinese, what measures, if any, have been taken to check the rate of natural increase? At a time when the country was beset by grave economic setbacks, in 1961, Chou En-lai dismissed population pressure, high densities, manpower deployment and shortages of arable land and grain supplies as problems confronting the country's planners. In the early 1950s birth control was denounced as simply 'a means of killing the Chinese people without shedding blood'. There was no mention of family planning in the text of the first five-year plan, 1953–7. It was during this time, however, in 1956, that the first campaign for family limitation was begun, and the following year the minister of public health declared that 'if our population growth is not in accordance with planned childbirth, it will prevent our country from quickly ridding itself of poverty and from becoming prosperous and powerful . . .'

Much more frequently, though, the necessity for birth control is rationalised by drawing attention to the improvements in maternal and child health and welfare and only by extension to 'the prosperity of the nation'. In any event at the time of the Great Leap Forward the campaign was abandoned. Instead it was argued that there was actually a manpower shortage: 'as we see it, the more people the better'. A second family planning campaign was instituted in 1962, coinciding with the economic difficulties. But the whole problem appears to have received little attention in the most virulent phases of the Cultural Revolution. although greater prominence has been given to family planning since 1969.

In the first campaign conventional western contraceptive techniques were used, late marriage was encouraged and abortion and the sterilisation of either partner were legalised. Also various herbalist remedies were advocated: 'Fresh tadpoles coming out in the spring should be washed clean in cold well water, and swallowed whole three or four days after menstruation. If a woman swallows fourteen live tadpoles on the first day and ten more on the following day, she will not conceive for five years. If contraception is still required after that, she can repeat the formula twice, and be forever sterile . . . This formula is good in that it is effective, safe, and inexpensive. The defect is that it can be used only in the spring.'

The importance of limiting the size of families to three, and preferably only two children, and of spacing births, has been stressed in each campaign. Intra-uterine devices and birth control pills have been made available on a limited scale in the second and third campaigns; and late marriage is still advised, about twenty-five for women and thirty for men.

To date, there is no indication that the Chinese have achieved a break-through in population control. On the contrary they recognise that they 'have been racing against time to cope with the enormous increase in population'. This is especially true when measured against the physical problems already outlined and against actual economic performance (see pages 98–99). A solitary and stark example illustrates this point. The Chinese claimed to have reaped a harvest of 250 million tons in 1958; in 1972 the harvest was 240 million tons, yet between 1958 and 1972 the population increased by well over 200 million.

3 Economic growth and technological change

The paramount significance of agriculture is best appreciated if it is understood that not only must China's fields produce enough food to feed the population, but also that the communes have to provide industrial crops and a surplus revenue for investment in industry. Moreover, unlike the Russian revolution, a proletarian uprising, the Chinese revolution was essentially a peasant movement. However, as after 1949 the Chinese copied the Soviet–Marxist blueprint for economic development, which favours the rapid expansion of heavy industry, the industrial programme is described before agriculture.

To provide a framework it is helpful to divide the 1949–73 period into planning phases. First came three years of reconstruction, 1949 to 1952, when a war-torn land was set painfully on its feet. The first five-year plan, 1953–7, registered considerable gains and confirmed the predominant role of industry, but in the process agricultural investment was disastrously neglected. Heavy industrial development lay at the heart of the second five-year plan, begun in 1958 – the year which also witnessed the Great Leap Forward and the establishment of the communes – and which ran nominally until the end of 1962. After only three years the Chinese claimed that they had met the targets set by the plan. In fact by the winter of 1960–1 the economy had run into serious difficulties, food was in short supply and factory output greatly reduced, and as a result China relied upon annual accounting between 1961 and 1965. Planning priorities were reversed in an all-out attempt to save agricultural production. A record harvest was claimed in 1966, the first year of the third five-year plan, and the year which marked the public phase of the Cultural Revolution. Further record harvests were reported in 1967, 1970 and 1971, the last year being the opening year of the fourth five-year plan, although the 1972 harvest fell back to the 1970 level, apparently because of natural calamities. Meanwhile industrial production made a comparatively good recovery to top the 1960 peaks by a growing margin in both 1971 and 1972.

Industrial location

Chinese policies towards industrial location are particularly important. Before 1949 factories were found mainly in the north-east and east, in Manchuria, Shanghai and Tientsin. Generally industry (mostly light industries such as textiles and food processing) was poorly developed, and was often financed or owned by foreigners. After 1949 the Chinese resolved to relocate industrial activity, to disperse it more evenly throughout the country. There were several reasons for this.

Firstly, the existing distribution was an unwanted reminder of the imperialist heritage. Secondly, over-concentration along the coastal fringe meant that the factories were vulnerable to attacks from the sea. Thirdly, plants could and should be sited more rationally, near to raw materials, power supplies, labour and markets. Lastly, it was intended to 'develop the economy of backward areas', which included national minority regions, where it was hoped economic penetration would result in tighter political control over the remoter parts of the country. The first five-year plan recognised, however, that 'the utilisation, reconstruction, and extension of existing industrial bases is a prerequisite for the establishment of new industrial bases'. Above all else, 'we must avoid over-concentration'.

The first five-year plan set out three broad locational aims. An integrated iron and steel works at Anshan, a second steel plant at Penki, the expansion of the coal centres of Fushun, Fuhsin and Hokang, a machine-building works at Shenyang and power installations in Kirin together formed a north-eastern complex which it was hoped would feed the construction of new industrial zones. This should be completed as far as possible under the first five-year plan. Also, new industrial areas were to be built in north, north-west and central China 'so that two new industrial bases centred on the integrated iron and steel works in Paotow and Wuhan can be established during the period of the second five-year plan'. Finally, but much less important, industrialisation was to be fostered in south-west China.

Thus under the 1953–7 plan, the northern half of the country, especially the north-east, received the lion's share of investment, and cities such as Peking, Paotow, Taiyuan, Sian and Lanchow, and the oil fields of Yumen (Kansu) and Karamai (Sinkiang) began to emerge as heavy industrial foci, while light industrial and handicraft centres were more widespread. The growth of southern centres like Hangchow

(Chekiang), Tayeh (Hupeh), Canton (Kwangtung), Liuchow (Kwangsi), Kunming (Yunnan), and Chengtu and Chungking (both Szechuan) was slower, although these cities were earmarked for future development. Meanwhile, Shanghai, by far the largest and most exposed single industrial centre, continued to outstrip all rivals.

From 1958 onwards the drive to relocate industry has continued, for if the scheme lost impetus during the difficulties encountered in the early 1960s, this was more than compensated for by the movement to set up small- and medium-scale enterprises which has intensified following the onset of the Cultural Revolution. 'The geographical distribution of China's industry has been brought into accord with the policy that a nationwide dispersal of enterprises should be accompanied by regional concentration. . . . China's industrial construction has also pursued the policy of integration of industry and agriculture and of town and countryside' (see pages 91–92). 'Many newly-built factories are scattered in the rural areas. This enables members of rural people's communes to take part in industrial construction and the families of workers and staff members to participate in agricultural production.' In this manner industry and agriculture support each other.

Recent estimates give some indication of success in shifting the balance of industrial production away from the coast. If 'coastal' is equated with the three centrally administered municipalities of Peking, Shanghai and Tientsin, and the seven maritime provinces of Liaoning, Hopei, Shantung, Kiangsu, Chekiang, Fukien and Kwangtung, then between 1952 and 1957 the inland zone increased in relative importance (measured in industrial output) from thirty-two to thirty-six per cent; by 1965 it had grown to forty-four per cent; by 1970 to forty-five per cent; and 'by 1975, more than half of the total industrial production will probably originate in the inland area'.

Curiously, there is a strange irony in all this, because having established atomic plants in the interior of the country, notably at Lanchow and in Sinkiang, strategic installations are now exposed to potential rocketry attacks from the Soviet Union. One western source even goes so far as to claim that in 1969 the Soviet Union seriously contemplated the 'nuclear castration' of China, and that it was only prevented from such action by United States' intervention.

Production performance

In the three years of reconstruction, 1949 to 1952, China equalled or improved most pre-1949 industrial production peaks. During the subsequent first five-year plan the central objective was 'to convert China, step by step, from a backward, agricultural country into an advanced, socialist, industrial state'. Heavy industry first, light industry second, and agriculture third was the order of priority. From 1953 to 1957 industry absorbed a massive 61.8 per cent of the investment funds, compared with a paltry, altogether inadequate, 6.2 per cent for agriculture. Agricultural output suffered as a direct result. Even more fundamentally, the Chinese failed to appreciate that the rate of industrialisation would be closely related to the expansion of agricultural production.

Industrial gains were impressive enough to persuade the Chinese that their policies were right, so that 'the central task of our second five-year plan' (1958–62) 'is still to give priority to the development of heavy industry', with further development of producer-goods at the expense of the consumer-goods industries.

The start of the second plan coincided with the Great Leap Forward. From 1949 to 1952 the industrial growth rate had averaged twenty-seven per cent annually, but of course conditions were atypical, because of war damage. Expansion had occurred at a rate of fourteen per cent a year between 1953 and 1957. The mean rate of growth for the three years 1958 to 1960 was twenty per cent – a leap forward of sorts, perhaps. But the average disguises an abrupt decline from thirty-one per cent in 1958 to twenty-six per cent in 1959, and only four per cent in 1960. Something was obviously seriously amiss.

A frequently quoted slogan at the time of the Great Leap Forward was that China would overtake Britain as an industrial nation within fifteen years; by 1972, for example, steel production would reach 40 million tons annually.* A peculiarly Chinese method, known as 'walking on two legs', was to have aided China in reaching these dizzy heights; indeed since then the techniques involved have become part and parcel of the Chinese model. The term 'walking on two legs' means the parallel development of large-scale, capital-intensive, scientifically sophisticated enterprises and small-scale, labour-intensive, self-sufficient schemes founded on local resources, manpower and expertise.

The year of the great leap saw the vigorous construction of 700,000 tiny back-yard iron-smelting furnaces, which employed a work force of some twenty million. 'Batteries of such furnaces, rising dramatically amid the fields of vegetables or cereals, became a distinctive feature of the countryside in 1958.' Anticipating the movement since 1966 to set up a comprehensive range of small industrial units, other

---

* In fact the 1972 steel figure was 23 million tons (compared with 18.5 million in 1960, only 10 million at a low point in the period 1966–70 and maybe even lower still between 1961 and 1965).

miniscule factories turned out fertilisers, sulphuric acid and ball-bearings. As it happened, however, the back-yard iron and steel proved to be virtually useless, except for tasks such as tipping agricultural implements.

According to the Chinese the slump in production mid-way through the second five-year plan was caused by three factors: firstly, bad weather and poor harvests (see pages 73–74); secondly, the withdrawal of Soviet technical assistance; thirdly, mistakes committed by the Chinese themselves which, as the Cultural Revolution unfolded, were largely identified with the misdoings of Liu Shao-chi and other 'capitalist-roaders'.

Certainly the fact that nearly 1400 Russian technicians left China in 1960, taking their blueprints with them, and that the Soviet government reduced the supply of equipment and cancelled over two hundred and fifty items of scientific and technical co-operation had serious short-term effects, as many key heavy industrial plants fell idle. There was a pronounced decline in industrial output in 1961, with a less marked drop in 1962, when production was probably somewhat above the 1957 level but only sixty per cent of the 1960 peak. On the other hand, with no other option open to them, the Chinese were forced to go it alone, and out of this situation was born a new and confident policy of self-sufficiency. Indeed, one measure of the relatively quick recovery was the fact that all Soviet loans (totalling 1406 million new roubles) were repaid by 1965.

And the recovery was made possible by a complete reversal of planning priorities, as an all-out effort was made to save the agricultural sector. Agriculture was to become 'the foundation of the national economy and industry the leading factor'. Investment plans were upended: first, agriculture, second, light industry, and third, heavy industry. Industry generally was to benefit from 'readjustment, consolidation, reinforcement and improvement'. Heavy industrial production was diverted into manufacturing chemical fertilisers, insecticides, irrigation and drainage equipment, and agricultural machinery and implements.

Thus, flying in the face of the traditional Marxist emphasis on heavy industry, the Chinese have implemented a programme in which industry aids agriculture. This pattern has lasted for over a decade and has even gathered momentum. Last year (1972), for example, a *Red Flag* article described how in the past few years about a third of the rolled steel in Honan has been used for agriculture, 'and thirty-five per cent of all capital construction funds were directly or indirectly invested in agriculture'.

Although there are no official figures for Chinese industrial output from 1961 to 1969, western estimates suggest that the economy began to pick up slowly between 1963 and 1965, industrial production growing by roughly ten per cent a year, perhaps topping 1958 levels immediately before the launching of the third five-year plan in 1966. Chinese sources claim that the Cultural Revolution acted as a spur to production, and actually led to a second leap forward in 1966. There are indications, however, of considerable economic dislocation, with workers and peasants leaving their jobs, ships stranded in ports, and transport links sabotaged.

In any event there was overall improvement during the third plan period, and Chou En-lai revealed that in 1970 the total value of agricultural output stood at US $30,000 million, and that of industrial output exactly three times as much, or value of agricultural output stood at $90,000 million.

In general terms, the available statistics reflect the comparatively impressive growth of Chinese industry during the 1950s, the difficulties experienced in the subsequent decade, and the expansion of the agriculture-supporting industries, such as fertilisers. Nevertheless it must be stressed that whereas certain items exhibit striking growth, *per capita* output remains relatively low and total production falls a long way short of national requirements. Hence there is a constant conflict between high levels of technological competence achieved in various industries, and low levels of production. Furthermore, even within the industrial sector some of the investment decisions which have been taken are questionable.

Industrial trends

Together with many other developing countries the Chinese spend vast sums on a defence budget, money which might otherwise be used for housing, education, health or public transport. A Soviet source states that China spends more than one-eighth of its national income on 'preparations for war' (which roughly tallies with an American estimate of between five and fifteen per cent of the GNP), and that the amount is on the increase. Defence expenditure helps to maintain conventional forces, including a standing army of between 3 and 3.5 million men, and a costly nuclear weapons and missile development programme. This uses not merely funds but also resources, such as the electricity generated by the Sanmen project, and, even more significant, chronically scarce scientific manpower.

A related example, 1967 vintage: 'Chinese scientists announce the completion of a giant new-type transistor computer suitable for all purposes . . . the new computer is of vital importance in the fields of atomic energy, rockets, and space flight, as well as in various spheres of the national economy . . . To express their infinite love, loyalty, faith, and admiration of Chairman Mao, the makers built the computer in such a way that every time the machine starts work a portrait of Chairman Mao apppears together with the words "Serve the People" in a facsimile of his handwriting. It also plays the tune "The east shines red, the sun rises, there emerges in China a Mao Tse-tung".' And yet China, unaided, launched its first satellite in 1970; and also possesses nuclear weapons. China conducted her fifteenth atmospheric nuclear test in June 1973.

Sometimes the emphasis is difficult to accept. While China's fields cry out for additional fertilisers, and current domestic manufacture and foreign imports fail to provide even half the optimum requirement of fifty million metric tons, there was, during the Cultural Revolution, a remarkable diversion of the chemical industry, so that it produced materials 'required in the manufacture of paper, printing ink, binding material and plastic covers for the publication of Chairman Mao's works'. In three years, from 1966 to 1968, 740 million copies of the Little Red Book (*Quotations from Chairman Mao Tse-tung*) were published, approximately one copy each for the entire Chinese nation, although not all copies were intended for domestic consumption.

One important lesson, apparently well-learnt from the experience of the great leap, is that quality is every bit as important as quantity. Thus growing self-sufficiency, or 'relying on our own efforts', goes hand in hand with not only 'greater' but also 'quicker, better, and more economical results'.

The manufacture of an increasing range of electronic equipment by a 'mature and powerful industry' is a measure of the degree of sophistication attained very rapidly, though its strategic role gives this branch of industry priority.

The stress on economy drives is characteristic, too, in keeping with Mao's injunction that it is urgently necessary to 'combat waste', and that China will only become rich and powerful through 'diligence and frugality'. At national and provincial level major savings occur with the co-operation of the individual factories and communes. The Talien cement plant is a case in hand. Rising production increased the need for more cement bags, so the sales office decided to collect used bags. 'At one construction site, they discovered that, instead of opening the bags at the sewn end as indicated, people thoughtlessly disembowelled the bags with a thrust of the shovel.' After it was explained 'that every bag saved meant a saving in state funds', the construction workers were careful to preserve the bags whole, and even kept the pieces of string used to sew up the bag. 'Within a short time, the cement factory had recovered forty million paper bags and 12,000 kg of cotton string from the construction sites.'

The interrelation of all forms of economic activity is critical. Industry supports agriculture and agriculture feeds industry. Industry also supplies railway lines and rolling stock for the transport network; the spread of the communications web itself aids the resiting of industry.

Transport

Extension of the railway, road, water and air transport network has proved necessary both for economic reasons and to strengthen political control over the outlying regions. Railways now serve every major administrative area apart from Tibet, and since 1949 the railway grid has been increased from only 13,000 miles in service to over 22,000 miles. There are tremendous construction and maintenance problems, as with the Lanchow–Sinkiang line, which stretches up into the Karamai oilfield (but which has not been linked with the Soviet system as originally planned), and which crosses extensive desert tracts where shifting sand presents a constant threat; or the two great bridges built across the Yangtze at Wuhan in 1957, and at Nanking in 1968.

Before 1949, water transport provided the main means of carrying goods; since then, both rail and road freight have become more important. The Chinese counterpart of the Soviet-tractor-and-opening-up-of-virgin-lands is perhaps the long-distance lorry. From the mid-1950s, Chinese juggernauts (in appearance much more like the American trucks of the second world war than the monsters now threatening European cities) have been able to select one of three different highways into Tibet. At the other end of the scale, carrying-poles, handcarts, pack animals and the bicycle are used to move goods and people. In 1969 a Yugoslavian source reported that China has 300,000 kilometres of 'all-weather' highways, and nearly 500,000 kilometres of secondary roads, which have no hard surface and are suitable for traffic only in good weather.

China also possesses about 100,000 miles of navigable waterways, a quarter of which can be reached by river-going steamers. The Yangtze and its tributaries account for forty per cent of the waterways aggregate; in the high-water season 10,000-ton sea-going ships can reach Wuhan, over 600 miles upstream, and steamers sail to Ipin, which is 1740 miles from the sea.

While various international airlines have been busy cancelling options on the Anglo–French Concorde, the Chinese have created a stir by confirming an order for three aircraft, because they are anxious to establish an international airline of their own. A fairly rudimentary domestic system presently links seventy or so cities, providing a passenger and freight service. Also, light aircraft are engaged in a series of economic tasks: rain making, bombing glaciers, crop spraying, reafforestation, dropping fish fry, geological prospecting, aerial surveying and photography, and weather charting.

Taching: an industrial model

One feature of economic development which is unique to China (if not wholly in concept, then certainly in the intensity and comprehensiveness of the propaganda) is the relevance of the *model settlement*, and Mao Tse-tung's admonition in 1964: 'In industry, learn from Taching.'

Before 1960 'China's oil industry was . . . very backward and imperialism and modern revisionism tried to use our shortage of oil to put pressure on us.' But in 1959 a new oil field was discovered at Taching (near to Harbin) in Heilungkiang. Initially a new oil city of at least 100,000 people was planned. Then it was realised that such a city would be parasitical rather than self-reliant. Instead, Taching has developed from a worker-peasant settlement described as 'a village-like town' into 'a rural city'. At first all that mattered was the quest for oil. 'Oil first. The workers let housing go and lived in tents, old cowsheds or shacks. Some dug underground shelters to sleep in . . . With the oilfield started, the Taching people turned to the problem of housing. . . . Everyone . . . went out to dig earth and build tamped-earth houses, small and simple beside the growing buildings and refining towers of the oil base. Even today, when Taching has become a huge modern oil complex, the workers choose to live in these earthen houses. "Our houses may be low," they say, "but our sights are high."' It is this 'spirit' which must be imbibed by all Chinese workers, just as they all must wave the 'red banner' of Taching and seek to overtake and outstrip the oilfield's performance. Taching wine is heady stuff.

Indeed, 'a new, communist type of person is being forged in the revolutionary crucible of Taching; they are able to fight the enemy, both with guns in hand and with pens in hand through their writings. Differences between workers and peasants, between town and countryside and between mental and manual labour are being gradually narrowed.' While the men-folk tend the oil derricks their wives and dependants cultivate the surrounding fields, so that Taching has become self-sufficient in food production. 'Rows of oil wells in cultivated land make a beautiful pattern of the Taching oilfield. There are no crowded cities here but scattered clusters of housing units with both urban characteristics and rural flavour, linked by a network of motor roads. Today, Taching appears as a rudimentary socialist industrial and mining area, combining industry and farming, city and country.' And, as far as the Chinese are concerned, it is the Taching message that will give the ultimate boost to industrial production.

A rural interlude

Whole worlds, as well as over two thousand years of history, separate the Taching worker and a Sung peasant. 'There was a farmer of Sung who tilled the land, and in his field was a stump. One day a rabbit, racing across the field, bumped into the stump, broke its neck, and died. Thereupon the famer laid aside his plough and took up watch beside the stump, hoping that he would get another rabbit in the same way. But he got no more rabbits, and instead became the laughing stock of Sung.'

This anecdote symbolises the interaction of man and nature, which the Chinese leaders seek to control, the rigidity, fatalism and intractability of peasant attitudes which they seek to reshape.

Over the centuries millions of peasants eked out an existence, rarely with enough to eat, poorly clothed, and living in simple homes. Yet families were often large, as many children, especially sons, were needed to help in the fields. In consequence land was subdivided into tiny, scattered strips of land. Large numbers of peasants were tenant farmers and landless labourers. Farm equipment was crude, draught animals few, and soils exhausted. Also there were long periods of inactivity during the agricultural calendar. Frequently the peasants were heavily taxed, many years in advance, and so they accumulated crippling debts.

Often there was a fierce hatred of the landowners. A peasant from a village in northern Shensi recalls how in 1920, when he was only twelve years old, a local landlord took him to the sheep pastures. 'We went eight *li* from the village. At dinner-time I was sent back to fetch his food. First he took off my shoes, and he pissed in them, then he said: "You must be back with my food before my piss has dried." It was a hot summer and I had to run barefoot across sand and I could not stop and rest on the way. I ran as fast as I could, but when I got back the landowner's piss had already dried, because the sun was strong and (he) beat me after he had eaten.'

This type of episode, often repeated, created a tremendous reservoir of resentment in the Chinese countryside; China's revolution was a peasant movement, born of misery and superstition. At harvest time the peasants ate in the fields. Before touching the food they propitiated 'the god of the crops' by offering grain, spreading out a quantity on the ground – otherwise the god would beat the crops with a small whip, so that nothing would grow.

The communist road to power lay in capitalising on peasant discontent, and destroying the old gods. As far back as 1927 Mao Tse-tung asked: 'The gods? Worship them by all means. But if you had only the Lord Kuan* and the Goddess of Mercy and no peasant associations, could you have overthrown the local tyrants and evil gentry? The gods and goddesses are indeed miserable objects.' Change, radical change. there had to be; change which would embrace the wide variety of agricultural landscapes.

Agricultural land-use patterns

There is a basic division between the agricultural areas of the south and east, and the pastoral regions of the north and west, where livestock raising predominates and oasis cultivation is practised around the desert edges. In the agricultural parts of the country, the principal distinction is between the rice grown in the south and the wheat of the north. Over ninety per cent of the paddy acreage is planted south of the Chinling range, on both the plains and hillside terraces; while about sixty per cent of China's wheat is found between the Chinling mountains and the Great Wall, although there is considerable overlapping of the two main staple crops. Rice may be triple-cropped in the lush tropical zone in the southern parts of Kwangtung, Kwangsi and Yunnan where cash crops include citrus fruits, rubber and sisal hemp. Two crops of rice are produced in the subtropical zone, extending northwards to the Chinling–Huai divide, with cash crops such as tea, tea-oil and tung-oil. In the warm-temperate climate of the middle and lower Yellow River and Tarim basin, winter wheat and cotton are typical crops. Spring wheat is produced in the temperate zone in the north-east, together with maize, millet, *kaoliang* and sugar beet. From 1949 onwards there have been important regional shifts in cropping patterns, livestock raising has increased in significance in parts of the south and east, and cultivation has spread into the pastoral areas. Quick-ripening

---

* Kuan Yu, AD 160–219, a warrior in the time of the Three Kingdoms, who was widely worshipped by the Chinese as the God of Loyalty and War.

rice strains are grown as far north as Heilungkiang and Sinkiang, for instance, whilst hybrid *kaoliang* now extends into the hill country of southern China.

Collectivisation

Before the setbacks of the early 1960s, change came to the Chinese countryside mainly as a result of attempts to rationalise deployment of the labour force. Collectivisation, and ultimately communisation, introduced a common organisational form which cut right across the diversity of landscapes and farming systems. Subsequently, there has been greater recognition of the importance of local conditions and initiatives, investment has been stepped up substantially, and agricultural technology extended.

In 1949 landlords and rich peasants owned over seventy per cent of the cultivated land, although they accounted for less than ten per cent of the population. To gain the support of the peasants the land was commandeered, given to former tenants and landless labourers, and ownership by the peasants was guaranteed. Under the land reform movement, by 1952 300 million landless peasants received 700 million *mou* of land, and also homes, draught animals and farm implements. Rentals due to the landowners were abrogated but new taxes were introduced.

At first the peasants were organised into mutual-aid teams. Already by 1954 there were ten million teams, covering sixty per cent of the rural population. The major features of the mutual-aid teams were the pooling of labour, farm implements and animals, mainly at sowing and harvest-time, in the case of the 'temporary' teams, and on a more general basis where 'permanent' teams were set up. Elementary production plans were formulated. Most property was privately owned, and the teams usually consisted of up to ten households.

Shortly afterwards permanent mutual-aid teams were consolidated into agricultural producers' co-operatives (APCs). By the end of 1956 ninety-six per cent of all peasant households belonged to APCs. Under the lower-stage APCs the land remained in private hands, but it was pooled and run by a central management. Peasant income was decided according to land and work contributions. The lower APCs frequently coincided with existing natural villages, and included maybe thirty to forty families. Under the higher-stage APC, however, land became the property of the APC, together with draught animals and the larger farming implements. Private plots, large enough to grow a few vegetables and raise a hen or two, were kept by individual members. Later these plots were to become a serious bone of contention, because all too often the peasant cared more for his plot than for the collective land. Remuneration – the accumulation of work-points – was now related solely to labour contributions. Manpower was divided into brigades of perhaps twenty families. A typical higher APC might include one large or several smaller villages, about 160 households, and cover about 400 acres.

The universal nature of collectivisation, the manner in which virtually all peasant opposition was silenced and undue blood-letting was avoided, and the rapidity with which it was instituted, are among the more extraordinary aspects of the campaign. Clearly, Mao Tse-tung had given tremendous impetus to the programme in July 1955: 'Throughout our countryside a new upsurge in the socialist mass movement is in sight. But some of our comrades are like a woman with bound feet, tottering along and constantly grumbling to the others: "You're going too fast." ' In this speech Mao urged full collectivisation by 1960; in fact it was completed by 1957.

But the comet of institutional change had only crossed a segment of the rural firmament – the heavens were still not fully ablaze.

Communes

Then, in 1958, the 'three red banners' of the general line, the Great Leap Forward and the setting-up of the rural people's communes were unfurled. The commune provided an organisational vehicle for carrying out Mao's recommendation that industrial, agricultural, commercial, educational, health and militia functions should be combined. Apparently, the APCs had shown themselves 'increasingly inadequate for large scale production'; smaller co-operatives merged into federations during the winter of 1957 to summer 1958, often embracing townships, so that the co-operative's managing group joined with local government, forming a political and economic unit, which became 'the prototype of the people's commune'.

By the end of September 1958, over 26,000 communes had been established, covering more than ninety-eight per cent of the peasant population. The following year, consolidation took place, reducing the number of communes to 24,000, averaging 5000 families in size. There are two types of subdivisions within the commune, called production brigades and production teams. In 1959 there were half a million brigades, usually equivalent to the higher APC, with from 200 to 300 families; the three million teams each had up to forty households. In 1962 the communes were generally reduced in size to about one-third, as they were increased in number to nearly 75,000, with an average of 1800 households each, divided among nine brigades and seventy-five teams.

Apart from planning the agricultural year, the commune controls nearly all other economic tasks throughout the Chinese countryside. Also, the commune is responsible for assuring the 'seven guarantees' covering food, clothing, housing, education, medical care and child-birth, marriages and funerals. Indeed, early in their history they were acclaimed as the ideal system for speeding up the pace of 'socialist construction, for transforming socialist collective ownership into socialist ownership by the whole people* . . . and for the transition from socialism to communism in the future'.

Such enthusiasm was premature. To begin with many mistakes were made. Virtually all private property was abolished, for example; mass labour projects, political study, and paramilitary training were too demanding; and family life was disrupted by the introduction of in-adequate communal dining halls and a crèche system which deprived parents of their offspring for unreasonable periods.

After the excesses of the opening months, conditions were relaxed, but it was too late to prevent production chaos. Thus by the end of 1959 organisation was at brigade level, roughly equivalent to the higher APC. Some family property and private plots were restored. Work pressures were eased, although large-scale, labour-intensive water con-servation and afforestation projects continued in slack agricultural seasons. As the economic crisis of 1960 deepened the team, rather than the brigade, was made the basic accounting unit by the end of 1961. To all intents and purposes, control was at lower APC level once again, frequently coinciding with the natural village. The commune, as origin-ally conceived, remained in name only.

Occasionally there were quite extraordinary happenings. In one Shantung commune in 1962 local youths damaged farm property, cut down standing maize, and threw 'lighted firecrackers among penitents at self-criticism meetings'. The ringleader perfected a trick of 'stealing peaches at night and imitating the grunting of a pig when footsteps approached, so that the innocent and useful pigs in the commune pens were blamed for his depredations'. The Youth League committee decided to intervene after the roll of honour of model overtime workers had been 'wickedly defaced'. The culprits were made to pass their leisure time reading, writing and even dancing 'but the errant lads showed little interest and many slipped away to insincere pranks'. Finally, the youths were introduced to a programme of Chinese folk-songs. Sur-

* Meaning state ownership.

96

prisingly, after this they were 'receptive to the normal curriculum of culture, education, party morale and love of labour'. There were incidents, too, where the members of one commune would raid the grain stores of a neighbouring commune, as a means of helping them meet production quotas set by the state.

Documents marking the tenth year of the communes stated that they made it possible to utilise manpower, land, animals and implements more rationally, to build large construction projects, and to 'engage in intensive and meticulous cultivation. This has enabled agricultural production to advance rapidly.' In the mid-1960s, however, it was known that 'the team is the unit for labour management; the brigade for the crop programme; the commune for the external relations of the group, for investment projects, and for industrial enterprises ancillary to agriculture'.

Currently, the team 'handles its income and distribution independently, bears its losses itself and keeps most of the profit . . . At present, undertakings run by the production teams account for the biggest proportion of the total assets of the communes.' As the wealth of the teams increases, 'in time the production brigade, and eventually the commune, will become the basic accounting unit'. No one knows just when this will occur. In the meantime, providing the 1970 to 1972 grain production claims are reliable, it would seem that progress has focused upon the natural village and has occurred in spite of, rather than because of, communisation. If this is the case, agricultural expansion must have resulted from the more recent technological improvements introduced into the village fields.

Technological changes

An 'Eight-Point Charter', introduced in 1958, is intended to bring a comprehensive series of improvements to the rural areas: soil amelioration; increased use of fertilisers; water conservancy and irrigation; seed selection; close planting; plant protection; field management and better farming implements.

Given China's huge manpower reserve, agricultural mechanisation raises both physical and ideological problems. Nevertheless, mechanisation is being promoted, on a 'step-by-step' basis, founded on local self-reliance and initiative as opposed to state aid. Broadly, what is at stake is the mechanisation of cultivation in north China and of irrigation and drainage in the south.

According to the Chinese in 1962, it was estimated that large-scale mechanisation would take at least twenty to twenty-five years. This is probably an underestimate. For instance, a recent western study calculates that from 1958 to 1971 China produced fewer than 188,000 conventional tractors (used mainly in the extensive farming areas in the north-east and north-west) and about 85,000 hand-operated tractors; whereas Japan, with only thirteen per cent as much paddy, has several million hand-operated tractors.

Improved food and cash crop seed strains are another example of technological innovation. Agronomists are even using atomic energy in agriculture, and in the last ten years have produced over forty new rice, wheat, soya bean and other crop strains by mutation through radiation. Imported seeds are being popularised: wheat from Chile in 1959, and barley from Denmark in 1965, are cases in hand.

Just before the advent of the Cultural Revolution it was revealed that 'electricity is now available in most of the villages in over half of China's 2126 counties. It is used for irrigation, drainage, processing farm produce, and lighting peasant homes, schools, commune offices and clubs. Rural consumption of electricity (in 1965) is twenty-five times what it was in 1957.' Furthermore, between 1965 and 1971 rural consumption of electricity doubled.*

The cumulative impact of such technological changes must have been considerable, and the direction in which they are being channelled appears to have altered too. Throughout the 1950s and into the 1960s attention was given to the pioneer fringe and the opening up of land which was in varying degrees, marginal. Since 1964, in contrast, there has been a rapid rise in the amount of stable, high-yield farmland. From 1957 to 1963 the area grew by only 1.1 million hectares, from 6.5 to 7.6 million, yet by 1971 the area had increased to thirteen million hectares, equalling twelve per cent of the total cultivated land; and it may prove possible to triple this figure in the years to come.

Production

What has all this organisational and scientific upheaval meant in terms of agricultural production since 1949? Output of grain increased from 154 to 185 million tons between 1952 and 1957 (compared with a pre-1949 peak of about 140 million tons). Then, seemingly, the impossible happened. In the great leap year of 1958 it was claimed that grain production had more than doubled to reach 375 million tons. In fact, the 1958 figure was revised to 250 million tons in 1959, when the harvest

---

* In 1969 rural consumption totalled four billion kwh, or eight per cent of total production, compared with only four per cent in 1962.

was said to have totalled 270 million tons. Even these last two totals were exaggerated.

Probable production in the Great Leap Forward years fell within the range of 195 to 205 million tons in 1958, 170 to 190 in 1959, and as low as 160 to 170 million tons in 1960. Between 1961 and 1965 there was gradual improvement to about the 1957 level of 185 million tons; while both 1966 and 1967 were described as record harvest years by Chinese sources. There were good harvests, too, in 1968 and in 1969, when according to a Yugoslavian source 230 million tons were harvested.

Then came the first official statistics since 1959. In 1970 the grain harvest was 240, and in 1971, 246 million tons. Chou En-lai predicted that the 1972 harvest would top 250 million tons, thereby breaking all previous records. However, it was later estimated officially that the harvest was the same as in 1970, or 240 million tons, because China 'suffered the most serious drought in several decades in 1972' (compare pages 73–74) although the reduction may in fact have been as little as a 'mere 2 million tons' according to Li Hsien-nien (a vice-minister), allowing for a total of 244 million tons.

Additionally, increased yields are reported for other food and industrial crops and for livestock, though there are no supporting figures for these reports.

Yet factors other than state procurement quotas must be taken into account. For several years 'many northern areas which used to get grain from the southern parts of the country to make up their deficiency have now become self-sufficient or even grain surplus areas. There are now only a small number of areas which still cannot meet their own needs in food grains.' For instance, 'particularly noteworthy is Hohengcheng production brigade of the Shangcheng people's commune in Hopei province which had record cotton *and* grain harvests (in 1972), exploding the fallacy that such a thing could not be achieved in north China'* (italics added).

Again, huge central food reserves – as much as forty million tons by late 1970 – have been built up, in addition to the food stock-piled by the communes, for Mao Tse-tung urges the population at large to 'store grain everywhere . . .' Most important of all, in 1973 the Chinese generally are demonstrably better fed than at any previous time in history.

---

* The harvest included an average of 170 *jin* of ginned cotton on 1200 *mou* of cotton fields and 1740 *jin* of grain on 800 *mou* of cultivated land.

Village—city stresses

Above all else China is a land of villages, with eighty-five per cent of the population living in the rural areas. This nevertheless leaves a figure of roughly 140 million people living in towns and cities, which from the Chinese point of view is unfortunate, because the Chinese dislike the city. To them the city means only one thing – pre-liberation Shanghai.

'Old Shanghai was known as the "adventurers' paradise" and Avenue Joffre was a microcosm. In those days lurid foreign advertisements marred the skyline. Shop windows were crammed with foreign goods such as lipstick, perfume, nail polish and other expensive cosmetics. Even most of the cigarettes and toilet paper were imported. The Jai Alai Auditorium, the Candidrome, the bars, dance halls, night clubs and other dubious businesses run by foreigners raked in fortunes while they undermined the spiritual well-being of the people. A tiny minority who had money rolled in luxury, guzzling and leading licentious lives while the working people had only the barest necessities. One could always see swarms of ragged beggars in the street and, not uncommon in winter, their starved frozen corpses huddled up on the pavement.'*

Naturally life is very different today, where the same Shanghai street is called Huaihai Road. At the time of the Spring Festival 1973, 'China-made cars streamed by in an endless flow. . . . Happy crowds packed shops, parks, theatres and cinemas.' But a strong philosophy of anti-urbanism nevertheless persists, which has economic as well as ideological implications: hence the unshakeable determination to iron out the difference in living standards between town and countryside.

Tachai: an agricultural model

This explains why the name of a small northern village, Tachai (in Shensi), is known throughout the length and breadth of the country, but only since Mao Tse-tung's 1964 dictum: 'In agriculture, learn from Tachai.'

The Tachai production brigade is located in the rock-strewn Taihang mountains, at a height of about one thousand metres. Tachai has eighty-three families and a population of about 430 people. The village

---

* Compare Chengtu, Szechuan, before 1949, where 'bureaucrats, landlords, warlords and wealthy merchants . . . wallowed in sensual pleasure while the working people lived in misery.'

has triumphed over both a bitter historical record and a harsh physical environment, so that while most of the country was battling with the severe economic difficulties of the early 1960s, Tachai moved from victory to victory, reaping record harvests, which it has continued to do ever since. The peasants of Tachai 'have brought into play their revolutionary drive and creativeness and relied on their collective strength to remake nature. They have transformed barren mountains into terraced farmland that gives high and stable yields. A poor hamlet before liberation, Tachai is now a thriving new socialist village . . . The village has taken on a new look. Blocks of new houses and stone-walled caves have replaced the earthen caves, and electric light and tap water are supplied to every household. The brigade has ample grain reserves and public accumulation funds and every household has bank deposits and its own grain reserves.'

Once again the grand design for both north and south China emerges, as brigades seek to emulate Tachai, particularly since the winter of 1970. 'On the plains in the north, the peasants deep-ploughed the fields, improved the soil and levelled the land. They also sank wells and built small- and medium-sized reservoirs. Those in the mountain areas built terraced fields and check dams across gullies and led water uphill for irrigation. The peasants in southern China transformed low-yield fields, expanded the paddy fields and raised the rate of land utilisation. In the coastal areas they reclaimed land from the sea to grow food grain.' In little more than a year some ten thousand brigades and communes had become advanced Tachai-type collectives, 'and many counties (were) swiftly marching towards this goal'. Thus Tachai is to agriculture what Taching is to industry.

A new folk-song from Anhwei, sung while transplanting rice, runs:

> Chairman Mao showed us Tachai's road,
> Everywhere songs of a bumper crop;
> What we're planting is a magic herb
> Whose fragrance will fill the hills.

China is surely at a crossroads. The notable progress of the early phase of development, before the Great Leap Forward, appeared to be in danger of being submerged in the early 1960s. But the ship has been steadied, and the mid-term prospects of the fourth five-year plan seem good – good in terms of the striking improvements in standards of living and the day-to-day life of the vast majority. For there is agreement among most China specialists that living standards are far better than in pre-1949 days, with famine banished, inflation non-existent and commodity supplies at a reasonable level: '... the basic needs of the people are guaranteed. Universal employment, low prices, low house rent, no personal income tax and a low and stable cost of living guarantee a living standard which is gradually being raised.' All this represents very real achievement.

Can these gains be consolidated and improved upon?

At least several decades, and perhaps a considerably longer period of time is required before a conclusive answer will emerge. The struggle between man as economic and political agent and the environment remains unresolved. Also, there are so many imponderables: if population growth is checked ... ; if the weather is kind ... ; if China remains politically stable and in its present benign mood ... ; if the current agriculturally oriented investment policies are maintained. ... But many aspects of the Chinese model of development make sense (for example mass mobilisation of labour, self-sufficiency and frugality) not only within China itself but for other parts of the developing world, and the Chinese experiment is a valuable one.

This chapter began by establishing the traditional Chinese concept of the close and harmonious connection between man and nature. It went on to elaborate the ideological approach of present-day China to man's conflict with nature. It is precisely at this point that such contrasting views merge, for currently in China there is a fresh awareness of the interdependence of man and nature, the vital role which conservation must play in the careful husbanding of resources and in the protection of the human environment.

Part Three

The history of China to 1840

1 From prehistory to the Ch'in revolution

The common statement that China has four thousand years of history is not in fact correct. Two thousand years BC is well before any existing record which can be described as historical. On the other hand, the prehistory of China, as revealed by archaeology, indicates clearly that the human race has occupied northern China for 600,000 years, and that even the remote inhabitants of the caves near Peking, now known as Peking Man, had some particular physical characteristics which are found in the modern Chinese. China, in fact, has good reason to claim that its people have always been 'Chinese', and that the contemporary Chinese are, in part at least, descended from these very remote ancestors. Neolithic skeletons from north China show virtually no differentiation from those of the modern inhabitants of the same regions. There is also evidence from pottery and art of the prehistoric period displaying close links with the later culture.

Much, indeed until very recent years almost all, the evidence came from the northern half of the country. The prehistory of southern China was unknown. It might be established that the classical culture of ancient China grew from the neolithic of the same region, but this could not be claimed for the southern half of the country. Indeed, even in the early historical period, the Chinese records themselves testify to the alien character of the south; but without archaeological evidence there was little to demonstrate the characteristics of the southern prehistoric peoples.

Recent discoveries have shown that in some parts of the south, especially in the province of Hunan, which is inland far from the coast, there existed an art form, found in burials, which, while wholly unlike anything known from north China, has obvious affinities with the art which centuries later flourished in the islands of the Pacific, and was carried to New Zealand by the Maoris. Such motifs as the protruding tongue in human figures, and floral outgrowths from the limbs of such figures, are well known in Polynesian art, even if their ancient significance is lost. They appear in the wooden figures found near Ch'angsha, which can be approximately dated to the seventh to sixth centuries BC.

Already by that period the culture of south China, and of the kingdom of Ch'u, of which Ch'angsha was the capital, was increasingly influenced by the classical civilisation of north China. But it is clear that this northern influence was superimposed upon another tradition, which in some way survived and moved towards and then across the sea – although none of the ancient links can yet be identified. There are other southern regional discoveries which suggest that more than one culture, distinct from that of the north, had flourished in the south. In Yunnan, at a site not far from its capital, K'unming, bronze instruments and artefacts were found decorated with figures and motifs indicating a pastoral society unlike that of the agricultural Chinese. They are relatively late, of the second century BC, a time when Chinese influence was already present, as is testified by the use of cast bronze vessels, but they still preserve the art tradition of an earlier, non-Chinese culture.

In the neighbouring large western province of Szechwan, art objects found in tombs of Han dynasty date (202 BC to AD 220), an age when Szechwan had long been incorporated in the Chinese empire, show features unlike anything else of that date found in China, and suggest the persistence of an underlying local tradition. The progress of excavation and archaeological discovery in south China is likely to lead before long to very radical reassessment of the prehistoric period in this part of the Far East.

The classical culture of north China, from which the later and modern civilisation lineally descends, is shown by archaeology to have reached an advanced technical development well before historical record gives any information. Bronze casting of the period not long after 2000 BC was skilful, and had reached a level only a little short of the high quality of the earliest historical age. When the first inscriptions to have been discovered, dating from approximately 1500 to 1200 BC, were written, the art of writing had clearly been practised for a long period, during which it had evolved from simple picture records – of which evidence in the basic ideographs remains – to the real ideographic system, which can convey ideas as well as objects and indicate grammatical structure. On analogies with other civilisations it would seem probable that such a development must have required several centuries. But there is as yet no discovery of a truly primitive Chinese text.

Hsia and Shang

The Chinese had for more than two thousand years recorded what they believed to be the history of early China. The record begins with the type of cosmic legend of creation common to all cultures, but soon takes on the form of precise history. It gives the names of rulers and sages who civilised their people, details of their government, and finally the rather sketchy but complete and consecutive history of a first imperial dynasty, the Hsia, with the names of rulers and the dates of their reigns. Nothing of this can be confirmed by any archaeological evidence whatsoever. All that can be said is that the Chinese view of their origins is remarkably 'rational', and puts heavy emphasis on the leadership of sage rulers, while relegating the acts and interventions of deities to a minor role. Sages taught the Chinese to come down from the trees and live in huts on the ground, to sow and to plough, to build boats, gather in towns, clothe themselves with woven garments, make pottery, smelt metal and submit to the organised authority of monarchs. The same sage rulers, or rather the latter members of the series, defended their subjects against barbarian attacks – the first indication that there were some human beings who had not come under their beneficent rule.

Then came the Hsia dynasty, which introduced hereditary monarchy in place of the succession of sages who had been chosen without regard to relationship. Early Republican leaders in 1912 made much play with this tradition to prove that in the Golden Age itself, monarchy was elective, or selective, not dynastic. This Golden Age of the Sages, however legendary, has had a lasting importance on Chinese thought; believed to be authentic history, it was the model which all subsequent rulers should aspire to copy or to restore. The history of the Hsia dynasty is typical of the so-called 'dynastic cycle' in which future Chinese historians firmly believed. The first emperor is a sage or a hero; his immediate successors are worthy sons or grandsons, then come intelligent but indolent rulers; indolence gives way to vice, intelligence to careless indifference and then to outright tyranny. The people rise, a new hero appears, the dynasty is dethroned: the 'mandate of heaven' has passed. Yet all this is totally without any but literary substantiation, and the surviving texts date from the first century BC, the work of Han historians who collated ancient texts and surviving traditions.

It is immediately clear that the model of the past has been constructed on the reality of the present. The fall of the last rulers who preceded the Han empire is mirrored in the legends of a remote past.

The risk of decline and decay for the ruling dynasty is subtly suggested by the classical story of their far-off predecessors. The Hsia dynasty is portrayed as ruling an empire conterminous with that of the Han dynasty itself, although it should have been very well known that no such vast extent of territory, from Manchuria to Canton, had ever been brought under one rule before the time of the Han Emperor Wu himself (140 BC–87 BC), in whose reign this great historical reconstruction was undertaken. Chinese traditional orthodox history is thus a legend modernised in the first century BC to appear as authentic, datable history. When this was first realised by European scholars – after the uncritical acceptance of Chinese orthodoxy in the eighteenth century – the next dynasty, the Shang, was unceremoniously dismissed as just a further extension of the same legendary tale. But here archaeology produced, at a later time, a major surprise. The excavation of the site at Anyang in Honan province brought to light a quantity of oracle bone inscriptions, bones on which the questions asked of the oracle, and the answers, had been incised. The oracle was the deceased king, or an earlier deceased king. From these questions and answers there emerges a complete list of the Shang kings down to, but excluding, the two last. Their names, with one miswriting, are the same as those that the traditional history gives, as is their sequence. But the oracle bones of Anyang have lain in the ground for nearly three thousand years, and no Chinese historian, ancient or later, could have consulted this source. Anyang was shown to be a capital of the Shang kingdom, but it had been destroyed by a flood of the Yellow River in the time of the last king whose name appears on the oracle bones, which is why his two successors are not mentioned.

Thus rebuked, the historians must now approach the question of whether there was a Hsia dynasty with caution. The list of royal names is much the same in length as those of the historical Shang; their length of reign varies, and is never improbably long. The incidents, sparse enough, recorded of their actions are not, with rare exceptions, magical or fantastic. Had it been intended to construct a moral tale it would have been easy to embellish it with much more lively matter. It has more the character of a pedigree with a few details, handed down orally. It seems at least possible that the Han historian Ssu-ma Ch'ien had before him records of such an ancient, originally orally transmitted, pedigree. It is also known from the classical literature that the term 'all the Hsia' was used to indicate the total of the Chinese states of that age, and that their rulers mostly claimed traditional descent from the legendary period. The term Hsia was not an invention of the Han historians, though the interpretation of the surviving legends about a

Hsia dynasty was certainly a Han construction. The traditional account indicates the part of the country where the Hsia were said to have had their centre. Archaeology may yet confirm that such a local kingdom did in fact exist; it is quite certain that the wide imperial domain assigned to Hsia or to Shang is fictional. The Shang ruled a kingdom in Honan province extending up the Yellow River valley to an undetermined limit, but did not include direct rule over the modern province of Shensi nor reach to the eastern sea coast. The Yangtze valley and all to the south of it was far beyond Shang control.

What can be confirmed of traditional Shang history by archaeological discovery is little more than the names and sequence of the rulers and the fact that the capital was changed at least once, although the traditional record gives more frequent moves, due to destruction by flood. The oracle bone inscriptions are religious, not historical records, and few facts beyond valuable linguistic and ritual information can be gleaned from them. Slavery was an institution, and slaves were recruited from prisoners taken in war. In spite of the keen interest in this aspect of Shang society shown by communist historians, the evidence for the extent and importance of slavery is very scant, and on the whole seems to point to war captives as the main, perhaps the only, source of supply of slaves. It therefore seems improbable that the economy rested on slave labour to the exclusion of native serfs.

To the west of the Shang kingdom, in the valley of the River Wei, a tributary of the Yellow River, there was a semi-autonomous tribe, or fief, called Chou. The Shang claimed suzerainty, and it seems that this was admitted. Towards the end of the dynasty, when it had come under the rule of an evil king (according to the traditional story) the ruler of Chou rose in rebellion, marched east, defeated and killed the king of Shang, and set up his own dynasty in its stead, removing the capital from eastern Honan to his western stronghold, near the later city of Ch'angan and modern Sian.

The Chou dynasty

The fact of this overthrow of the Shang is certainly historical; the cause is not necessarily so, and some aspects of the Chou conquest have been revealed by the discovery in recent years of inscribed bronze vessels which show clearly that the pacification of the eastern territories of Shang took several years. All was not decided in one battle on the plains of Mu. The Chou kingdom was designed on what is familiar to the western world as the feudal system: the country was divided into fiefs whose rulers, more or less closely related to the monarch, had the duty of raising forces to fight for him and were also required to pay ceremonial visits to court. They were invested by the king, and records of some investitures exist on inscribed bronze vessels which seem to have been interred, perhaps with the founder of the line or by a later descendant.

The Chou kingdom was certainly much more extensive than that of the Shang. It reached to the sea coast of the Shantung peninsula, and included the modern Shensi province in the west, and the site of modern Peking in the north. The southern border was less well determined. Several smaller fiefs occupied the area down to the northern watershed of the Yangtze basin, but not all of these were at first under Chou authority. The term 'emperor', though often used for these early rulers, is not correct; the words which we have translated as 'emperor' were not used as a title until the end of the feudal system. In Shang and Chou times the supreme ruler was *wang*, the king, and no one else could use this title.

There is evidence that in its early years, and for perhaps some three centuries (1025 to 722 BC) the Chou kings really did have considerable authority over their vassals. Some of these had been close kin of the founder; others, such as the ruler of the eastern sea coast, the fief of Ch'i, were probably local rulers who wisely accepted a distant suzerainty and were given fictitious pedigrees connecting them with earlier ancestors of the royal house. The feudal system worked, it would seem, fairly well, so long as these family relationships were relatively close and cordial. But the Chinese from the earliest times practised exogamy: no man could marry a woman of his own paternal lineage, however remote. Wives must therefore come from another 'clan'. The Chou nobility was grouped in a rather small number of clans. Its members could not marry except within this group, but must exclude their own clan. Thus dynastic marriages of the type which in western feudalism were used to strengthen loyalty to the crown could not be practised in China. Most of the great fief holders were themselves of the same paternal descent as the king.

The decay of virility and character among the later Chou kings is the cause traditional historians assign to the disasters which occurred in the eighth century BC. The king made frivolous demands upon his nobles, succumbed to the whims of his favourite queen, and when the affronted nobility were summoned in a time of real peril, they doubted the genuineness of the call, and did not rally. A barbarian invasion overwhelmed the Chou capital, and the refugee king had to flee eastward to found a new capital at Loyang in eastern Honan.

The loss of the old western capital, and the records which it may have contained, has left a great deal of Chou history rather conjectural. The traditional story gives many details and incidents, some of which are very improbable, but on the whole it is not an incredible and fantastic tale. Archaeology has substantiated the fact of the feudal system of government. It is in any case clear that after the retreat to the east the kings never regained the degree of authority they had formerly held, and continued to lose power. The ancient home was made into the fief of Ch'in, and a warrior assigned the task of recovering it and guarding it from the barbarians.

The state of Ch'in

This was the origin of the state of Ch'in, which ultimately united the whole of China in the first real empire. The barbarians, going by many names in the long course of history, were always mounted nomadic raiders from the Mongolian steppe: 'Men with the hearts of beasts,' living in a country 'where not even an hair can grow.' The Chinese saw their fierce neighbours as a permanent scourge for which there could be no cure – no Chinese settlement of the steppe was practicable, and the only defence was constant vigilance on a long border. From these conditions the idea of walls to guard passes or accessible open stretches between the mountains arose, and were finally linked together to form the Great Wall of China.

Within the kingdom, the fief holders grew more independent and powerful. They absorbed pockets of so-called barbarians, hill and marsh folk, who had occupied areas less attractive to Chinese culti- vators. They also began to annex the many small fiefs which were embedded among the greater ones. Often the only historical record of these smaller fiefs is the fact and the date of their subjugation by a pow- erful neighbour. The age of the decay of the feudal system, the decline of royal authority and the beginning of a contest for supremacy among the greater states, the sixth and fifth centuries BC are also the age of the Chinese philosophers, and of Confucius himself. The Chinese world witnessed the concurrent phenomena of the break-up of the ancient political system and the rise of new intellectual doctrines interpreting the world and the role of man in a way wholly different from the antique tradition. There was a striking contrast between the increas- ingly militant and ruthless struggle for supreme power among the greater rulers, and the idealistic doctrines of philosophers and teachers who assumed a unity of the Chinese world which the political leaders were so violently striving to attain.

The age of the Warring States

Thus China slipped into the age of the Warring States (480–220 BC), which may be said to have begun shortly after the death of Confucius in 480 BC. That event was no outstanding landmark to his contemporaries; they would have stressed the increasing power of two 'outside' states – Ch'in in the north-west, Ch'u in the south – and their aggressive wars and intrusions upon the civilised Chung Yüan, the Central Plain, where the old centres of power and culture lay. The age of the Warring States, contemporary with the second generation of the great Chinese philosophers, has also remained famous in popular tradition as a period of ruthless and guileful wars, subtle conspiracies, loyalty and treason, fit subjects for romanticised history. It had this character; but it was also the period in which southern China, the Yangtze valley, came to play a very important part, and in the process of conflict and rivalry with the northern states to acquire their culture and art, and to adopt their literature and traditions. Ch'u was regarded as semi-barbarian in the time of Confucius; by the end of the Warring States it was a major contender for the supreme power in China.

In this age of strife all but a purely nominal authority was lost to the Chou kings, virtually segregated in the royal capital of Loyang. They were at first still useful to legitimise the usurpations and annexations of the great states. Confucius strove to uphold their authority, but few others cared what became of them. Late in the century all the rulers of the major contesting states, of which there were now only seven, assumed the royal title, in effect formally repudiating the remnant authority of the king in Loyang. Ch'u had never acknowledged it, and in his own land its ruler had always been king. When, in 256 BC, the king of Ch'in embarked on what were to be the really decisive conquests, he took Loyang and abolished the Chou monarchy. No other state yet acknowledged his right of succession, and for half a century there was no longer any supreme king. Ch'in gained mastery through strong organisation, a state dedicated to war, despising and indeed suppressing the culture of the east; and also profited from her strategic position in the north-west, ringed with mountains, a stronghold from which sallies and conquests to the east could be carried out without fear of attack from the rear. In the last years of the third century BC Ch'in, 'like a silk worm devouring a mulberry leaf', in the words of the Han historian, Ssu-ma Ch'ien, conquered all China. One by one, antagonistic to the last, the eastern states and Ch'u, the great southern power, succumbed. Their many attempts to combine in the face of common danger were frustrated by jealousies and dynastic ambition.

The Ch'in revolution

The revolution which followed this conquest was, until in our own times it was surpassed by one more profound, the only real transformation of Chinese society which has occurred. The feudal system was abolished. The new 'first emperor' – erstwhile king of Ch'in – ruled the whole vast territory through his own centrally appointed officers, and garrisoned it with his own Ch'in troops. Land was freed for purchase, and feudal privilege eliminated along with the feudal aristocracy itself which, when not exterminated, was concentrated in powerless poverty at the new capital, Hsienyang, near modern Sian in Shensi. A 'cultural revolution' took place: all books dealing with the history of the states, the teaching of the philosophers and anything not considered 'useful' by the magistrates of the new empire had to be surrendered for burning on pain of death. Fortunately, an imperial collection was exempt, but it is doubtful how much of this escaped subsequent calamity. Much was hidden; what we have of the ancient literature survived mainly in this way, but not all the rediscovered texts of the Han period can be treated as wholly authentic. The new régime enforced a single teaching, that of the School of the Law, long in favour in the kingdom of Ch'in. Law, in this sense, meant criminal law, to which all were subject without distinction of rank. It also meant suppression of all forms of literature not approved by the state, and these were few indeed. The theory was that given a rigid and enforced legal system it would not matter whether the king himself was competent or not, the law would ensure tranquillity. He must, however, have no rival, no near equal, and no fiefs would be given to his family: the royal power, or rather what may now be called the imperial power, must be wholly supreme. Many lesser ordinances enforced the new unity and smothered local autonomy. The Chinese world passed in a generation from a multi-state system, of equal or at least competitive kingdoms, to a uniform, total and all-embracing empire.

There can be no doubt that at this time the result was profoundly unpopular with the Chinese people. They might appreciate the end of warfare, but they deplored the harsh rule of Ch'in and the end of local loyalties. The first emperor, who expected his descendants and successors to be numbered in this way for 'ten thousand years' – for ever – reigned for eleven years. He travelled widely, but in conditions of rigid seclusion which made it possible for his few intimates to carry on intrigues and deceptions of which he had no knowledge. When he died on an eastern journey, near the coast of Shantung, his dead and putrefying body was conveyed by cart across the width of China without his attendant troops or any but his intimate eunuchs knowing he was dead. On their arrival in the capital the chief eunuch, a faithless intriguer, having contrived the death of the Crown Prince, put his younger brother on the throne as Second Emperor.

2   From the Han to the Mongols

The Han dynasty

The rule of Law was soon proved unable to conceal or mitigate the effects of the folly of an inexperienced youth under eunuch influence. Harsh taxation, now no longer backed by the iron will and power of the First Emperor, led to outbreaks of revolt. They spread rapidly: leaders from the old aristocracy, and others drawn from adventurers among the people, arose to lead the ever-growing rebellions. Before long they were almost as much concerned with their mutual rivalries as with the overthrow of the dwindling remnant of Ch'in authority. The Ch'in were eliminated; the founder of the Han, a wily man of peasant origin, kept as his part of the spoils the strong 'land within the passes' – ancient Ch'in, modern Shensi. From that base he waged for several years an often unsuccessful war against his chief antagonist, Hsiang Yu, an aristocrat from southern Ch'u, who for a time appeared to be the new arbiter of China's fate. Of Liu Pang, founder of the Han empire, it may be said he never won a battle (except the last), but rarely – if ever – lost a campaign. Cunning, patience, an ability to win friends and gain supporters, gave him the final victory. Hsiang Yu, defeated and a refugee, took his own life when all hope of escape was lost. The story of his fall remains one of the great Chinese operas to the present day.

The Han dynasty completed, with more caution and less cruelty, the revolution which the Ch'in had brutally inaugurated. There was a slight concession to feudalist feeling. Some fiefs were created – in favour of the royal family – but as time passed legislation to compel all princes to divide their fiefs equally among their sons fragmented the feudal holdings. These were also judiciously intermingled with districts ruled and garrisoned by imperial officers and troops. Within a few generations feudal privilege and power was no longer a reality. In place of it arose the social system which endured until the recent communist revolution. The freehold property in land meant the development of a landowning class, a poorer class of peasant farmers and a large class of landless tenants. When the peasant owner in the middle was too squeezed by the growth of landlordism on the one side and tenantry on the other, revolt was never far away. The unification of the empire, and the comparative freedom from wars which followed the Han victory, brought about profound economic changes beyond the sphere of land tenure. A money economy arose, and this new phenomenon, difficult to manage and wholly unfamiliar even to the educated class, produced some serious crises. It was discovered that to permit the owners of copper mines to mint as many coins as they pleased led to inflation. To restrict the coinage unduly, by rigid government control, had other unfortunate results. These problems arose mainly in the reign of the Emperor Wu (140 to 87 BC), one of the great dynamic figures of Chinese history. Warrior (usually by delegation to his generals), administrator, religious innovator and economic experimenter, he dominated his age. The historian Ssu-ma Ch'ien disliked him, and felt himself wronged by the Emperor. He has successfully introduced into his history some concealed snide criticisms, and it is said that in a 'lost' section he was still more outspoken.

The historians and the scholars, whose training and outlook were inspired by a reverence for the remote past, and the classical age of Confucius, neither understood nor liked the task of grappling with new economic problems. The Emperor Wu therefore turned to the merchants, who did understand business. This action was stringently condemned by the scholars, but solved the economic crisis. The Emperor Wu also achieved by border warfare a long-lasting, but not permanent, control over the nomadic raiders of the steppe, then known as the Hsiung Nu, who may have been the ancestors of the Huns who invaded Europe five hundred years later. As a by-product of these campaigns the Chinese found the land route across central Asia and made contacts with the Greco–Macedonian kingdoms in the eastern part of what had been Alexander's empire. They also sent envoys to the Roman empire; descriptions of Ta Tsin, which was Rome, are preserved in the Han histories. They are reasonably accurate, with some confusions, and do at times indicate the observations of one who was present, not only recording hearsay.

The Han Empire thus corresponded in many ways to the almost exactly contemporary Roman Empire in the West. This has led to the view that they were in other respects similar societies, and shared a like fate. Yet the differences are profound. Rome was the outgrowth of a city state; the Han Empire the amalgamation of ancient kingdoms already of great area. There was a unity of speech, custom and ethnic character in China far greater than that of the Roman world. The Han empire was a land mass to which maritime communications were of secondary importance. The theory of society, the enlarged family with joint responsibility, the emperor as the head of the human race in a paternal as well as in a political sense, the secondary importance of his military role and the primary importance of his religious function, are all features of Chinese society which are sharply different from those of the classical West. They have also proved more enduring.

Conscious both of the new character of their régime and of their own rather obscure origin, the Han emperors gave a great emphasis to the establishment of an orthodox doctrine to justify their system. Confucius and his teaching, so centred on loyalty, was the most suitable and also the most widespread current doctrine; the Han emperors, after some hesitation, put the seal of their approval upon it. History could be encouraged especially as it showed, or sought to show, that the unified empire was really the norm of the Golden Age, and the feudal system a decline from that happy state. The Han had restored the unified empire. Thus was created the tradition of legitimacy which continued to inform all Chinese historical writing. It was necessary to establish which contesting prince was the legitimate heir; then his side was on the right, was moral, was sanctioned by heaven, and his opponents were evil, ambitious, depraved and cast out by heaven. Especially if they lost.

The Han dynasty is usually divided into two eras, by, first, the usurpation of Wang Mang, which lasted from AD 9 to 25, after which the second, a collateral branch of the imperial family, was able to recover the throne, and moved the capital from the old centre at Ch'angan (Sian) to Loyang. Called for this reason the Eastern or Later Han, the dynasty and empire enjoyed a new lease of life for two centuries, during which the empire was expanded by the incorporation of central Asia (modern Sinkiang) and much of what is now Russian central Asia, as far as the shores of the Caspian Sea. These farther limits were rather fleetingly maintained, but a Chinese administration in Sinkiang was solidly implanted. One consequence of this colonial empire was closer contact with India, and the spread of Buddhism by pilgrim monks along the great 'silk road'. Buddhism is first officially mentioned in Chinese historical record in the Eastern Han period, but it is probable that official notice had been preceded by several years of private preaching.

The internal weakness of the empire in the political sphere was due, both in the early and later Han periods, to an unexpected consequence of the united empire. The sovereign had no equal, and his family no peers. But he could not marry a girl of his own patrilineal descent. So he must marry the daughter of a subject. There were no civilised foreign powers with whom to make matrimonial alliances, as had been done between the rival Chinese kingdoms. The daughter of a subject would become empress, and mother of the heir, either because she was very beautiful, or because her family were very influential. In either case the consequences were inconvenient. The family of a pretty but obscure girl at once rose to wealth, power and arrogance. They were intolerable to the established ruling class, but secure as long as the emperor lived. If the family were already influential the added status of being the consort family made them most dangerous, and they became greatly feared and hated. The solution was to try to get such power that another girl of the consort family could be made the bride of the heir to the throne – for Chinese exogamy did not forbid such unions. Everyone at court other than the relatives of the consort family itself was determined to prevent this: hence a series of sanguinary *coups d'état*, assassinations and exterminations of the fallen consort family. Hardly one escaped this fate. Some famous consort families did manage to impose themselves for as many as three generations, and in each case the succeeding repercussions were the first cause of the downfall of the Western and then of the Eastern Han.

Except when these dislocations had already become serious, the administration of the empire had succeeded in avoiding unrest in the provinces. The great peasant rebellions of the Han period, the Red Eyebrows at the end of Wang Mang's usurpation and the Yellow Turbans in the last years of the Eastern Han, arose as a consequence of the disorder in the central government. The Han dynasty was thus brought down in the last years of the second century AD by violent palace conflicts between the eunuchs and the army, themselves the outcome of family feuds between consorts and their enemies. In the disorder of these days the administration was torn apart by conflicts between the supporters and clients of the court eunuchs, who had the ear of a very foolish emperor, and their opponents, who increasingly gained influence in the army. The army massacred the eunuchs; the emperor was carried off and was passed from one military commander to another; a complex civil war developed, with the peasant Yellow Turban rebels as a background. Finally, three major contestants emerged, none strong enough to destroy both rivals, none trusting enough to combine to destroy the third. China was divided into the Three Kingdoms: Wei in the north, Wu in the south, and Shu Han in the far west. This last, the smallest and weakest but ruled by a prince who claimed to belong to a remote collateral branch of the Han imperial family, has always been the favourite of the historians and, through this tradition, of popular legend and romance also. Legitimacy must be upheld.

In fact the Chinese historians have never been able to decide that there was any legitimate successor to the Han, that any prince had received the unqualified mandate of heaven. So alone in Chinese history this period does not have a dynastic designation, but only the name 'Three Kingdoms' (*San Kuo*). The period has greater fame in literature and drama, from the many versions of the *Romance of the Three Kingdoms* (*San Kuo Chih Yen Yi*), than it deserves. It was brief and turbulent, and ended in another reunion of the empire, the Tsin dynasty, which itself proved but transitory.

The invasion of the northern barbarians in AD 316 was a catastrophe more than comparable to the Vandal sack of Rome. Loyang was destroyed, and it is probable that more books were lost in this disaster than in the Ch'in persecution. The whole of China north of the Yangtze was overrun, but the Tsin princes rallied at Nanking, and regained the Yangtze valley and all south of it. China was now divided between Tatar dynasties ruling in the north and the Chinese empire in the south. For seventy years the north was an unstable chaos of warring tribes from which no effective government developed. Then the invasion of another, the Toba, brought all the north under one rule, the Toba Wei dynasty, which gave stability and allowed civilisation to revive.

The Empires of North and South

For two hundred and seventy-three years China remained divided between north and south. In the south, at Nanking, dynasties rose and fell, at rather brief intervals, barely surviving the lifetime of the forceful man who had founded them. The Wei dynasty was more enduring, and rapidly adopted the civilisation and even the language of its Chinese subjects. As time passed, the distinction between the two races faded. Tatar surnames retained an alien sound, but those who bore them spoke, wrote and thought as the Chinese of the educated class and were indistinguishable from their Chinese counterparts.

There had been a great emigration from the north at the first shock of invasion, but millions remained, and among them, where local circumstances favoured them, men of influence and standing from the old Chinese society of the late Han and Tsin. These became, with their Tatar colleagues, a new type of aristocracy, which dominated northern society and had some reflection in the south also. The essence of the new order was that power did not depend on office held from a weak dynastic ruler, nor from large fiefs, but upon a following of armed men who could be called up either to defend or to subvert the imperial government. This was no doubt a legacy from the tribal origins of the Tatar aristocracy, but it related to the conditions under which the Chinese had produced a similar caste in the confusion of the last age of the Han and Three Kingdoms.

The emperor of the day, and his weak dynasty, depended upon the support of these military leaders. He rewarded them with the high ranks and titles of the imperial civil service, now ineffective beyond the capital unless acting with the approval of some military potentate. Many of these were interrelated; they combined, feuded, fought and quarrelled without any serious regard to the authority of the emperor, unless the throne was occupied by the one among them who was for the moment stronger than the others. Their struggles were usually short and only their professional followers were involved. The mass of the people remained outside the dispute, if suffering from the disorders it caused. It is never clear that any local patriotism for northern or southern régimes was a strong motive. Both sides aspired, in theory, to a reunion of the empire; neither conceded legitimacy to the rival. War between north and south was sporadic but endemic. Border fortresses multiplied along the rather indeterminate frontier to the north of the Yangtze.

The Chinese call this period the Empire of North and South or the Six Dynasties (from the number which reigned in the south) but it is also the 'Age of Confusion', which has led some Western scholars to characterise it as a Chinese 'dark age', like that which followed the extinction of the Roman Empire of the West. This is far from true. The Six Dynasties, particularly the southern dynasties, produced some of the finest of Chinese poetry, and there were major developments in religion and in art. Nanking was a sophisticated, even decadent, city of luxury and arts. History was written, the script was never lost, literacy did not decline.

The spread of Buddhism during these centuries, likened to the conversion of the Roman and barbarian worlds to Christianity, was also different in operation and in effect. Buddhism came from a foreign land, India. Its scriptures were only translated from Sanskrit into Chinese by the laborious efforts of generations of scholars, and its doctrines for many centuries reached only an élite. Buddhism is not a socially-orientated religion. It values individual enlightenment, study, self-perfection, and withdrawal from the world. It carried no message for mass interpretation and did not seek power or try to oust earlier deities.

118

It was not concerned with secular education. Consequently it grew on the Chinese civilisation like ivy on a great tree: it neither disturbed the roots nor affected the growth of the major branches.

The introduction of Buddhism and its gradual penetration, first of the educated, much later of the populace, is the very reverse of the growth of Christianity in the Roman Empire. Its effects on art were important and lasting, it profoundly influenced the development of the other native Chinese religion, Taoism, but its secular impact was muted. The institutions of the Chinese state, the teaching of the schools and the literature of the orthodox philosophy were not significantly touched by Buddhist influences.

The period of the Empires of North and South was thus a formative one, not one of declining civilisation. It was also a turning point in Chinese history. Had the division become lasting and established, it seems probable that the differing character of the two regions, emphasised by the existence of separate political systems, would have in time given birth to two, or perhaps more, nation states. The unity of the Han Empire would have been a memory of something no longer attainable, as the Roman Empire became in Europe. This did not happen. The prime cause was the lack of any defined border between north and south. The Yangtze is not a frontier, but an artery; the frontier lay to the north, in low mountains or marshy plains, no real obstacle to advancing armies. As soon as one power became strong enough to win victory, reunion was certain.

The break-up of the Wei dynasty in the north delayed this for half a century. The decline in effectiveness and power of the southern empire, under weak dynasties, presented the opportunity to the first strong ruler to rise in the north. This was the founder of the Sui dynasty; a Chinese on the paternal side, he was related through his mother to the reigning dynast, whom he dethroned and who was of Tatar descent. The new Emperor rapidly unified the north, then struck south and swiftly overthrew the weak Ch'en dynasty in Nanking. In AD 589 China was once more united in a single state. Although there have been many changes of dynasty, and some partial foreign conquests, the unity rebuilt by the Sui and T'ang dynasties has endured ever since. It became the norm; division was chaos, to be deplored as fatal to peace and prosperity.

The T'ang dynasty

This outcome cannot have seemed very probable at the time. The Sui dynasty reunited the empire but, in the second reign, engaged in a prolonged and repeated attempt to conquer the northern kingdom of the three into which Korea was then divided. These efforts failed; the extravagant conduct and megalomania of the Emperor Yang Ti led to revolt, and soon the new-found unity collapsed in a welter of civil war. From this emerged, in six years, the T'ang dynasty, which gained control of the whole empire, and endured for three centuries, from 618 to 906. The T'ang thus did for the Second Chinese Empire what the Han had done for the First. In both cases union was achieved by a short-lived and harsh régime; in each case the union was consolidated and developed by a long-lasting dynasty pursuing moderate and skilful policies. This reconstruction of an empire which had disappeared three hundred years earlier can be likened to the possibility that Charlemagne could have restored a real Roman Empire in the West. In China the dream became fact, in Europe it faded.

It can be argued that the development of a culture is actually helped by diversity rather than unity, and that had the Chinese world continued to be divided the later qualities of Chinese civilisation would have been enriched. The Chinese themselves have never accepted this view. To them unity is the first essential; within the empire – or whatever the state may be called – local diversity is desirable, and a subject of pride. But unity must come first. There can be no doubt that it was the astonishing vigour and achievement of the early part of the T'ang dynasty which implanted this conviction. The real founder, Li Shih-min, who succeeded his father to reign as T'ai Tsung, is accepted by traditional historians (if not always by contemporary ones) as the outstanding monarch of Chinese history. Brilliant as a general, at a very early age, he was equally or better known as an administrator and an innovator in the structure of the imperial government. He was an active historian, and his calligraphy is still a model. T'ai Tsung only lacked sons worthy to succeed him. Instead, he was to be followed by the fifty-year rule of his erstwhile concubine and daughter-in-law, the Empress Wu, who dominated the prince, whom she seduced into marrying her. After his death she dethroned her own son, and for the last years of a long life reigned as monarch in her own right; the first and only occasion on which the Chinese throne was occupied by a woman.

Had these remarkable changes of role been all that the Empress Wu accomplished, she would be a curiosity of history; in effect she exercised a lasting formative influence, partly in order to secure her own strangely illegitimate position. Under the measures which this able and ruthless woman put into effect the military aristocracy, of the type described as characteristic of the northern empire, and to which the

T'ang imperial family themselves belonged, was steadily deprived of power, virtually decimated, and eliminated as a major political force. The Empress Wu achieved what T'ai Tsung could only cautiously begin to do, which was to break the power of those clans and families who would inevitably prove a source of danger to the new dynasty.

The political and social changes which Empress Wu promoted gave the new empire a stability in its social and political structure which had been lacking since the decline of the Han. Abroad, the frontiers were rendered secure, the nomads repelled and Korea, after a long war, finally conquered and occupied. This rather useless exercise in imperialism was later modified into the suzerain-tributary relationship which endured under changing dynasties until the Japanese domination at the end of the nineteenth century. One lasting consequence of the Chinese conquest was the unification of Korea into one kingdom, which also endured until modern times.

The creation of an effective civil service administering all parts of the vast empire was more than a restoration of the Han system. From the time of T'ai Tsung onwards the new principle of entry into imperial service by public examinations was followed, being free, with some few exceptions, to all who could compete. The Chinese thus invented the examination; one of the more controversial of their contributions to the world which many centuries later adopted this method of determining qualifications. Its purpose at the time was to substitute another stream of imperial officials for the hitherto exclusive reliance on the clients recommended by the powerful aristocracy. The two systems continued in use under the T'ang, the new steadily replacing the old one, until recommendation faded from normal practice. Thus the T'ang period, particularly in the late seventh and first half of the eighth centuries, was an important period of social change in which the aristocratic nature of society was transformed slowly into a bureaucratic order recruited from a much wider field of literate gentry, the sons of the minor land-owning class, who did not command military or civil power. For its time, the T'ang bureaucracy was highly organised and efficient. It introduced and operated a more sophisticated system of revenue collection, relegated the army to the frontiers as a professional force divorced from political authority, and was on several occasions able to carry out a census of the population which, as discoveries of contemporary documents prove, was no mere estimate of taxpayers but a detailed record listing men, women and children in individual families. The figure for the year 754 was 52,880,488.

It was, curiously, the throne itself which was less stable than its own administration. The Empress Wu, at a great age, and ill, was forced in the year 705, a year before her death, to hand over to the son whom she had deposed. He governed foolishly under the influence of an ambitious wife who hoped to emulate the mother-in-law she hated. Overthrown by a palace revolution, another son of the Empress Wu was put on the throne by his sister, the Princess T'ai p'ing, who also imagined herself to be the obvious heiress of her mother's unique position. A granddaughter had already aspired to the same heights, and had fallen by the way. Women hoped for a degree of liberation which was still many centuries ahead. It was the grandson of the Empress Wu, later known as Hsüan Tsung, or by his nickname Ming Huang – the Brilliant Emperor – who deposed his sister, and soon after succeeded when his ineffective father gladly abdicated. Ming Huang was not, however, the Crown Prince but a younger son: his eldest and other elder brothers did not contest his accession, and the brothers lived in good friendship for many years, a fact which orthodox Confucian historians found consoling in view of the obvious breaches of convention and morality in the T'ang succession.

Thus, including the great T'ai Tsung himself, not one of the emperors of the first 150 years of the T'ang period, its finest age, were the legitimate heirs of their fathers. No crown prince came to the throne. Under these circumstances it might be thought that experience showed that some form of selective succession among the imperial family would be a wise innovation, rather than leaving such selection to the violent fortunes of palace revolution. This was not possible, or not thought possible, in a society dominated by Confucian ethics, even if these were so often honoured in the breach. The reign of the Brilliant Emperor, of nearly half a century, was indeed a period which is still seen as a time of cultural splendour and outstanding achievements. The greatest of the T'ang poets, Li Po, T'u Fu and many others were contemporaries of Ming Huang; the first development of the drama arose at his court; in art the painters – whose work is known only through early copies – were esteemed in later ages as models of near-perfection. In many other arts – Buddhist and lay sculpture, the first true porcelain, and very fine silver ware, the early T'ang period is supreme. In the T'ang period the Chinese civilisation was more open to foreign influence and to contact with foreign peoples than it was to be for the next thousand years. A poet like Li Po could speak Persian; Islam was first introduced by the large Arab trading community in the southern ports; Nestorian Christianity enjoyed the tolerance, indeed the favour, of the court, and left a celebrated contemporary monument recording these facts. At almost every point the origin of some later development of Chinese civilisation is found in the age of Ming Huang.

The reign of the Brilliant Emperor ended in disaster. His infatuation with his famous, if hardly girlish, concubine, Yang Kuei Fei, caused him to ignore the ambition of the commander of the northern frontier army, an officer (like many others) of Turkish origin. An Lu-shan revolted, and found that the only opposition was the feeble defence put up by the palace guards, who were more ornamental than militant. Ming Huang had to flee to remote Szechwan in the west, sacrificing the concubine Yang Kuei Fei to appease the mutinous troops, who demanded her death. This episode, the theme of the poet P'o Chu-yi's epic written a few years later, has been one of the most celebrated tragic stories in Chinese literature and drama ever since. The dramatic and poetic versions tend to gloss over some less romantic aspects; the Emperor was seventy-two at the time, Yang Kuei Fei over forty, and she had originally been the concubine of one of the Emperor's sons.

A long civil war followed before the dynasty, ultimately victorious, recovered Ch'angan, the capital to which the aged and broken Ming Huang returned, shortly to abdicate in favour of his eldest son. An Lu-shan had already been assassinated and succeeded by another rebel; victory was attained by using foreign mercenaries, the Uighur tribe, who were Muslim, and partly by winning over and pardoning prominent rebel commanders. The skill and devotion of the imperial commander-in-chief, Kuo Tzu-yi, who was claimed by the Nestorians to be their friend and patron (and conceivably convert) was also a major factor. Even in disaster the prestige of the T'ang imperial family was enough to win support and to retain control of south China, which was not a battlefield of the civil war. The restored dynasty did not, however, regain that unquestioned authority and control which the first emperors had exercised. The great provincial military governors, whether ex-rebel or loyalist, had to be humoured, and sometimes took up arms. They also impaired the authority of the civil service in their domains. Politics became a game of checks and balances; the aim of the court to reduce, or at least contain, the power of the military governors; the objectives of the latter to maintain their positions and if possible pass them to their heirs. In the latter aspiration they were frustrated by skilful court policy, but the later emperors could never get rid of the system which was the legacy of the revolt of An Lu-shan. For another century relative stability and peace were achieved on these terms; it was not an age of growing disorder and showed no diminution in the standard of literary eminence and art. But politically it slowly weakened. The short lives and brief reigns of the later T'ang emperors, perhaps due to unwise experimentation with 'drugs of immortality' – which secured rapid immortality in the next world rather than in this one – contributed to political decline. No military governor really attempted to usurp the throne, but nor did any of them lose power in the provinces in favour of the court.

The influence of palace eunuchs has often been cited as a cause of the T'ang decline, and with weak and sick emperors, sometimes minors, the opportunity for such influence was considerable. But, unlike the Han period, it was not possible for the T'ang eunuchs to exercise much influence beyond the capital. Military governors were not dependent on their favour for survival even if it was worth their while to bribe them for minor advantages. The civil service was now too powerful an organisation; its members were no longer the clients of some great family whose fall would involve the ruin of many officials. Eunuch power was pernicious at court, and possibly contributed to the weak health of successive late T'ang emperors, but it was not a decisive factor.

Careless administration, allowing distant armies to go unpaid, corruption and self-seeking, were the fatal flaws. The fact that the army stationed on the frontier between what are now Tonking and Yünnan (the former area then a Chinese province, the latter the hostile kingdom of Nanchao), was still an imperial army paid by the court, proves that even by the middle of the ninth century the central government had much power. Unfortunately, it neglected to pay this army; in the year 868 it mutinied, abandoned its post and started to march home, looting on the way. The leader was a new, later a familiar type, the 'failed candidate for the civil service'. Huang Tsao was thus an educated man, but his army was a professional one, and gained recruits from a wide assortment of malcontents as it marched north. The military governors in his path usually preferred allowing the rebels go on, as long as they went into the domain of the next governor; thus they were not seriously opposed, but for some years wandered about central China, plundering, blackmailing the governors and gaining strength. The apparent inability of the court to mobilise effective power to suppress them finally convinced Huang Tsao that he had nothing to fear from a bold assault on the capital itself. He was right; a sudden rapid march was hardly resisted, Ch'angan fell, the reigning emperor fled to the west, and in 881 China dissolved into anarchy.

The Five Dynasties

For several years the confusion grew worse. The rebels were defeated but the victors promptly started to fight each other; some rebels became 'loyalists', but only to further their own ambitions under this cover. The

124

powerless emperor was restored to the capital but was controlled by whichever satrap was momentarily in power, and fell under the domination of the next one to gain the prize. Finally one of alien origin, as many were, and more brutal than the others, deposed and massacred the imperial family, destroyed the great city of Ch'angan, and in 904 set up his own 'dynasty' in the eastern city of K'aifeng, which had been his headquarters. The southern governors repudiated him, as did others, and each and all claimed the throne; there were 'emperors' on all sides. Gradually some system evolved. The south broke clean away to form several states, whose rulers took the imperial title but left each other alone. In the north the unstable Five Dynasties controlled sometimes all, more often parts of the country. They were founded by military commanders, and usually endured no longer than the lives of these founders. Territory in north China, including the passes of the Great Wall and the site of modern Peking, was ceded to the northern Tatar kingdom of Liao, established in 936 in what is now Manchuria. In the north-west, Kansu, another alien régime called Hsi Hsia set up an independent kingdom.

The Chinese orthodox historians treat the Five Dynasties as continuing the legitimate line of authority, although they were brief, turbulent and often alien. But they did control greater areas than any of the southern states. Thus, while in the period of division after the Han the unified south was considered to be the legitimate state, in the period of similar but far shorter confusion after the T'ang, it was the relatively more powerful northern states which are listed in the dynastic sequence.

It was, indeed, from the north that the restoration of unity and strong government was to come. The founder of the Sung was a general in the service of the brief Later Chou dynasty. The ruling emperor was a child, heir to the deceased 'strong man'. The officers of Chao K'uang-yin, dissatisfied with this situation, one night roused their commander and threw a dragon robe – imperial costume – round his shoulders, telling him he must either accept the throne or be killed. Chao K'uang-yin accepted. This curiously Roman episode, so common in the history of the Roman Empire, is unique in Chinese history.

The Sung dynasty

The sequel was also not on the Roman model. Chao K'uang-yin, founder of the Sung, was a very skilful politician, moderate and merciful, with a fine sense of timing and an understanding of the limitations of his power. This he built up both in the face of his southern rivals and in the internal situation. He was a Chinese, and this recommended him to those who had tired of 'barbarian' commanders turned emperors. He invited the smaller southern kingdoms to surrender their independence, promising comfortable immunity and wealth to their rulers. They trusted him, and he kept his promises. Much of the south submitted, state by state, without resistance. Where it was attempted, it was easily crushed, but the Sung emperor was still merciful to the conquered. He was acting in tune with a widespread feeling and belief now dominant among the Chinese people, or at least among the literate class: that unity was the only way to prosperity and peace; separatism was not to be admitted. When the major state of the south at first pleaded that it was in itself worthy to remain independent, the Emperor remarked: 'And what crime have the people of Kiangnan committed that they should be exiled from the Empire?'

On the other hand, Chao K'uang-yin decided not to try to restore Chinese authority in Vietnam (then confined to the northern part of that country) which had been a T'ang province. The Vietnamese had revolted after the fall of the T'ang. They set up their own kingdom, and the Sung were content to treat it as a tributary state, like Korea, a position which the Vietnamese accepted, and which became henceforth the long-lasting relationship between the two countries. The Emperor was shown plans to conquer the south-western kingdom of Nanchao in Yünnan, ever hostile to the T'ang and ruled by a dynasty of Thai origin, although the country was culturally much under Chinese influence. He refused, stating that he did not regard Nanchao as part of the empire. It remained independent until conquered by the Mongols.

The Emperor also succeeded in disbanding the army and reducing the great authority of the generals, thus breaking the vicious circle of usurpation and conspiracy of which his own elevation to the throne was the last example. Whatever troubles his dynasty was to encounter from foreign enemies, it is a fact that the Sung were less affected by internal revolts than any other Chinese dynasty of long duration. It became the age in which the civil service, now wholly recruited from the gentry by public examinations, ruled supreme. There were frequent and prolonged policy conflicts between different groups, but although imperial favour was given and withdrawn, the party out of power was neither persecuted nor imprisoned, executed or exterminated (as had been the usual fate of the fallen statesmen), but merely exiled to take charge of distant magistracies in the far-off provinces, sometimes such as had a reputation for a bad climate. For their age, the Sung were humane. The problem which beset the dynasty, and which was never solved, was posed by external enemies. The configuration of power in the steppes beyond the northern frontier had profoundly changed in the late T'ang and Five Dynasties period.

From the time of the Sung onward the danger did not come from that part of the Mongolian steppe directly north of China, as it had done for centuries, but from what is now Manchuria. The Three Eastern Provinces, as the Chinese call them, are not semi-desert, but fertile and in parts forested country, capable of sustaining a large population and a settled agricultural economy. They had developed in this way largely as a result of contact with China, and the Tatar dynasties which ruled these countries benefited from much greater resources and manpower. The Liao dynasty had already exacted the cession of the north-east of China proper from one of the weak Five Dynasties, and the Sung were never able to regain it, meeting disaster when they tried. This gave the northern neighbour the entry into the North China Plain through the passes north of Peking. The Hsi Hsia in the north-west, though also established in what had been territory of the T'ang empire, were not so powerful, if just as hostile. Foreign dangers were the constant preoccupation of the Sung emperors.

For rather more than 150 years the Sung held their own, and this period was marked by great intellectual and artistic activity. It was the age when Confucianism was reshaped to meet the ideas of a more sophisticated period and acquired the form and doctrine which it subsequently retained. At the same time a very intense political contest raged between two groups of scholar officials (often at the same time protagonists of differing philosophic interpretations of the Confucian classics). On the one side were the followers of Wang An-shih and his reforms, which were both economic and political. He sought to make the empire strong enough in material power to resist the potential invaders. His plans envisaged an active participation of the government in the direction and financing of agriculture by advancing seed grain loans to the peasants, who would repay at harvest, and above all by diminishing the power of moneylenders who drove the peasants into debt. Other reforms aimed at greater internal security by mutual surveillance and guarantees among neighbours in villages and cities. This, which lent itself to the activity of the informer, was the most enduring of Wang An-shih's policies. The reform policy was applied, repudiated, reapplied and modified on several occasions, depending on the personal views of the reigning emperor. The monarch was assailed at all times by the reproaches and exhortations of the opponents of the reforms, led by a famous historian and statesman, Ssu-ma Kuang. The objection of these opponents was twofold: firstly – of great appeal to conservative Confucians – that the policies of Wang were new; secondly, that they overturned established customs and were concerned with economic questions which should not be the business of the emperor or his officials.

Wang An-shih has been called a socialist before his time, but this is really an anachronism. Much of his policy was highly authoritarian and aimed at strengthening the power of the government rather than giving power to the people – an idea which would never have entered his head. On the other hand, the characteristics of the diehard are very conspicuous in some of the arguments used by his opponents. Whether the Sung régime profited more from the sporadic enactment of the reforms, or lost more through the contests and distractions of the quarrel might be as questionable today as it appeared to contemporaries.

One feature of this period was the comparative freedom from palace intrigue and plotting which marked the involvement of the throne in this long-lasting dispute. The Sung emperors were temperate men, not with conspicuously brilliant minds but neither lazy, corrupt nor erratic. The last of those to reign over united China, Hui Tsung, was an artist of great renown and talent, but unfortunately not very much interested in politics and inept at administration. He also had the misfortune to reign when the neighbour to the north, the Liao, had just been replaced by a more militant Tatar people and dynasty, the Kin of the Jurchen tribe, remote ancestors of the later Manchus. Having conquered the Liao, the Kin moved south to invade China. The Sung court unwisely decided that the Liao having fallen they, the Sung, were entitled to recover the lost territory in northern Hopei province. The result was a disastrous defeat, the siege and fall of the capital, K'aifeng, the capture of the emperor Hui Tsung, and the loss of the northern half of China.

This event, in 1121, marks the division of the Sung period into what is called Northern Sung, when the dynasty ruled all China, and Southern Sung, when it was confined to the south, with the capital at Hangchou. The Sung retained the Yangtze valley, and the south was now a much richer and more developed country than it had been five or six centuries earlier at the time of the Northern and Southern Empires. It had largely escaped both the troubles at the end of the T'ang dynasty and the rebellion of An Lu-shan. New industries such as silk weaving, tea growing and above all porcelain were concentrated in the south, particularly in the south-east part of the country. This soon became, and remained, the richest region in China.

It was during the Southern Sung period that active commerce with the lands to the south of China, and also with Japan, developed far beyond its former importance. In the Southern Sung the revenue from excise and customs exceeded the land revenue, which has never been the

Above: This pottery bowl, found in Kiangsu in 1963, dates from the late fourth or third millennium.
Right: A tripod pottery jug from the third or early second millennium, found in Shantung in 1964.
Below: The funeral suit of Tou Wan is made of jade sections 'scwn' together with gold. It dates from the late second century BC.

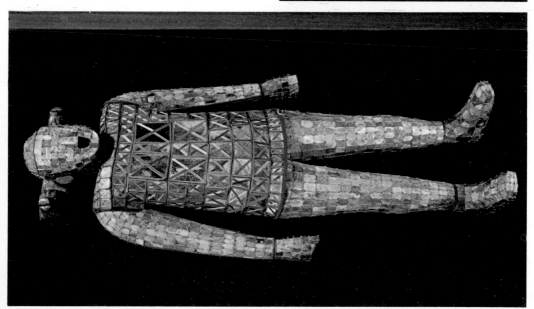

Facing page: A twelfth-century AD celadon tripod vessel from Shensi.

Left: A superb bronze galloping horse of the second century AD. Below: A model of a horse and carriage, complete with driver and attendant. This bronze group also dates from the second century AD.

Overleaf: A traditional opera performance at Peking. The personalities of the characters are indicated by the different colours of make-up used and the parts of the face covered.

Facing page: The Temple of the
Ancestors, Canton.

Above: Harvesting a fodder crop.
Left: A typical scene – bicycles,
buses, but no cars – on the
avenue into Tien An Men,
Peking.

The entrance to the former Imperial Palaces in Peking.

case before or since. Navigation had improved with the invention of the maritime compass, originally designed by Taoist priests to determine the favourable aspect of buildings and tombs, but adapted to maritime use either by Arabs in imitation of the Chinese, or by contact among the seafaring population. To protect this commerce the Southern Sung developed naval power, virtually new to Chinese governments. It has been suggested that the advancing economy of the Southern Sung, its superb handicraftsmanship, the development of overseas commerce and the growth of industries such as silk and porcelain, which worked in large part for export and increasingly in concentrated centres of production, had reached a point where it would be natural to have been succeeded by an industrial revolution and the development of machine technology. The domination of land revenue and landowners was diminished.

The Yüan (Mongol) dynasty

If this could have happened, it was frustrated by new events in the north. The Mongols, under the redoubtable Chingiz Khan, had overthrown the Kin dynasty, and they too soon turned south to attack the Sung. Moreover, the Mongol conquest of the north was no mere change of régime. It was accompanied by the most extensive devastation and wholesale slaughter which China had known. Vast areas of the northern provinces were virtually depopulated, and some parts remained in this condition as 'hunting parks' for the Mongol rulers until well into the fifteenth century. The north-west, the kingdom of Hsi Hsia, was almost exterminated and never fully recovered. The Southern Sung had to turn all their resources to a desperate and prolonged defence. It lasted forty years – whereas the Mongol conquest of great kingdoms in western Asia took barely as many weeks. The Sung stubbornly defended the maritime cities and the great centres on the Yangtze where their naval power could operate. It was not until the Mongols outflanked the empire by moving down the far western marches of Tibet to invade and conquer the Nanchao kingdom in Yünnan that the Sung defences began to crumble. The navy was the last support of the falling dynasty, and the last Sung emperor perished in a naval battle near the modern city of Hong Kong.

Kublai Khan, who was already ruler of the north for several years, now became sole emperor in all China; he is perhaps the best-known emperor of China to the western world. He was not, of course, Chinese. He ruled the empire with a mixed civil service of foreign officers and Chinese civil servants. One of the former was the Venetian Marco Polo, who spent seventeen years in his service, and on his return to Italy wrote his famous book, which revealed for the first time the character of the Chinese state to a largely incredulous Europe.

Kublai was a prodigious figure to Polo, but to the Chinese he and his dynasty were alien and oppressive conquerors. The Chinese educated class felt ignored and neglected; although, towards the end of the Mongol dynasty, the civil service examinations were re-established, they had lapsed for nearly a century or more, during which time administrative power had largely been in the hands of the foreigners whom the Mongols enlisted in all parts of their huge empire and from beyond its borders. Muslims from central Asia were more prominent than the few Europeans, and were notorious for their corruption and disdain for the Chinese. The Mongol rule was thus never popular in China, and failed to win the co-operation of the educated classes.

By contrast, Kublai continued, or tried to continue, the vast schemes of conquest which his predecessors had carried out. He had already added the south-western kingdom of Nanchao, in modern Yünnan province, to the Chinese empire; after his complete conquest of the Sung he turned his attention to overseas objectives and to Vietnam and Burma. None of these ventures was a lasting success. His invasions of Vietnam, at first victorious, were later opposed by tenacious resistance in the jungles, and ultimately the Mongol forces withdrew, accepting the old relationship of suzerain and tributary, which they could have obtained without an invasion. In Burma the Mongol destruction of the Burmese kingdom was followed by a withdrawal brought about by the climate, which was unhealthy for the northern armies; the country was left in confusion under a number of mutually hostile and turbulent principalities, mainly ruled by alien Thai princes. An expedition to Java, also successful at first, ended with a well-planned local revolt which compelled the Mongol armies to leave the country.

The most spectacular failure was the attempt to conquer Japan. It was renewed after the first defeat; on this occasion the tenacious resistance of the Japanese feudal levies was aided by the 'Divine Wind' – the typhoon which wrecked much of the Mongol fleet and brought the invasion to an end. It seems possible that Kublai still planned another invasion, but he died before it was launched, in 1294, and his successor abandoned the project. The fleet used in the expeditions to Vietnam, Java and Japan was in effect the successor to the Sung navy. It was Chinese-manned, in part commanded by Chinese officers, and used the technical skills which had been developed in the preceding period. It also seems probable that the Chinese-commanded fleet, and the Korean component which took part in the campaigns against Japan, had very slight commitment to the policies of the alien court, and did not exert themselves unduly in its service.

It is one of the ironies of history that the best-known emperor of China was a foreign conqueror, not a Chinese, and that the Chinese have often been, and are still today, saddled with a reputation for following aggressive policies towards their neighbours which were in fact Mongol policies, for which there is no Chinese historical counterpart. No Chinese dynasty ever planned an invasion of Japan or Indonesia, and their direct rule in Vietnam had been abandoned three hundred years before the age of Kublai. Nor had any Chinese army been seen in Burma.

After the death of Kublai the Mongol dynasty, which in China is known by the dynastic title of Yüan, declined swiftly. The later emperors had short reigns and little competence. Only the last, Tohan Timur, had a long tenure of power, from 1333 to 1368, but it was marked by the increasing confusion and spread of the Chinese revolt which was to end Mongol rule and force the last Mongol emperor to flee from Peking in 1368. Had the Chinese revolt come under a single leadership from the beginning it is probable that victory would have been won several years earlier. In fact there were numerous revolts which were not only uncoordinated but mutually hostile. Much of the long war was fought between Chinese rivals, and had the Mongols possessed the leadership and qualities of their ancestors they should have profited from this situation to suppress all the rebellions.

Two major revolts stand out as historically significant. The first was the rebellion in the southern coastal provinces, led by a man with knowledge of the importance of sea power, who deprived the Mongols of their naval supremacy and thus effectively dislocated their communications with the south. The other, the ultimate victor, was the rebellion which was led by Chu Yüan-chang, the founder of the Ming dynasty. A native of the south-east, the region around the mouth of the Yangtze, he began life in the poorest possible circumstances. His parents, driven by famine from their farm, sold him as a boy to a Buddhist monastery. This life as an unconsidered novice he abandoned to become a beggar and then a bandit. From this occupation he rose, naturally in a time of disorder, to the position of a rebel commander, and then to supreme leader of the revolt which, having overcome all rivals, including the rebels of the southern coast provinces, was crowned with complete victory over the Mongols, the capture of Peking and the flight of the emperor to the lands beyond the Gobi desert.

3 From the Ming to 1840

The Ming dynasty

The Ming dynasty, almost alone (with the possible exception of the Early Han) was founded by a man of the people, illiterate, without any education, but of a most forceful character and great ability. Since he had held no title, he for the first time gave his dynasty a name without local territorial meaning, calling it 'Ming' – Brilliant. He fixed his capital at Nanking, in the region where he was born and from which he had drawn his strength. It was his son who moved it north to Peking, the former Mongol capital, which he rebuilt in the form which the older part of the modern city still retains today. The new Ming empire was more extensive than the Sung had ever been, or the T'ang either. It included the province of Yünnan which the Mongols had conquered, incorporated south Manchuria, as part of the province of Shantung across the sea, and also exercised suzerainty over the northern part of Manchuria. In central Asia the Ming controlled the oasis of Hami, but did not extend their authority to Kashgar and the western part of modern Sinkiang. The reasons may have been twofold. Firstly, the central Asian region was still strongly held by Mongol khans descended from the conquerors of Chingiz's time; secondly, the importance of the overland trade route to western Asia, the old silk road, had declined with the improvement in navigation techniques which had made the sea route more valuable and also safer. Marco Polo, with his uncles, came to China by the land route; seventeen years later he went back to Europe, by way of the Persian Gulf, by sea. Mongol devastation of the northwest, the kingdom of Hsi Hsia, had also contributed to the decline of the land route, and Sung power in south China had enhanced the importance of the southern provinces and their sea communications with India and beyond.

The most dangerous rival of the founder of the Ming had been the leader of the south coastal revolt. His power was largely naval. The Ming learned this lesson and from the first proceeded to build a navy which would surpass all previous attempts. The Ming Precious Ships, what may be called capital ships, were much larger than any previous naval constructions. They carried crews of a thousand men, they had watertight compartments – the earliest record of this device – and they were navigated in the open ocean with the compass.

Under the Emperor Yung Lo, son and second successor to the founder, between 1405 and 1433 the Ming fleet set out on a series of great maritime expeditions, six during Yung Lo's reign and a seventh under a successor, which have no parallel in earlier, or later, Chinese experience. They were not expeditions of conquest and invasion, although they carried up to sixty to seventy thousand soldiers. They annexed no overseas territory, nor did they establish fixed bases under Chinese rule. Their bases, principally Malacca, were the territories of allied states. At a later date orthodox Chinese historians, who as officials disliked the naval expeditions, succeeded in obscuring their real purpose with slanted propaganda descriptions. It was said that they were prompted by the Emperor Yung Lo's obsession with the fear that the nephew whom he had dethroned, and who had disappeared when Nanking fell, had taken refuge overseas and might there organise a restoration. In fact the youth had been concealed by eunuchs and later became a Buddhist monk, in which character he lived on, wandering over China for fifty years, until in old age he was recognised and was allowed to spend his last years in retirement in a monastery near Peking. By that time Yung Lo had long been dead and his great-grandson reigned. Unlikely in itself, this explanation becomes absurd when it is shown that many of the expeditions – all the later ones – were to such distant countries as Oman, the Hejaz, Somaliland and the western coasts of India, places where a Chinese fugitive emperor could not conceivably have won support or recognition. The second explanation vouchsafed by the orthodox historians was that the expeditions were sent to these far-off places merely to collect strange and curious objects for the diversion of the ladies of the harem. Yung Lo was not a man of this frivolous disposition, but a very experienced soldier and administrator.

It emerges from modern research that the main purposes of the great expeditions were quite different. Firstly, perhaps, it was to impress upon the rulers of the overseas countries the power and also the goodwill of the new dynasty ruling China. In contrast to Mongol armed invasions, the Ming came in peace, and brought valuable gifts for well-disposed sultans and kings. These gifts were in fact part of the second, probably more important objective, which can be defined as imperial monopoly trade suitably disguised. The Emperor sent showy, prestigious, but not really very costly gifts, and in return took as reciprocal 'tribute', as Chinese etiquette defined it, really valuable imports: copper from Thailand, ivory from Africa, timber from the Indonesian isles, and a wide variety of goods from all over the coasts of the Indian Ocean. These the imperial court sold in China. No one else was allowed to engage in overseas trade. The great voyages were also a way of training the navy to navigate great ocean distances by compass.

The opposition which finally, under Yung Lo's successors, brought an end to this remarkable efflorescence of Chinese sea power came from the civil service, for more than one reason. Firstly, the navy was not a regular branch of the imperial service, but a court-organised activity commanded by court eunuchs. Cheng Ho, the famous admiral who navigated and commanded all the great expeditions, was not only a eunuch but also a Muslim, from the inland province of Yünnan. It seems a strange choice, but Yung Lo had his reasons. The eunuchs, entirely subservient to his will and without any status other than that of his favour, could be trusted, when ambitious military commanders might not be so reliable. The expeditions were to lands largely under Muslim rulers, and the commander-in-chief must be as much a diplomat as an admiral. Hostility in Aden or Hormuz could have jeopardised a fleet thousands of miles from its home base. A Muslim and a eunuch, granted his competence, was a wise choice: acceptable by religion and skilled in negotiation. The civil service hated the eunuchs, who were beyond their control, overriding the authority of regular officials and in the past, as in Han times, becoming a potent political menace. This was not likely under Yung Lo, but under successors it could easily become so.

The second reason was that the civil service, the educated Confucian scholar class, disapproved of trade by persons such as the monarch. 'The Sage takes no account of gain and loss' – only of virtue and vice. It was morally wrong for the emperor to be concerned in a disguised but lucrative trading venture. Thirdly, both the expeditions and the navy were financed by a source which the civil service did not control. The Mongol emperors had left huge areas of north China desolate after their invasion, and designated them as imperial hunting parks. When the Ming came to power they took these lands as crown property and, not needing them for such extensive hunting, sold them off to landlords and settlers – at a handsome return. These funds built and maintained the navy and provided for the great expeditions.

After Yung Lo's death the opposition managed to stop the expeditions, but as his immediate successor only reigned ten months the last of the series was sent out by another young ruler, who listened to different advice. That however, was the end. Opposition prevailed, and the land revenue funds ran out. The navy was allowed to decay, just sixty-five years before Vasco da Gama rounded the Cape and sailed into the Indian Ocean. Had the Chinese empire set up bases and colonies in such countries as the Philippines, where they would have met no resistance, or developed a lasting connection with Malacca, with which they had a close and friendly alliance, the whole enterprise of the Portuguese east of India might have been frustrated, with incalculable consequences for the history of Asia.

The Ming dynasty suffered after the reign of Yung Lo from a rapid succession of short-lived and youthful monarchs. This, as always, meant uncertainty in policy, regencies, and increasing eunuch influence. Before the end of the fifteenth century the Ming were no longer a formidable enemy to the Mongol tribes to their north, and the Manchu tribes in northern Manchuria were becoming restive under Chinese suzerainty. There was, none the less, much internal stability, although none of the later Ming emperors was an outstanding ruler or even a strong personality. The civil service was the instrument of government and it had now restored and perfected its own system of recruitment and administration. Bureaucracy reigned supreme: it did not matter too much if the monarch was frivolous or indolent as long as he left the essentials of government to competent and experienced senior officials. Trouble came when the influence of eunuchs on emperors who had no experience of the world beyond the palace, and no intimate companions since childhood other than the eunuchs who attended them, became dominant and noxious.

The Ming dynasty endured for two hundred and seventy-six years; and only the last decade of this period was truly plunged into disorder. The splendid treasures of art interred with the Emperor Wan Li in 1620, only twenty-four years before the end, prove the wealth of the empire, if they also testify to the waste of these resources on unproductive luxury. Unlike the Sung, the Ming had little to fear from alien enemies. The Mongol power never again threatened the Chinese empire. Tamerlane is said to have planned to invade the empire to avenge the fall of his distant kinsman, Tohan Timur. He died before his plans were ripe, and no other west Asian ruler ever attempted a conquest of China. Japan produced a minor menace, the pirates who infested the sea coast aided by Chinese *confrères* from the coastal provinces: they made the seas unsafe, a direct outcome of the unwise decision to let naval power decline. But the Sino-Japanese pirates were not the armed forces of an enemy state, and their activity was reduced and finally controlled by an enforced depopulation of the coastal villages; only towns with garrisons remained inhabited. The appearance of European seafarers, Portuguese at first, in the southern ports at the end of the sixteenth century was a portent for the future, but not a matter of concern to the Ming court. There was one enemy to the north: from the end of the sixteenth century the Manchu tribes repudiated Ming suzerainty and, having come together to form a vigorous kingdom, began to encroach upon the territory of the empire in what is now south Manchuria. The Manchus had in fact learned too much from their Chinese suzerains; their kingdom was organised on Ming models, but had its own novel and effective military system.

Early in the seventeenth century the Manchus conquered the whole of the Ming territory beyond the Great Wall, south of Mukden. They set up their capital in Shenyang and their ruler took the imperial title, calling his dynasty Ch'ing – Pure. Chinese and Manchu, now written, were official languages, and the young Manchus were taught the Confucian classics. Many thousands of former Ming Chinese subjects living in this region became Manchu subjects and were admitted to the Manchu military system, the Eight Banners. But the frontier on the Great Wall was a very real obstacle to further expansion. Raiders might pass it, but to sustain an invasion it was necessary to hold the passes, very strongly fortified and garrisoned by the élite of the Chinese army. The Manchus had little prospect of such a success unless Ming power was disrupted from within the Empire. This is what happened.

For several years the Ming dynasty had been suffering the evils which have recurred throughout Chinese dynastic history: the accumulation of land in the hands of a smaller number of larger landholders, and the absenteeism and extortionate rents which followed from this; a weakness in physical stamina and moral fibre in the imperial family due to the corruptions of undue eunuch influence and unrestrained extravagance; and the debilitating effects of such eunuch power upon the efficiency and probity of the civil service itself. In some respects the history of the Ming is close to the model of the 'dynastic cycle' which orthodox Confucian historians expounded. In other respects it no more conforms with this model than does the real history of almost all the other dynasties. The Ming passed within three generations of monarchs from the austere and fearsome founder to indolent and foolish youths. They then produced relatively competent, if far from outstanding, monarchs for over a century. The last twenty years were marked by palace plots, sudden deaths and overweening eunuch influence. Disorder in the country and a major rebellion were the last consequences of the decline and the immediate cause of the fall; the reverse of previous experiences.

The Manchu Ch'ing dynasty

Drought, causing famines which were neglected, even within the limited capabilities to provide relief of a seventeenth-century society, produced a major rebellion which, in itself badly led and without any constructive programme, could have been suppressed by the imperial army had that force not been concentrated on the northern frontier against Manchu encroachment. Incompetence and indifference left the rebellion to thrive until, in a sudden unexpected sweep, its leader, Li Tzu-ch'eng, bore down on the capital, which had been left virtually defenceless. Peking fell; the last Ming emperor took his own life, and the rebel claimed the throne. All now depended on the attitude taken up by the commander-in-chief of the northern frontier army, Wu San-kuei. Had Wu submitted to the new 'Shun' dynasty, it is probable that that régime would have succeeded the Ming, although it might not have proved long-lasting. Li was a man of no education, and was certainly lacking in the ruthless shrewdness which had characterised the first Ming. The Manchus would have found no opportunity to enter China.

Tactless action cost Li Tzu-ch'eng the support of Wu San-kuei, who then made his terms with the Manchus. He was to chase away the rebels and avenge his late master; the Manchus were to enter China peacefully and their Ch'ing dynasty be accepted as legitimate successors to the Ming. Wu probably expected to crush the rebels first and then turn on the Manchus; if so, he miscalculated. He crushed the rebellion, and handed over Peking to the Ch'ing; then he was assigned the task of destroying Ming pretenders in southern China. Meanwhile, the Manchus consolidated their hold on the north, loading Wu and two other Chinese collaborators with high honours. South of the Yangtze the resistance of Ming partisans was prolonged for more than twenty years, and in the last stage Wu San-kuei himself, master of the southwest, did turn upon the Manchus and proclaim himself emperor. He died before the issue was decided, but he was not making great progress at the end. His son was soon crushed, and in the year 1662 the youthful Manchu Emperor K'ang Hsi was at last truly emperor of all China.

The different history of north and south China in this interim between the Ming and Ch'ing had long-lasting effects, perhaps only effaced as practical political issues in very modern times. The north had been occupied, not conquered; there was no deep resentment against the Manchus, and in any case the capital, as usual, benefited from the presence of the court and government, especially when there was full control over the provinces and their revenues. The south had fought to the bitter end, enduring sieges and massacres, and it was treated as a conquered, hostile country. When open resistance had to cease, secret societies pledged to 'expel the Ch'ing; restore the Ming' – a slogan they were still using two hundred and fifty years later – spread their clandestine power throughout southern society and exported it in the nineteenth century to the overseas communities in south-east Asia. The south could not be trusted; therefore no Chinese navy, necessarily based on and recruited from the southern coastal provinces, could be trusted either. The Manchus adopted the policy: 'Defence of the coast but no battles at sea'.

This fear of southern revolt vitiated Manchu rule; it led to an arbitrary division of candidates for the civil service. Half were drawn from the Manchus themselves – a mere ten per cent of the whole population. Half of the Chinese fifty per cent were recruited only from the northern provinces. The south, which contained the majority of the population, the wealthiest provinces and the highest proportion of educated people, was left with one quarter of the posts in the civil service. Only the most talented southerners could hope for success; many hundreds of able men were excluded. This was a certain recipe for unrest. The decision to raise no southern naval forces was to prove disastrous in the nineteenth century, when the pressure from the European powers became dangerous. The south was far from Peking; it did not benefit from imperial expenditure in proportion to the revenue raised from it; a sense of neglect and distrust by the ruling dynasty fostered revolutionary feeling. The south bided its time, but it had a long time to wait.

If there were basic flaws in the Manchu political system these were for the Ch'ing dynasty concealed for more than a century, for they enjoyed the good fortune of having three very unusually able monarchs in succession, whose reigns were long. K'ang Hsi was only sixteen when he came to the throne, following the first Manchu emperor of China, himself a retiring man who is said to have abdicated to become a Buddhist monk under cover of a false announcement of his death. K'ang Hsi ended the long civil war in victory, spent many successful years campaigning against Mongols and in central Asia, and reigned for sixty years. To the West he was known as the patron of Jesuit missionaries, until the condemnation of that Order by the Vatican in the Rites Controversy affronted a monarch who admitted no right by any foreign potentate to order the affairs of religion within his domains. K'ang Hsi left to his son, who reigned as Yung Cheng, an empire greater in area than any which had preceded it (unless the Mongol empire of Chingiz Khan, of which north China was only a part, can be counted as a Chinese régime – which it was not).

The Eighteen Provinces within the Great Wall were now only the inner region of the empire. All Manchuria, and the present Maritime Province of Siberia, with the territory on the left bank of the Amur, were the original Manchu kingdom's territories. Inner Mongolia was administered by vassal Mongol chiefs, Outer Mongolia by a Buddhist theocrat, who also acknowledged the suzerainty of Peking. Sinkiang, or Chinese Central Asia, was reduced to a province. Suzerainty was claimed and exercised over Korea, Tibet and Vietnam; asserted over, and acknowledged by, Burma, Thailand and the RyuKyu Islands. Taiwan, the last stronghold of Ming partisans, had been occupied and reduced to obedience. It is to be observed that, with the single exception of the RyuKyu Islands, this pattern of suzerainty was confined to countries which either had a direct land frontier with China or, like Thailand, could be reached by land. The Manchus made no claims on Indonesia, where the Dutch were already becoming established, or over the Philippines, where the Spaniards were in partial occupation, nor were even theoretical claims pressed against Japan. The Ming had made such claims, although the Japanese never accepted them.

The reason why the Manchus had been able to establish such a wide domain, and why before them the Ming had also greatly enlarged the empire, lie partly in the facts of demography. By the late Ming period the population of China exceeded one hundred million; by the middle of the Ch'ing, in the eighteenth century, it was more than double that figure; by the nineteenth century the estimate, rather than the enumeration, of four hundred million, was to prove too low when in the twentieth century a modern census was at last taken. Under competent government, China was now too strong for any neighbour; there would never again be nomad invasions, and there need never have been invasions from seafaring nations either, if adequate defences had been maintained.

The Manchus neglected the navy, but they had a strong and for many years efficient military machine. The Eight Banners enrolled every male Manchu, and also the Chinese from the land beyond the Great Wall. In addition the Green Banner Army, raised in China, was distributed in garrisons throughout the country. It was not organised in mobile formations, a precaution against rebellion. So long as the Manchu Bannermen and Chinese auxiliaries who fought with them were constantly exercised in the far-off border wars of Outer Mongolia, Sinkiang and the frontiers of Manchuria, they retained their fighting quality. But in the reign of Ch'ien Lung, grandson of K'ang Hsi, another very able ruler who also occupied the throne for sixty years, there were no more worlds to conquer, at least in the eyes of the Manchu emperors. The nomadic menace was for ever ended, partly by Manchu conquest and partly by the concurrent advance of Imperial Russia into Siberia. As yet the western seafarers were few in numbers, not hostile, and seemingly harmless. Japan had withdrawn under the Tokugawa Shoguns into strict isolation. Russia appeared, even in K'ang Hsi's reign, as a remote nuisance. Russian claims and exploration along the Amur led to a sharp clash, in which the Manchu army won the day, followed by a treaty which defined the limits of the Chinese empire. These were fixed north of the left bank of the Amur, but this remote territory was a tribal region, more under suzerainty than under direct administration. Yet the Treaty of Aigun was the first that the Chinese empire ever signed with a European state; for the first time the Manchus acknowledged, if indirectly, that there existed another state, bordering on their own empire, which must be counted as civilised and powerful, even if its centre of power was very far from China. No one in that age paid much attention to this event; but China had got rid of the nomads only to acquire a new and ultimately much more formidable neighbour.

Neither the subsequent progress of Russian arms in Siberia and Central Asia, nor the British conquest of India, nor Dutch expansion in Indonesia, disturbed the Chinese court. It seems today that these able and intelligent men, such as Ch'ien Lung, were remarkably blind to important changes and developments in their own world. This may be partly explained by the fact that the extent of British power in India, or Dutch in Indonesia, was not very conspicuous until Ch'ien Lung was a very old man. Late in his reign he could still send his armies over the Himalayas to conquer Nepal, a feat never performed before. The cost was very great and impoverished the treasury; the returns – acceptance of tributary status – hardly matched the outlay; and one significant aspect of the cost was the scandalous corruption of the supply services. In the last years of Ch'ien Lung his power of surveillance over the administration began to fail; his favourite, Ho Shen, originally a soldier of the imperial guard, was given almost boundless authority and used it to amass one of the largest fortunes in specie and jewellery, property and land, which history records. All was seized by Ch'ien Lung's successor as soon as the aged, and now abdicated, emperor was dead.

Ho Shen's fortune, like the tomb treasures of the Ming emperor Wan Li, attest the wealth of the empire after one hundred and fifty years of unbroken internal peace; and also demonstrate clearly what was now going wrong. Lord Macartney, George III's ambassador to China, who visited Peking in the last years of Ch'ien Lung's reign, was not deceived by the outward magnificence, nor by the actual efficiency of the arrangements made for his journey overland from Canton to Peking. China, he said: 'was a great ship, now far gone in decay, which can never be rebuilt on the same bottom'. It was a prophecy which took more than a century to verify, but it was right.

The three great Ch'ing emperors, so outwardly successful and in practice so secure, achieved much which none of their predecessors had accomplished. No rebellion broke the peace until the last years of Ch'ien Lung. Population increased, and the area of the empire was greatly expanded. Intellectually the age was distinguished by the depth of its classical scholarship and the development of a new and sophisticated 'higher criticism' of the ancient texts. Not until this age did Chinese scholars begin to doubt, and then to prove, that some of the ancient texts were partial reconstructions and that others could not be attributed to the traditional authors – including some traditionally believed to be from the pen of Confucius himself. There was no lack of ability, no loss of scholarship; but it was directed on a narrow beam, the focus entirely on classical studies. One of the characteristics of the age was this introspective conservatism, at the very period when elsewhere in the world a thrusting generation of extroverts was challenging all old orders.

The Manchu dynasty may be said to have been ultimately ruined by its early successes. The long peace which the three great rulers so admirably maintained led to a great increase of population and strong pressure on arable land which could not be increased proportionately and was not relieved by industrial development. The success of these scholarly autocrats in winning the allegiance of the Chinese educated class was paid for by adopting without reservation the most conservative interpretation and outlook prevalent in this class of men educated only in a very restricted field. The Manchus opposed new ideas in literature, politics or philosophy. They feared being judged 'barbarians' if they did not uphold the most cherished of Chinese ancient traditions. The examination system was continued on Ming models up to the end, and paid no attention to such mundane matters as mathematics, economics or physical sciences. This attitude retained the allegiance of the elderly but was to lose the respect of the young.

The conquest of the nomads led to the decay of the armed forces and a failure to recognise that their equipment was out of date, just as their original task was now long since performed. Clinging to the traditional claims of the Chinese monarch to be the sole sovereign ruler in the world, to whom all others paid tribute or, if they did not, were remote savages of no importance, they simply ignored the changed international situation which was bringing far-off countries into closer relations, first by trade, later by political pressures. Ch'ien Lung, in his letter to George III brought back by Lord Macartney, could still in all sincerity, at the very end of the eighteenth century, refer to the English king as 'dwelling in the depths of the sea' – a remote unreal figure, deserving of a courteous reply and some fine gifts for having taken the trouble to send tribute across such vast distances.

These early successes and their resultant unexpected unfavourable consequences were compounded by one major failure of the Chinese society and its rulers. Population increased, agriculture developed the use of new crops, such as the potato and sweet potato, maize, and new strains of wheat, but there was no development of industry. Mines remained primitive, shallow, hand-worked holes. Silk and porcelain, the two great exports of earlier times, were produced in handicraft workshops smaller in scale than they had been in the Sung dynasty. No technical improvement had been made to navigation or to shipbuilding since early Ming times. The Chinese had long ago invented the horse collar, which gave so much more power to horse-drawn transport, but they had not developed any other source of power beyond water and wind mills, nor did they rush to copy the new steam when it appeared in the West. Overseas trade was restricted by the Manchu rulers to the one port of Canton, and the effects of even this limited contact made them deeply suspicious of the evil foreign influences which might, and did, infect the Cantonese. The merchant class, which was ready and certainly able to develop modern capitalist forms of production, was harassed and oppressed, without any security of property. This blighted the enterprise and destroyed the confidence of the one group which could rapidly and successfully have assimilated the science of the West.

Trade was regarded with disdain by Confucian scholars, even when in fact they protected merchants and permitted them to break the law by purchasing land and thus entering the scholar-landlord class. Like the Jews of eighteenth-century Europe, the merchant class was at once protected by patrons from the official ranks and persecuted by the governments which these officials served. The scholar should also be an artist: he might handle the brush for painting as well as for writing, but he did not handle a chisel, still less a spanner. Technical knowledge was for craftsmen; even the exquisite porcelain of the period remains virtually anonymous work – the director of the kilns may be known, but not the potters or the artists. A society so closed to a whole range of skills in which, as a people, they have great natural ability, was ill adapted for the changes of the coming century.

The old explanation of the dynastic cycle does not truly fit the Manchu Ch'ing case any better than at other periods. The dynasty came to power by an accident, a by-product of a Chinese civil war; its first ruler in China was a minor at the time and never an effective ruler. Twenty years later K'ang Hsi, also a youth barely out of boyhood, proved himself a man of exceptional ability and robust constitution, which gave him a very long reign. His son, Yung Cheng, was a cold but very competent character, well fitted to consolidate. Ch'ien Lung, who also reigned for sixty years, was able, intelligent, a good poet, a keen student of history, very industrious and until almost senile in full command of the immensely laborious task of supreme autocrat. The dynasty had inherited from the Ming, and then enhanced, the power of the emperor. Everything devolved on him; his ministers advised, but he alone decided. The considerable powers of the old supreme council of the emperor in T'ang and Sung times had waned away when the counsellors were no longer great and influential men from powerful families, but bureaucrats risen from relatively simple origins by successive examinations. The Manchus stood in the relation of master to slave in respect of their own Manchu people – hardly a relationship which makes for frank criticism. They did not treat their Chinese ministers as slaves, but they tended to distrust them if they were really able.

The fortune of three exceptionally capable men: father, son and grandson, concealed the fact that the imperial work load was now much more than any ordinary man could hope to discharge adequately. At the same time the habit of leaving everything to His Majesty meant that the ministers of Ch'ien Lung's successors were not well trained to guide a less capable autocrat. Thus the Manchu dynasty started with a brilliant promise, fulfilled it for 150 years, and then in one century swiftly declined to impotence and collapse. Yet the unfortunate sovereigns of the first half of the nineteenth century were all hardworking; one a miser, the other frugal, only the third rather profligate.

The Manchu dynasty had tried to avoid the perils of dynastic intrigue for the succession by abolishing the ancient position of crown prince, held by right by the eldest son of the emperor if he was born by the empress and not by a concubine. Instead the Manchu monarchs made no choice, publicly, until they lay dying. Then a trusted minister, or more than one for security, was given the key to a locked casket in which the emperor had written the name of the son whom he chose to succeed him. The system may have worked sometimes; it is possible that Chi'ien Lung was so indicated by his father Yung Cheng, and he in turn may have nominated Chia Ch'ing, his own successor. But there has been a strong belief, sustained by some evidence, that Yung Cheng was able to manipulate the choice in an unauthorised manner.

If faction was avoided by this system it was still unable to provide suitable choices in the later period. Chia Ch'ing, who followed Ch'ien Lung, was a mediocrity anxious to amass wealth, and quite unable to assess the dangers which were approaching. He dismissed the embassy of Lord Amherst with much less courtesy and still less contact than Ch'ien Lung had accorded to Lord Macartney. But in Macartney's time England was still heavily engaged in the wars with France. When Lord Amherst came to China the war was won, the British navy really ruled the seas, especially the eastern seas, and China was dealing in this cavalier manner with the power which was to be dominant in Asia for the next hundred years. Ch'ien Lung had been very old, and was brought up in a world which barely reckoned with the existence of Europe. Chia Ch'ing should have been trained to take an acute interest in events which had changed the whole configuration of world power.

Chia Ch'ing's son Tao Kuang came to the throne in 1840. A well-meaning, frugal, not to say parsimonious man, hard-working, but of limited intelligence and wholly insufficient education for his enormous responsibility. He found himself compelled to grapple with the new problem of British sea power, the opium trade, demands for an opening of China to foreign trade, diplomatic relations on the western model and other unheard-of innovations. He blundered into the Opium War, of which the consequences were disastrous, both immediately and remotely, to the survival of the Manchu dynasty and, as it proved, to the ancient institution of Chinese monarchy itself.

The success of the three great rulers and the failures of their successors alike prove that the system of autocratic monarchy had outlived its function. If it required very exceptionally able men, and the good luck to have three successive rulers of this quality, to make the system work, then it had little prospect of success when operated by more ordinary men. The empire had grown vast, and the number of the emperor's subjects far exceeded the population of any other state in the world. Yet the means of communication were still no better than they had been in the Han period. Months passed before orders from Peking could reach the governor of Yünnan. Officials were transferable from post to post from one corner of the empire to another; in theory no local power could thus remain long enough to plot sedition, but it also meant that transferred officials spent months on the road between the capital and their new or old posts. The number of regular members of the civil service was surprisingly small: at most some four thousand men actually held offices. Much of the clerical work at the capital, as in the provincial governments and district offices, was performed by men outside the regular service, who were employed *ad hoc* and were also paid by the official magistrate. His own salary was almost nominal; he paid his way, and his staff, by retaining a part of the revenue which it was his duty to raise and send to the capital. This was accepted as inevitable, but it meant connivance at a form of corruption which could not be controlled.

A system of supervision, called the Censorate, was supposed both to control the civil service and advise, even admonish, the emperor himself. History records the valiant actions of censors who performed this last action, which indeed was often their last. As the power of the throne increased, the effectiveness of this system declined. No real changes had been made since the Sung period, when recruitment by examination had wholly replaced recommendation. No form of representative institution had ever been proposed.

China truly was a fine old ship which could not be rebuilt on the same bottom, for the bottom had decayed, and the fundamental assumptions on which the system had always rested were no longer valid. It had evolved as a 'world state', the sole civilised power in a barbarous universe. As such it had great claims to respect and supreme moral authority. When the surrounding conditions ceased to fit the original model, the Chinese imperial system became increasingly anachronistic. It failed to evolve any system of diplomatic relations, since the very idea of an equal power was ruled out. Suzerain and tributary were the only conceivable relationships. Embassies to China were recorded – as tribute missions. Embassies from China are never directly acknowledged in the orthodox histories. The Son of Heaven did not send missions to lesser beings.

It would seem doubtful whether the later reformers who hoped to save the monarchy by modelling it on British practice or European examples could have succeeded, even if their efforts had not been fatally hampered by two facts: the dynasty was Manchu, alien, and hated in the south; and in its last fifty years it was ruled by a reactionary woman as regent for a succession of minors. The consequence of the fall of the monarchical system, the only system that had ever been tried or operated in China, was to leave a gap in the political understanding of the people which it has taken nearly sixty years to fill. Legitimacy had been associated with the 'mandate of heaven' passed from dynasty to dynasty; if there was no dynasty, no emperor, who held the mandate of heaven, who could be seen as a legitimate ruler? For many years this psychological problem lay at the root of the instability of successive régimes. Today, the people take the place of heaven; they have given their mandate to the Communist Party, and the effectiveness of its rule is the guarantee that it truly holds the mandate.

Part Four

The modern history of China

1 Introduction

Much of China's dynastic history down to the nineteenth century demonstrates, as the earlier chapters show, a remarkable degree of continuity in government, society and culture. This is not to go so far as to say that the idea of a *changeless* China founded on Confucianism is a wholly accurate characterisation of the period, but its history does reveal that no matter how prolonged the interdynastic crises, how bitter the rebellions, how brutal the conquests and how sharp the feuds, China's political institutions and, with them, China's traditional civilisation survived. When we come to consider the modern history of China, covering the period from 1840 to the present day, the old characteristic of stability and continuity in political institutions no longer applies. Not only is the dynasty in decline – a feature that would by itself be of no special consequence, for dynasties by their nature rose and fell in a fairly regular cyclical pattern – but along with dynastic decline emerge signs of progressive decay in traditional Chinese society. Eventually, the wane of the dynasty developed into the wane of the whole of the traditional civilisation in the wake of a social and intellectual revolution on an unprecedented scale. However, the chief characteristic of modern Chinese history is not only the long process of decline in China's traditional civilisation; the most distinct feature of the period is that the transformation of dynastic decline into the decline of China's traditional civilisation took place at a time when militant western expansionism brought about the violent intrusion of the western powers into the internal affairs of the Chinese empire.

Given the scope of the changes that have been wrought in China since 1840 and the complexity of the circumstances in which they came about, it is hardly surprising that their real nature should be the subject of controversy. A view advanced during the period of the political domination of Asia by Europe claimed that what was happening was simply a long process of westernisation. In times of change politically, this came to be regarded as a flagrant oversimplification, and it has now been superseded by the view that China has been modernising under western stimuli. Thus an important approach to the modern history of China has been to attempt an analysis in terms of China's response to western contact. For example, in the successive stages of confrontation with the West from the Opium War of 1840 down to the turn of the century (by which time a modernising Japan enters the scene) this response, meaning the proclaimed views of China's leading reform-minded officials, took three main lines. These were the need to acquire western arms, the need to promote the industrialisation of China using western technology and, ultimately, the need to reform China's political institutions. This approach notes at the same time the gradual transformation of China's world outlook as traditional sinocentric culturalism gave way, under the combined challenge from the West, Japan and Czarist Russia, to modern nationalism.

Another important approach to China's modern history is that employed by Chinese Marxist historians. This sees China as having passed through primitive, slave and feudal societies, the impact of the West occurring, however, before the onset of the capitalist stage of society. Chinese feudalism having been interrupted by the western intrusion, China then enters on a period of semi-feudalism and semi-colonialism during which the principal features are the people's struggles against domestic reaction and imperialism. In place of the emphasis on response to the West there is, to cite one suggested periodisation, firstly the period of struggle against the intrusion of foreign capitalism, and of domestic rebellion, from 1840 to 1864; secondly, the period of struggle against the semi-colonial, semi-feudal state and the carving up of China by the imperialists from 1864 to 1901; and, thirdly, the period of anti-feudal democratic revolution from 1901–19. Both this Marxist approach and the 'response to the West' approach contribute considerably to our grasp of the real nature of the changes during the modern period. But by highlighting the role of exogenous forces it is implicit that indigenous forces on balance played a less important part. While the available evidence does not yet justify upsetting this general conclusion, it may be that historians will in future uncover evidence to support the view that internal changes already in motion and governed by indigenous forces played a more significant role than is at present recognised. For this reason, even though the point of departure for the modern history of China is firmly fixed at the Opium War of 1840, it is none the less important to start by noting the principal characteristics of Chinese society and government on the eve of the western impact before considering the response it provoked.

2 1840–60: Foreign wars and internal rebellion

By the beginning of the nineteenth century, the Manchu régime had passed the peak of its power and was faced with problems traditionally associated with the decline of a dynasty. Its administrative inefficiency, widespread corruption and peculation, 'strained' treasury and incipient economic crisis arising from pressure of population, all pointed to the fall of the dynasty in the not too distant future. A clear sign of what was in store came with the White Lotus Rebellion (1796–1804), whose adherents claimed that official oppression had forced the people to rebel. That was to be the first in a long series of destructive rebellions punctuating the history of the nineteenth century. But the most intractable of these problems, and the one from which most of the others to varying degrees stemmed, was the population explosion. The century of peace and prosperity, the period of *Pax Sinica* lasting from the suppression of resistance to the Manchus in 1683 for most of the eighteenth century, saw China's population grow from between 100 and 150 million to 300 million. Unfortunately, this growth was not matched by a proportional increase in cultivable land. In fact, while the population rose by about one hundred per cent, arable land only increased fifty per cent (from 549 million *mou* to 791 million *mou*, one *mou* being approximately one-sixth of an acre). By the turn of the century population growth had attained such momentum that even when social and economic conditions were less favourable, it reached 430 million in 1850.

The immediate impact of the population explosion was felt by the peasants, who found it difficult to eke out an existence on the land and cope with taxes and rent. In due course government revenues were affected and it became difficult to maintain the surpluses needed to tide the country over short-term emergencies such as natural calamity, war and rebellion. The upshot was that many peasants became dispossessed and in the absence of alternative means of employment added to an existing pool of potential political dissidents. Here, then, were emerging most of the ingredients for the fall of the old dynasty and the rise of a new dynasty. The period of the great Ch'ing dynasty had almost turned full cycle: state power was waning, and along with it the ability to levy taxes and maintain garrisons and armies; landlords and petty officials could defy the power of the government and, standing between it and the peasants, they could syphon off much of the surplus product of the land with impunity. It was only a matter of time before an oppressed peasantry, finding the burden intolerable, would rise in savage rebellion, overthrow the old dynasty and found a new one.

Left to its own resources China might have solved the problem in that way. However, the Ch'ing dynasty was not to be allowed to complete such a cycle, and this confluence of internal events in the first half of the nineteenth century was to be greatly complicated as a new challenge emerged in the form of militant western expansionism. The intrusion of the West into China's affairs had by this time undergone a qualitative change to reach this stage. For instance, the early Portuguese, Spanish and Dutch merchants had mainly wanted to buy items on the Chinese market that had luxury or rarity value; the Catholic missionaries arriving at the same time principally aimed to win converts while acquiescing in Chinese practices and standards of conduct. By contrast, at the turn of the century the English, by now the most numerous of the foreigners on the China coast, not only aimed to open up the Chinese market to manufactured goods exported from England but also, through the Non-Conformist Protestant missionary movement, threatened to convert the Chinese to a creed that regarded as repugnant much of China's existing social system. It is not surprising that China resisted these attempts at subversion.

The Macartney and Amherst embassies of 1793 and 1816 had failed to make any impression on the Chinese resolve to keep the British merchants in a sort of traders' quarantine in Canton, the port farthest away from the capital, Peking. What appeared to be an obstinate and unreasonable refusal to face reality when both China's own 'junk' trade to south-east Asia and Britain's trade in Canton had shown that the tribute relations theory was outworn, was regarded in a wholly different light by the Chinese court. What the British were seeking had no precedent in the tribute system on which east Asian foreign relations were based. In fact, although Chinese rulers, depending on the actual balance of power in east Asia, had at their disposal a whole repertoire of means to use in conducting foreign relations, ranging from military conquest of non-Chinese peoples at one extreme, through controlled administrative assimilation and acculturation to the other extreme of avoiding contact altogether, at no point was there provision for contact with China on the basis of equality among sovereign states. That would lead to the negation of the entire Chinese world order, which was an extension of China's own internal hierarchical system and as such involved, besides an acknowledgement of the position of the emperor at the apex, a degree of ideological commitment to orthodox Chinese beliefs.

Meanwhile, however, despite Chinese obduracy, the dynamism of the Industrial Revolution was having its effect on the entire British mercantile system, which was to have consequences for the character of the trade conducted at Canton. This trade had always been difficult to balance. Despite the feeling in Britain that there would be a suitable outlet for manufactures in China, sub-tropical Canton went in a big way neither for Lancashire cottons nor, understandably, for Yorkshire woollens. Eventually the need to use silver bullion was largely obviated by balancing the trade with raw cotton exports from British India. Thus there developed a triangular India–China–England trade pattern in which private traders – with the co-operation of the East India Company, which had monopolies in India until 1813 and in China until 1834 – imported raw cotton at Canton, the proceeds from the sale of which they used to buy the Company's bills of exchange payable in London or Calcutta. This triangular trade provided the company with funds in Canton to buy tea, which had become a national drink in Britain in the seventeenth century. It also provided an outlet for Indian produce, the profit from which could be remitted to India. At the same time, the Company maintained a channel for the remittance of profits from India to London through Canton.

The British government was not unhappy with this arrangement: tea was highly taxed and produced considerable revenue. However, this system continued to evolve, and two developments that took on particular significance in the early nineteenth century were to set Britain and China on a collision course. The first was the growth in private trade, spurred on by the spirit of private enterprise and the dynamism of the Industrial Revolution: private traders increasingly dominated the Canton trade once the Company ceased to monopolise British trade in India. The second was the increase in the consumption of opium in China. Since opium could be cultivated cheaply on a widespread basis in India the private traders sought to import greater and greater quantities at Canton to balance the existing trade and to meet the growing demand as the habit-forming narcotic took its toll.

The spread of opium addiction in China can be related on the one hand to the private traders seeking single-mindedly to exploit a commercial opportunity, and on the other to the degree of connivance, official and private, of the Chinese at Canton. Fortunes were at stake and the distribution networks and vulnerability of the population constitute convincing evidence of the degree of dynastic decline already present. The government's policy on opium had been, from the early eighteenth century, to ban it. That policy had always been undermined, however, as officials connived in its import and cultivation. The combined effect of three factors ultimately made it imperative to act decisively. The first was the number of addicts, which some estimates place at ten million in 1830; the second was the reduction in Peking's revenue from the Canton trade monopoly as the co-hong–East India Company system was supplanted and more funds syphoned off locally; the third was that from the 1820s China began to suffer a net outflow of silver bullion through payments, mainly taken to India, to meet the cost of the increasing opium imports. The last was a decisive factor in spurring China to action, because it made silver dearer in terms of copper cash and exacerbated an existing fiscal crisis arising from the debasement of copper cash, counterfeiting and the resultant tendency to hoard silver. The combined effect of these factors had been to increase the burden on the people, in particular the peasants, since the exchange rate between cash, the medium for everyday transactions, and silver, the medium for remitting taxes and government fiscal operations, rose.

By now, Britain's commercial expansion in China had become dependent on the opium trade and China was convinced that the fiscal crisis was to a large extent a result of the outflow of silver, caused by the opium trade. At the same time the ending of the Company's monopoly had brought about, as a result of a request from the Canton governor-general, the appointment by the British government of a Superintendent of Trade to control the foreign merchants at Canton. Not so intended by the Chinese, who simply wanted a head merchant (*Taipan*), this nevertheless had the effect of substituting confrontation between officials for that between the Chinese government and the Company, with all the attendant repercussions in terms of national honour and prestige. Lord Napier, appointed in 1834, had no success whatsoever in placing Britain on an equal footing with China through conciliation, which was the gist of Palmerston's instructions. He in fact died shortly after his arrival, and was replaced by George Robinson in 1835, whose meek policy did not satisfy the traders and led to the appointment of Charles Elliot in 1836. It was at this juncture that the idea of legalising the opium trade under strict tariff and barter conditions to reduce smuggling, combined with a severe ban on its use by scholars, officials and soldiers, was mooted by realistic Chinese officials. In anticipation, the traders began to prepare for even larger imports of opium, but the legalisation plan was rejected by the Emperor and China embarked on a vigorous crusade to exterminate the opium evil. At this juncture, the Chinese world and the British world stood in opposition: China sought to suppress opium and maintain the tribute system of foreign relations; Britain, so long as the struggle against the tribute system, which prevented free trade, continued, was hopelessly dependent on opium to balance the trade.

The man chosen to lead the crusade was Lin Tse-hsü, who arrived in Canton in 1839. Before he arrived, the local governor-general had brought the Chinese side of the trade to a standstill with repressive measures. To bring the smuggling to an end Lin demanded the surrender of opium stocks at the trading posts and a guarantee, on pain of death, that the traders would not pursue the illicit trade. To enforce his demands he detained the community, including Elliot, for six weeks, an act regarded by the British as piracy against liberty and property, but by the Chinese as a rightful enforcement of law. The detention ended when Elliot decided to assume ownership of all the opium on behalf of the Crown and surrender it to China under duress. This move, regarded as 'statesmanlike' by some of the traders, since it rendered China 'liable to the Crown', was also motivated by the fact that the stockpile was soon to be replenished by large consignments from India, ordered when the rumour was about that China would legalise the opium trade. Once liberated, the British community left for Macao, from where they were expelled shortly after because of Elliot's refusal to submit a sailor involved in a murder case to Chinese jurisdiction, finally withdrawing to the barren island of Hong Kong, ninety miles from Canton. There they awaited the arrival of a British expeditionary force, whose despatch Palmerston had ordered in response to a campaign for action launched by nearly three hundred firms in London, Manchester and Liverpool connected with the China trade.

The Opium War

A British expeditionary force of warships, transports and some 4000 soldiers arrived in China in 1840 under Admiral Elliot, cousin of Captain Charles Elliot. His instructions were to get satisfaction for the illegal detention and assurances as to future security, compensation for the surrendered opium, the abolition of the monopolistic system of trade at Canton and the repayment of debts incurred by the mono-polists, the so-called co-hong. A blockade along the China coast was to be employed to urge China to enter into meaningful negotiations. The stage was now set for the ensuing three-phase Opium War.

The first phase, from June 1840 to January 1841, saw the British seize Chusan south of Shanghai, blockade ports from Ningpo to the mouth of the Yangtze and then advance to the Pei-ho near Tientsin, thus threatening the security of Peking itself. These moves brought two results: firstly the Emperor, alarmed at the scale of the threatened reprisal, lost faith in Lin Tse-hsü, sacked him and banished him to dis-tant Sinkiang; secondly, the British, mollified by assurances from the governor-general at Tientsin, Ch'i-shan, as to the Emperor's desire to settle matters, withdrew to the south. There they entered into negotia-tions with Ch'i-shan. So far Ch'i-shan had succeeded in removing the barbarian threat to Peking without firing a shot. Once the negotiations began, however, he was in difficulty and his refusal to yield to demands for the ceding of Hong Kong caused Captain Elliot, now prosecuting the British case, to order an attack on the Ch'uan-pi forts. This forced Ch'i-shan to sign the draft Ch'uan-pi Convention providing for an indemnity, a 'settlement' on Hong Kong, direct contact between officials and the re-opening of trade at Canton. This draft was promptly rejected by the Emperor for what it yielded to the barbarians, and the unfortunate Ch'i-shan was exiled to the far north-east. More omi-nously, Palmerston also rejected it for the insufficiency of the indemnity and its woolliness over the British rights to Hong Kong, and Captain Elliot was replaced by Sir Henry Pottinger in 1841 for not having maximised the opportunities provided by the presence of the expedi-tionary force.

By the time Pottinger arrived the war had passed through its second phase, precipitated on the one hand by the Emperor's decision to appoint I Shan as imperial commissioner and general-in-command of barbarian suppression, and on the other, Elliot's decision to regain the initiative. The British besieged Canton and retired only when a large ransom had been paid and Chinese troops evacuated. An indication of the enmity that now existed between the Cantonese people and the British occurred when a large crowd harassed British troops during their withdrawal. Pottinger eventually arrived in August 1841 with instructions to negotiate only when the court had consented to a re-appraisal of Anglo-Chinese relations. In the autumn, with only 2500 men, he occupied positions along the China coast; once reinforced by some 10,000 men from India in the spring of 1842, he extended his activities by occupying Shanghai, cutting the Grand Canal where it crossed the Yangtze, thus interrupting north–south traffic and threatening Nanking. The Manchus had no force to match his in either organisation or weaponry and were compelled to negotiate. The outcome was the Treaty of Nanking (1842) which completely changed the international status of China. Under its provisions, China indemnified Britain for military expenses, confiscated opium and merchants' debts to traders, abolished the co-hong monopoly, opened five 'treaty' ports to trade and residence, ceded Hong Kong, agreed to communications on the basis of equality and to the principle of a fixed tariff.

The full extent of the international consequences of this wedge driven in by the British only became clear in 1844. By then China had agreed to the Supplementary Treaty of the Bogue (1843) with Britain and treaties with the United States and France in 1844. Since they were all subject to the principle that any privilege extended to one must be enjoyed by all, the 'most-favoured nation' clause, these treaties and those signed later constituted a comprehensive single system of treaty law. Under it China lost her tariff autonomy and the right to jurisdiction over the activities of foreigners in certain localities. The loss of tariff autonomy (which was not restored until 1930) not only opened the way to the penetration of China by foreign manufactures, which damaged the handicraft industry, but also prevented the framing of tariffs in the national interest, such as those to protect developing industries. By agreeing to extra-territoriality, China sanctioned the development of international settlements and the granting of concessions which not only gave foreigners political power and economic leverage in China, but encouraged what from China's point of view was a non-functional concentration of industrial and commercial activity, since the overriding consideration was accessibility to foreign-owned steamers. The equally damaging 'most-favoured nation' clause was further evidence that China and the West were still not in the same universe of discourse. China believed firstly that with trade being finite in quantity, the more nations sharing it the greater the likelihood of their fighting each other and therefore the easier the problem of control; and secondly that the Chinese emperor, being a 'universal' monarch, should look on all barbarians with equal benevolence.

Most of the provisions of the treaties were imposed and they have therefore been correctly stigmatised as 'unequal treaties'. Significantly, mention of opium, the immediate cause of the war, was avoided for obvious reasons. But this omission actually highlights what the ultimate causes of the war were. This confrontation was between civilisations, between self-sufficient agrarian China on the one hand and industrialised and expanding Britain on the other. China could not accept the

British concepts of international relations, free trade and jurisprudence any more than Britain, as part of Europe and Christendom, in which nation states enjoyed sovereignty and mutual independence, could stomach either the theoretical assumptions on which the Chinese world order was based or their practical manifestation in the system of tributary relations. This has given rise to the view that some sort of confrontation was inevitable. Unfortunately, the bitter experience of the war did not shock China into the dynamic response that subsequently followed the opening of Japan. Instead, China's response, having been compelled to take the first steps towards joining the international community, was characterised for two decades by anti-foreignism and non-cooperation. There is a view that this amounted to lethargy, a failure to grasp the urgency of political and military reform. But this is seeing the problem through western eyes. The Manchus were clearly far too preoccupied with internal problems to contemplate change of that dimension, even assuming that they would have wanted to have much more to do with the barbarians on the maritime frontier.

The Taiping Rebellion

There was, as we have seen, a symbiotic relationship between the opium trade and China's internal crisis. Apart from the problem of widespread addiction, it had exacerbated the plight of the peasantry by contributing to the rise in the exchange rate between copper cash and silver bullion. But this was only one of the many factors contributing to a situation conducive to rebellion. The events surrounding the First Treaty Settlement and its outcome, though they were to have far-reaching repercussions, were not immediately as important to the dynasty as the domestic crisis brewing for half a century. Westerners have understandably focused attention on the new institutions of the Treaty Ports, which we now know contained the embryo of great change. The rise of a new business class, the *comprador* bourgeoisie, much maligned for its collaboration with the foreigners, pointed to fundamental shifts in business activity. Missionary work in and around the settlements was increasing. Similarly, the fact that large numbers of Chinese were emigrating, particularly in response to the discovery of gold in California and Australia in 1848 and 1851, albeit under the appalling conditions of contract labour, suggested that China had become irrevocably more involved with the world than ever before. However, the impact of all these developments was for the future. For the present, while the Manchus had not stopped the import of opium

156

they had settled the problem on their maritime frontier according to the institutional precedent usually employed in dealing with barbarians on the inner Asian frontier, and attention was focused on the problems of rebellion.

These problems became outright challenges to the dynasty in the series of mid-century rebellions that followed. From 1850 to 1864 the Taiping Rebellion affected much of the rich productive heartland of the lower Yangtze provinces. From 1853 to 1868 control over the southern part of the North China Plain, between the Huai and Yellow rivers, west of the Grand Canal in an area straddling the borderlands of Kiangsu, Anhwei, Honan and Shantung, was wrested from central government officials by the Nien Rebellion. In Yunnan province Chinese Muslims were in rebellion from 1862 to 1873, while another Muslim rebellion took place in Shenshi and Kansu, the arid panhandle strip that provided the corridor for communication with Turkestan, from 1862 to 1873. And between 1854 and 1873 Miao tribesmen were in rebellion in the mountains of western Kweichow. The scope and duration of these mid-century rebellions show just how close to collapse the dynasty was. In its endeavour to survive and reaffirm its mandate to rule, as the history of the Taiping Rebellion reveals, it was to appeal to the loyalty of the educated élite of scholar officials to the state and to the Confucian order.

The Taiping Rebellion centred around the disaffection of a group of Hakkas (descendants of early migrants from north China who survive as a linguistic group) led by Hung Hsiu-ch'üan. The genesis of the rebellion was in part due to the decline in central authority and the vulnerability of the populace to illegal pressures, which explain the tendency to form 'militia' groups for self-defence and ultimately to resist corrupt administration, and in part to inspired leadership. Hung's motivations were primarily nationalistic and anti-Manchu, but are blurred on the one hand by his faith in a distorted Protestant fundamentalism, gleaned from missionary contacts in Canton and bad translations of the Bible – a faith that led some westerners at the time to see a Christian revolution in the offing – and on the other hand by his mental illness. The latter had caused the hallucinations that he claimed were visions, revealing he was the younger son of God and brother of Jesus. By 1851 this anti-Manchu religious–military group had control of much of Kwangsi and in 1852 they moved north, capturing Nanking in 1853. There they established themselves, neglecting the south and having been repulsed in a drive to the north. The rapid success of the campaign can be attributed to two factors: the wide spectrum of disaffection that existed in China, and the general appeal of their reform programme. The latter comprised a blueprint for a new society based on a system of primitive communism incorporating measures to equalise land use, operate a common treasury and carry out social restructuring, including an improvement in the status of women and the administration of justice. Clearly, this programme amounted to a rejection of the entire Confucian tradition and it is no surprise that it alienated the landed class, the officials and the educated Confucians – in fact the entire ruling group.

If this programme had been practicable, if the Taipings had made alliances with other rebels such as the Nien and the Triads, a secret society fomenting sedition in Amoy and Shanghai, or supposing they had sought direct foreign aid, what was a rebellion might have become a revolution. In the event, reforms were not implemented, revolutionary zeal was squandered and the rebellion degenerated by stages through internecine power struggles, profligacy and corruption. Meanwhile, China's scholar-official class had rallied to the cause of Confucian tradition, showing its opposition to the prospect of government by heterodox rebels by helping to create a new kind of army. This was based on the idea of a paid, disciplined and trained local militia, many small units of which already existed, and the first example was the Hsiang army formed by Tseng Kuo-fan. Initially the aim was to create an effective defensive force; eventually they proved strong enough, as regionally-based gentry-led striking forces, to take the offensive. Ultimately they proved the means of quelling the rebellion.

Before China was to quell the rebellion another confrontation with the foreigners was to place the dynasty once more between the twin threats of internal rebellion and foreign aggression. The powers, having vacillated about shifting to a coercive policy to enforce the treaties lest it prove counter-productive by increasing chaos and reducing trade, eventually sought negotiations for the treaty revision scheduled for 1854. They were rebuffed and, convinced that the treaty system was in jeopardy, Britain and France used two minor issues, a controversy concerning jurisdiction over a boat flying the British flag, and the murder of a missionary, to send a combined expedition north to Tientsin. There, in June 1858, they secured agreement to the Treaty of Tientsin providing for resident ministers at Peking, ten new Treaty Ports, limitation on inland transit dues on foreign imports, an indemnity, arrangements for travel in China for foreigners, and freedom of movement for missionaries. However, the struggle to get representation at Peking was not to be won so easily: when the time came for ratification in 1859 the Emperor had had second thoughts and the foreign expedition was repulsed off Tientsin. It was not until 1860, when the expedition under Lord Elgin and Baron Gros had been greatly reinforced and had advanced on Peking, that the 1858 treaties were ratified. Additionally, new conventions were signed with Prince Kung, representing the Emperor, who had fled, opening Tientsin to foreign residence, increasing the indemnity, securing the Kowloon Peninsula opposite Hong Kong island for Britain and permitting French missionaries to own property in China.

The Second Treaty Settlement had manifold repercussions. The means to secure it were brutal, including the razing of the Summer Palace, and the treaties are consequently stigmatised as 'unequal'. In practical terms, the semi-colonial status of China was consolidated with the loss of sovereignty over navigable water, internal tariff autonomy and the debilitating indemnity. At the same time pressure on the maritime frontier was now matched in a kind of gigantic pincer movement on the north-east frontier, when Russia seized the opportunity to consolidate its invasion of the Amur region and acquire the whole of the territory between the Ussuri and the Pacific (founding Vladivostok – 'rule of the East') under the Treaties of Aigun (1858), Tientsin (1858) and Peking (1860). But its biggest repercussion was in the court, for it irreparably damaged the anti-foreign war clique headed by the Hsien-feng emperor, who died in 1861, and enabled Prince Kung to emerge at the head of a faction whose priorities were to quell the rebellions and to co-operate in a limited way with the treaty system: the rebels were a 'disease of the vitals', the foreigners an 'affliction of the limbs'.

3 1860–95: Dynastic revival and self-strengthening

The Second Treaty Settlement was followed shortly after by a formal change in the Chinese leadership. The Hsien-feng emperor was succeeded by the T'ung Chih emperor who, as a child, was represented by a regency. After a power struggle the two empress dowagers, one of whom, Tz'u Hsi, was to dominate court politics for almost the next half-century, and Prince Kung were appointed co-regents. This marked the start of a new phase in the modern history of China during which the country underwent a process of dynastic revival and self-strengthening. This process, the first decade of which has come to be called the T'ung Chih Restoration, was promoted largely by Prince Kung who, having tided China over the crisis of 1858 to 1860, had reached the conclusion that the traditional attitude of 'using barbarians to control barbarians' was manifestly bankrupt. In his view, what was now needed was a respite in which to build up China's military strength; this would be the key to dealing with both the rebels and the barbarians. Western aid would be needed for this to succeed, and with such a strategy in mind it would be necessary to take tactical measures to accommodate the West diplomatically.

For their part the foreign powers, having squeezed concessions from the Chinese government, realised the futility of excessive coercion. Instead, they shifted to a policy whose rationale was to sustain and to help modernise the régime the better to promote prospects for trade. Britain supported the government on these grounds in the final stages of the Taiping Rebellion, having hitherto maintained strict neutrality. By 1864 foreign representatives in China, supported by their home governments, were committed to a 'co-operative policy' towards China. The main planks of this were co-operation among the powers, co-operation with Chinese officials, the recognition of China's legitimate interests and the just enforcement of treaty stipulations.

160

China's self-strengthening movement can be divided into three main periods. The first, from 1861 to 1872, saw the introduction of new methods for dealing with foreigners as well as substantive attempts to apply newly-acquired scientific and technical knowledge to build up military strength. It led to the establishing of the Tsungli-Yamen in Peking in 1861 to handle foreign affairs at the capital, and to the appointment of two commissioners under the Yamen's jurisdiction to handle foreign affairs in the provinces. The latter was a skilful attempt, in the event foiled by diplomats and traders, to reduce the need for diplomatic activity in the capital. To the foreign community the Yamen became known as 'the foreign office'. Indeed, its organisation and functions bore much more resemblance to later Chinese developments than to the traditional institutions for conducting foreign affairs. However, its activities, until its gradual decline after 1870, when provincial officials began to wield much more power, covered a very wide range of subjects. Besides conducting China's foreign relations, at the peak of its influence it promoted schools, the acquisition of scientific learning and its application to industry. It also had attached to it the offices of the inspector-general of customs and the Interpreters College.

Both these offices were in themselves important innovations. The appointment of Horatio Lay as the first inspector-general of customs signalled the formation, from the *ad hoc* foreign inspectorate that had functioned since 1854, of the foreign-dominated Maritime Customs Service. By 1875 this Service had brought order out of chaos in the collection of duties on foreign trade, and employed 252 British and 156 other westerners. Despite criticisms levelled at it and at the successive inspectors-general, on account of whose ambiguous role Britain was able to exert considerable leverage in the Yamen, it was producing almost one quarter of all the central government's revenue in the 1890s. The Interpreters' College was in fact an early beneficiary of this added source of revenue. In the years after its establishment in Peking in 1862 it formed the precedent for similar colleges in scientific and general studies, which also functioned as institutes from which foreign knowledge could be disseminated.

These efforts to regularise diplomatic contacts and promote western learning were paralleled in this period by substantive developments aimed at strengthening China through industrialisation and western armaments and the despatch of a few Chinese students to study abroad. Supported by the modernising influence of the Yamen, despite conservative opposition this category of innovation is particularly significant, not only for the emphasis on government-run military industries but also for the close associations of such developments with

China's provincial leaders. This was to confirm men like Tseng Kuo-fan, Tso Tsung-t'ang and Li Hung-chang in provincial power bases reinforcing the tendency towards regionalism. This was the price that the centre had had to pay for the quelling of the Taiping Rebellion by regionally-based armies. For example, the Kiangnan arsenal was established at Shanghai in 1865 by Tseng Kuo-fan and Li Hung-chang; the Foochow dockyard was set up in 1865 by Tso Tsung-t'ang; the Nanking arsenal established in 1867 by Li Hung-chang.

A fortuitous confluence of Chinese and western interests after the bitter history of the two treaty settlements provides the background to these first tentative steps towards modernisation. With the West temporarily appeased, China's new provincial leaders, whose regional armies now had modern arms and employed improved methods of logistical support rather than the old practice of living off the land at the expense of the unfortunate peasantry, systematically extinguished the rebellions excising what Prince Kung had called 'the disease in China's vitals'. The quelling of rebellion was of course only the first step to recovery. The social and economic consequences were daunting. It has been estimated, for example, that some twenty million people perished as a result of the Taiping Rebellion alone. At the same time there had been an almost total collapse of civil administration in the regions worst affected, one aspect of which was the forced suspension of the examination system for recruiting officials. This further aggravated China's mid-century weaknesses: economically, administrative neglect was the deadliest foe in a country in which the peoples' livelihood depended on hydraulic agriculture necessitating meticulous care of man-made measures for water control and conservation. The calamitous effects of the flooding of the Yellow River, when it changed course to flow north of Shantung, illustrates what happened when the dikes were neglected. The problem that faced China's provincial leaders as they reversed the cycle of rebellion was essentially how to translate military success into dynastic revival.

The main feature of the policy to cope with the aftermath of the rebellions involved the restoration of regular civil administration with the utmost urgency. The examination system for recruiting men of talent into the administration was restored. This was backed up by the reopening of local academies and the printing of texts and so forth to ensure standards of ideological orthodoxy among candidates. In the areas where civil administration had been restored, the scholar-generals heading the provincial administrations and their official colleagues turned once more to the gentry, who had previously responded to their call to form regional armies, to support their efforts.

The gentry, degree-holders themselves and almost invariably land-owners too, constituted the key link between the lowest echelons of formal government and the people. Traditionally they carried out the tasks of population registration and tax collection. They were also the group most responsible for rebuilding administrations in the traditional mould after the fall of dynasties. Now they were being summoned, by a dynasty that had apparently miraculously escaped the consequences of its decline, to reintegrate China's ravaged countryside. Working through the gentry, the provincial administrations implemented a programme providing for the remission of agricultural taxes, the distribution of seeds and tools and the resettlement of farmers. At the same time, the umbrella of defence provided by the militia and the regional armies was reinforced at the local level by the formation of the *pao-chia** system of mutual guarantee and collective security. The whole was cemented together by a vigorous reaffirmation of orthodox values stressing the need for frugality and austerity in times of crisis. Step by step China's scholar-generals restored the old Confucian system.

But what, in effect, did the T'ung Chih restoration achieve? Diplomacy had been used to repel foreign aggression. Modernisation restricted to considerations of self-defence had been used to suppress rebellion. The Confucian system had been restored as a means of national recovery. Clearly China had responded to the crisis by a reaffirmation of the past. In retrospect, the reasons for this are not difficult to understand. Having arrested a cycle of rebellion that would have led to social revolution, how could hard-won stability be subjected to the disruptive effects of anything more than this very limited programme of modernisation? The social system based on traditional Confucianism would not have withstood such an impact. Far from selling out to the forces of reaction and imperialism, China's leaders opted for stability within the only system they knew. For them it was an act of the possible.

The legacy of the T'ung Chih restoration is to be seen in the second and third phases of the self-strengthening movement. While it solved some problems, it created others. The regional leaders became more entrenched in power bases with their own private armies, modern arms industries and hand-picked bureaucracies in which they patronised officials from their own provinces. They had sources of revenue

---

* The *pao-chia* was a traditional institution for registration, surveillance and crime reporting. Ten households formed a *p'ai*, ten *p'ai* a *chia*, ten *chia* a *pao*. It was an important external control mechanism.

163

they could control such as the Likin*, a tax on the movement of commodities, the collection of which could be supervised by the gentry.

Although their loyalty to the throne was never in doubt, the question of keeping a balance between traditional central power, wielded largely by the Manchu court under the influence of the dowager empress Tz'u Hsi, and these new regional interests which, since the Taiping Rebellion had become overwhelmingly Chinese, was constantly under consideration. The career of Li Hung-chang, governor-general of Chihli and commissioner for the northern ports from 1870 to 1895, is the outstanding illustration of this phenomenon. Inevitably such powerful leaders ultimately determined the features of China's development.

As the second phase of self-strengthening (1872–85) shows, the trend was to maintain defence-orientated industries, including the despatch of personnel to Britain, France and Germany for training, but at the same time to diversify the range of industry to include profit-orientated enterprises. The institution known as *kuan-tu shang-pan* (literally: 'supervised by government and undertaken by merchants') was developed to attract merchant capital without yielding actual control to merchants. This highlights just one of the many dilemmas presented by modernisation. Ideally, to maximise efficiency and profit the merchants should have enjoyed rights to management. After all, it was their money that was at stake. But that would have eroded the influence and prestige of the scholar-official class *vis-à-vis* the merchant class under the traditional Confucian system. Kuan-tu shang-pan was therefore a compromise, with antecedents in the traditional institutions of government monopoly, the prime example of which was the salt industry, that tapped merchant capital while upholding the old prejudices and discrimination against the merchant class. With all its deficiencies in terms of inefficiency and nepotism, it became the main model for new industry in this phase. Example of government-supervised merchant undertakings, which made up an important part of Li Hung-chang's industrial empire, are the China Merchant's Steam Navigation Company (1872), the K'ai-p'ing Coal Mines (1877), the Shanghai Cotton Cloth Mill (1878) and the Imperial Telegraph Administration (1881). Besides these and other industrial developments such as a machine factory in Szechuan (1877) and a textile factory in

---

* Launched during the Taiping period, this tax had an advantage over the land tax, whose rate had been made immutable by imperial decree, in that it was comprehensive yet minute (one thousandth *ad valorem*) which meant the prospect of greater revenue in periods of stability with little incentive for evasion. However, it was wide open to peculation and became a disincentive to commerce.

Kansu (1878), a group of seven officers were sent to Germany in 1876, a naval academy was established at Tientsin in 1880 and plans adopted for a modern navy, and a short railway was laid north of Tientsin in 1881.

The third phase of self-strengthening, from 1885 to 1894, witnessed a continuation in the search for a positive programme for national defence. Significant achievements included the organisation of the Board of the Admiralty under Prince Chün, the emperor's father, in 1885 and the formation of the Peiyang fleet in 1888 under Li Hung-chang's control. He was also responsible for the setting up of a military academy at Tientsin in 1885. By now, Chang Chih-tung had emerged as another leader of the self-strengthening movement. First, as governor of Kwangtung in 1887 he established a mint (Li established a mint in the same year at Tientsin, where he was governor-general of Chihli and commissioner for the northern ports); in 1890 as governor-general of Hukwang he inaugurated the Ta-yeh Iron Mines, the Han-yang Iron-works and the P'ing-hsiang Coal Mines to form a composite iron and steel industry, and made plans for a trunk railway to connect Peking with the Yangtze. Between 1884 and 1891 the energetic governor of Taiwan, Liu Ming-ch'uan, who also had a military background, carried out a construction programme comprising railway and mining developments, facilities for the export trade and fiscal innovations. This phase is also notable for the additional diversification of industry as part of China's effort at increasing national wealth and the ability to cope with foreign economic competition. For example, a range of light industry producing consumer goods was set up, including cotton mills and textile plants, a paper mill and match factories. There were attempted innovations, too, in the organisation of the new enterprises as merchants, whose capital was constantly sought, endeavoured to gain more control. The organisational concepts of *kuan-shang ho pan* (joint government and merchant enterprise) and *shang-pan* (merchant enterprise) were advanced but, in the face of official preference for government-supervised merchant undertakings and continued discrimination against merchants, made little headway.

The continued restriction on free merchant enterprise throughout the three phases of self-strengthening epitomises the spirit in which it was conducted. The T'ung Chih restoration had seemed to work in that the threat from internal rebellion was removed, the foreigners were appeased and the traditional Confucian system was restored. Thereafter, with the occasional exception, the innovations of most reform-minded officials were, as we have seen, severely limited in scope and designed not to disturb the new equilibrium. Since the proposals, even though they were modest, had to run the gauntlet of criticism from the reactionary elements in the court, many of whom had not been near a Treaty Port or a barbarian, it could be argued that reforming zeal was inhibited. In fact this was not true. At the time, reformers and reactionaries sharing a common tradition were part of the same spectrum of Confucian opinion separated by differences of degree, not of basic outlook. The fundamental problem, as international relations during the self-strengthening period demonstrate, was that Chinese conservatism promoted a static view of the world scene rather than a dynamic view of constantly changing international relations. The result was that China prepared for the confrontations of the 1880s and 1890s on the basis of demands made by foreign powers in the 1840s and 1850s. In other words, having spent two decades without any positive practical response other than regular manifestations of xenophobia, China then spent three and a half decades preparing for the next round of international conflict, which would determine the success or failure of self-strengthening, strictly on the basis of past experience.

During the T'ung Chih restoration and the 1870s China's foreign policy, like its domestic counterpart, was tested and found reasonably adequate. If relations with Britain and France were not altogether smooth they brought at the most gunboat diplomacy and anti-foreignism rather than the bitter showdowns that had punctuated the earlier period. Britain's failure to ratify the Alcock Convention* of 1868, the crisis over the murder of the British official Margary on the Sino–Burmese frontier† in 1875 and the subsequent Chefoo Convention in 1876‡ demonstrated that a new *modus operandi* had evolved for this type of confrontation. Similarly, the Tientsin Massacre of 1870, a violent expression of the offence that Christianity was giving to entrenched Confucianism, in which ten nuns, two priests and two French officials were murdered, severely strained Sino–French relations though the deterioration stopped short of war. Further evidence of the positive

---

* The Alcock Convention emerged from a review of the Treaty of Tientsin. On balance favourable to China in that it raised the import duty on opium and export duty on silk, besides stipulating that in future if Britain availed itself of the 'most favoured nation' clause relevant obligations as well as rights would be incurred, it was not ratified by the British government because of opposition from merchants and traders.

† Margary, with the permission of the Chinese government, was exploring a possible trade route between Burma and China.

‡ The Chefoo Convention, negotiated in 1876 but not ratified until 1885 because of opposition arising from foreign interests, British traders and the Indian government, was drawn up after Britain had used the crisis over Margary's murder to open up discussion on a wide range of subjects besides compensation. It provided for four more Treaty Ports, the limitation of Likin free areas to Treaty Ports and a code of etiquette for diplomatic relations.

aspects of China's new diplomacy could be seen in the opening of legations in London, Paris, Berlin, Madrid, Washington, Tokyo and St Petersburg just a decade after the first envoys had ventured on a fact-·finding trip abroad in the company of the American diplomat Anson Burlingame. These contacts suggest that although China was still the victim of unequal practices, limited modernisation within the Confucian vision could cope with situations which, not so far back under the traditional tribute system, would have precipitated armed confrontation.

The first ominous signs that future challenges to China would not take precisely the same form as their predecessors, which had stimulated and set limits to the self-strengthening movement, came in the early 1870s. While China was preoccupied with the Margary affair, the rebellion of Yakub Beg* in Sinkiang and associated Russian pressure on Ili, Japan evinced designs on the Ryukyus and Korea, two of China's most regular tributary states. Japan had in the past been tributary to China, and it was this that had prevented China from offering no more than a commercial treaty to her in 1871 lest an undesirable precedent be established under which former tributaries enjoyed equality of status. By now Japan was modernising under the Meiji restoration, having been opened by the West in 1854. This probing into the zone whose states had traditionally recognised China's suzerainty soon became a pattern involving Britain and France as well as Japan. Britain's main interest lay in Burma and France's in Annam (Vietnam). By the end of the decade China's tributary system, the bone of contention in the opening of China, had become the centre of a new challenge, with France having declared Annam a protectorate in 1874, Japan having 'opened' Korea in 1876 and annexed the Ryukyus (Okinawa) in 1879.

China was unable to devote attention to these efforts at detaching her tributary states until Sinkiang had been pacified. The decision to suppress Yakub Beg precipitated a full-scale debate over the allocation of resources. Eventually, frontier defence gained priority over maritime defence (the naval programme) on the grounds that to ignore the rebellion would be to invite further Russian encroachment, and that whereas the maritime powers sought ports and trading rights Russia, sharing a long common frontier with China, sought territory as well as trading

---

* Sinkiang had been governed as a military colony by China after the Ch'ien Lung emperor's conquest. As imperial control waned, the local Uighur population had rebelled and Yakub Beg, supported by Britain as a counter to Russian expansionism, had by 1870 established himself as ruler of Kashgaria and part of northern Sinkiang. Russia used this 'threat' to the frontier to occupy Ili in 1871 until such time as imperial authority was restored.

rights. Tso Tsung t'ang was put in charge of the campaign and succeeded in defeating Yakub Beg in 1877. China resorted to diplomacy to recover Ili from Russia, succeeding in 1881 under the Treaty of St Petersburg. This was a major feat, since the treaty nullified the Treaty of Livadia of 1879, when the Chinese negotiator, seeking to retrieve Ili, to the dismay of the court actually put his initials to an agreement ceding seven-tenths of the territory in question. It is presumed he did so in ignorance, though there is the suggestion that the ignorance was due to his being at the time in too much of a hurry to get home.

Buoyed by this success, conservative elements advocated taking a tough line with France over Annam, since to make an example of one aggressor would deter Japan, Russia and Britain in Korea, Manchuria and Burma. Li Hung-chang and Prince Kung, however, counselled caution pending the completion of the naval programme and sought, unsuccessfully, to get French agreement to making Annam a joint protectorate. When Chinese troops suffered a defeat there, the dowager empress Tz'u Hsi ordered Li Hung-chang to seek a settlement. The outcome, the so-called Li-Fournier agreement of 1884, pleased neither side; before China had evacuated her troops a further clash occurred which precipitated the Sino–French war over Annam. This was the acid test for the self-strengthening movement, and in the first major engagement, in August 1884, twelve French ships attacked Foochow, sinking or damaging eleven Chinese warships and destroying the dockyard which, ironically, had been built with French aid during the period of co-operation. After three months of military deadlock in Tongking and a French blockade of the Yangtze, the two sides finally reached a settlement on the basis of the Li-Fournier agreement. Although China inflicted a major defeat on French forces at Langson before the signing of the treaty the war, besides being very costly, had revealed that the limited diplomatic, military and technological modernisation had not made China sufficiently strong to meet the new challenge to her tributary states.

This vulnerability did not go unnoticed. Britain made Burma a protectorate in 1885 and attention now focused on Korea. Japan, having been informed by the Tsungli Yamen in 1875 that Korea, though a tributary state, enjoyed autonomy in internal and external affairs, proceeded to 'open' Korea in 1876 in the fashion of a western maritime power. The annexation of the Ryukyus further alarmed China, and Li Hung-chang urged Korea to balance Japanese influence by entering into treaty relations with other powers; at China's behest treaties were signed with the United States, Britain, France and Germany in the early 1880s. China's position was now somewhat restored, formal cognisance of which was reflected in a commercial treaty and the appointment of Chinese advisers, including Yuan Shih k'ai, who was to train the Korean army. But the existence of a strong pro-Japan faction in the Korean government rivalling the pro-China faction enabled Japan, after sponsoring an attempted *coup* in 1884, to have this expressed in a formal agreement with China. This not only reduced Korea almost to the status of a joint protectorate but also brought about a significant surrender of suzerainty on the part of China. It also provided Japan with a pretext for armed intervention when Chinese troops put down an anti-government uprising in Korea in 1894. Diplomacy having failed to secure the withdrawal of troops, Japan and China declared war on each other on 1 August 1894 after the Japanese navy had sunk a steamer bringing Chinese reinforcements to Korea.

The first Sino–Japanese war was the last test for China's self-strengthening movement. On land, Li Hung-chang's Huai army was crushed at Pyongyang. At sea, his Peiyang fleet suffered an ignominious defeat. The expensive naval bases at Port Arthur and Dairen were captured by attacks launched from the landward side. Finally, in February 1895, the remains of the Peiyang fleet were destroyed when Japanese troops captured the forts at Weihaiwei and turned their guns on to the helpless ships in the harbour. China, humiliated, sued for peace. Li Hung-chang, whose war it had been, negotiated the Treaty of Shimonoseki signed on 17 April 1895. Its terms obliged China to cede Taiwan, the Pescadores and the Liaotung peninsula to Japan; to recognise Korea's independence; to pay a huge indemnity, open more ports and negotiate a commercial treaty that would give Japanese nationals the right to engage in industry and manufacturing in China.

Japan's victory signalled the opening of a new era in east Asian history. A new maritime power had emerged to rival Britain; a new land power to challenge Russia. But the implications were greatest for China. Defeated by a smaller Asian nation whose modernisation had been achieved as a result of the Meiji restoration that had begun only in 1868, all the shortcomings of the T'ung Chih restoration and self-strengthening had been mercilessly exposed. China's attempted modernisation within the limits of the Confucian vision had been a disaster. Foreign ideas and practices could not be grafted to the stock of China's traditional civilisation. If China had to undergo a process of regeneration it was becoming increasingly clear that it would have to take the form of revolution from below rather than limited reform imposed from above. From now on, China's reformers would take up more radical and more nationalistic positions. But they would have to contend with an unprecedented degree of international rivalry over China as the flood-tide of imperialism rose.

4 1895–1912: Reform, reaction and revolution

China's humiliating defeat in the Sino–Japanese war of 1894–5 had immediate repercussions at home and abroad. In internal affairs, with Li Hung-chang in disgrace, Yuan Shih-k'ai and Chang Chih-tung became pre-eminent, Yuan having responsibility for military training affairs and Chang being the new expert on foreign matters. But the main development was the upsurge in the clamour for reform. The war had shattered all illusions. Whereas the earliest leaders of self-strengthening, men like Tseng Kuo-fan and Tso Tsung-t'ang, had prescribed strong weapons and efficient guns; and the second generation, whose representative *par excellence* was Li Hung-chang, had added economic wealth to that prescription, there now emerged a third generation aiming to make China strong and prosperous by new means. Their prescription, which gave priority to administrative and institutional reform, had hitherto uncharted implications for the monarchy and China's traditional civilisation. As for China's external relations, Japan's victory had dislodged the keystone of a carefully constructed structure that could never be rebuilt. Its place was to be taken by a series of bilateral arrangements as empire vied with empire in a battle for concessions that led to the division of China into spheres of interest. At the same time as China was trapped in these two vortices the persistent undercurrent of peasant unrest was once more gathering momentum as the direct and indirect consequences of foreign pressure on the Chinese economy began to have effect.

For the foreign powers, the immediate cause for concern was Japan. Shortly after the treaty, Russia, France and Germany, using open threats, prevailed on Japan to return the Liaotung peninsular to China. Russia, who felt most menaced by the presence of Japan on the mainland, instigated this intervention and, though Japan only conceded at a price, enjoyed a brief advantage in dealings with China over railway concessions in Manchuria. China's relief, however, was temporary. Within two years Germany had seized Kiaochow as a naval base and forced China into a ninety-nine year lease that included concessions on railway construction in Shantung; Russia compelled China to sign an agreement to lease Port Arthur and Dairen for twenty-five years and to grant railway concessions in Manchuria which, together with Mongolia and Chihli, became a Russian sphere of influence; Britain secured Weihaiwei on a twenty-five year lease, the hinterland of Kowloon (known as the New Territories) on a ninety-nine year lease along with a promise that the Yangtze valley would remain a British preserve; France leased Kwangchow bay for ninety-nine years and carved out a sphere of influence in Kwangtung–Kwangsi–Yunnan, adjacent to its protectorate in Indo-China; and Japan, not to be left out, secured Fukien as a sphere of influence. Only Italy, perhaps too new to the role, failed when attempting to secure special rights in Chekiang. Meanwhile the United States, preoccupied with the Spanish war and the annexation of the Philippines, did not enunciate its policy until 1899. It did not seek to participate in direct imperialism, but rather to keep rivalry under control, to prevent the acquisition of exclusive rights, lest these inhibit trade and block outlets for capital investment, by promoting a movement for equality of commercial opportunity in China. This idea, actually originally conceived and secretly promoted by Britain, was elevated into the celebrated 'Open Door' policy which subsequently checked the movement that seemed to forebode the imminent dismembering of China.

Within China, the humiliating defeat and crippling indemnity, amounting to three times China's annual revenue, brought vigorous demands for reform. These demands, some of which had been made at the time of China's defeat by France in 1885, intensified with the formation of associations and the publishing of journals and newspapers devoted to reform. Such methods, owing not a little to the influence of the West generally and of the missionaries in particular, contributed to the coalescing of demands for reform into the Reform Movement, 1895–8. So far, for over half a century, ever since the violent impact of the West, successive generations of Chinese reformers had grappled with the question of seeking ideological sanction for change from within their own tradition. As we have seen, the sanction for self-strengthening had been the need to adopt western ways to defend Chinese ways. In the 1890s this was still the position of the moderate reformers, one of whose leaders, Chang Chih-tung, had postulated the persuasive slogan 'Chinese learning for the essential principles, western learning for the practical applications'. His view was that

Chinese civilisation could not be supplanted by western science and technology, but that it could to advantage be supplemented by it. With the advent of the radical reformers like the young scholar Kang Yu-wei and his even younger disciple Liang Ch'i-chiao, however, this moderate position was rapidly overtaken. Kang's reinterpretation of the classics now provided a philosophical sanction for wide-ranging institutional reform. While his persuasive arguments shocked orthodox Confucian scholars, they were a vital factor in mobilising opinion for radical reform.

The mounting foreign pressure for concessions and spheres of influence that to patriotic Chinese seemed to forebode partition and dismemberment, precipitated the crisis that gave Kang Yu-wei the opportunity to get his views on reform through to the young Kuang-hsü emperor in January 1898. After six months in which he subjected the monarch to a barrage of memorials, Kang finally succeeded in convincing him of the need for fundamental reform, and the first decree was issued on 11 June. Shortly afterwards Kang, hitherto precluded as a plebeian, was granted an audience. From the date of the first decree to 21 September 1898 the Emperor, advised by Kang Yu-wei, Liang Ch'i-chao and others who had been placed in key positions, issued some forty decrees. Kang's long-term aim was to replace the imperial Confucian system with a constitutional monarchy; the measures of this short 'one-hundred day reform' concentrated on liberalising the educational system and improving the administration by abolishing sinecures and increasing efficiency, but they touched on many other subjects, including agriculture, industry and commerce, the law, the police, the armed forces and the postal service.

The reforms antagonised the entire conservative establishment. Indeed, most were either challenged or delayed, since the opposition knew that in the final analysis the outcome rested with the dowager empress Tz'u Hsi, the power behind the throne who, although ostensibly in retirement since 1889, had continued to hold the reins of government. For her part, though not averse to moderate reform she could now see her own position being eroded, and the issue of radical reform was soon translated into a power struggle with the Emperor. The reformers knew that reactionary suppression of their programme was likely and plotted to forestall it with the connivance of Yuan Shih-kai, who was training a modern army at Tientsin. Yuan, however, was far too cunning a politician and revealed the existence of the plot to the Manchu military commander, Jung Lu. With his support, Tz'u Hsi executed a *coup d'état* on 21 September 1898 to end the hundred days reform and virtually restore the *status quo ante*. All that remained of the programme were the university at Peking and some colleges and schools in the provinces, together with the abolition of certain sinecures. The Emperor was placed in detention; K'ang and Liang escaped to Japan, while other reformers were executed. Tz'u Hsi began her third regency and China embarked on a period of reform that was to end in revolution.

China's international relations and court history of this period interacted with equally critical developments in Chinese society. Although the T'ung Chih restoration and the quelling of rebellion had ushered in a period of stability in which dynastic decline was temporarily retarded, the livelihood of the Chinese people remained precarious. The new equilibrium took into account the growth that had occurred as a result of the mid-century rebellions in military and militia influence, and the lowering of the standards of the gentry whose ranks had been swelled by the sale of degrees. The quality of civil administration fell and the population was extremely vulnerable to natural calamity such as flood and drought. The great famine in north China between 1876 and 1879, when some twelve to thirteen million people perished, is stark evidence of the conditions that existed. Peasant unrest was endemic and easily aggravated by additional economic and political pressures. For example, sections of the traditional handicraft industry suffered because of increasing foreign imports; China, having surrendered tariff autonomy under the unequal treaties, could do little either to preserve them or to protect the development of indigenous modern industry. This unrest was fuelled by the gentry's objection to missionary activities that conflicted with traditional beliefs and challenged their traditional role as leaders of local society. In the new climate of nationalism that had been created by the war and the outrageous behaviour of the powers, it was neither difficult nor unreasonable that hostility should be channelled against foreigners.

This was the setting for the Boxer Rebellion of 1900. The Boxers* were a secret society associated with the White Lotus sect which rebelled in 1796–1804, and with other societies. When they emerged in the late 1890s most of China's provinces were affected by disorder. Their sudden rise in Shantung can be linked, however, not only to economic and political conditions caused by Yellow River floods and famine but also by the gouging out of a sphere of influence there by Germany. Although initially anti-dynastic in the tradition of peasant

---

* The Chinese name of the society was 'I Ho Ch'uan', usually crudely rendered as 'Righteous and Harmonious Fists'. It practised a form of calisthenic military art. Hence the popular name 'Boxers'.

rebellions, by the end of 1899 the Boxers had become anti-foreign and pro-dynastic*, enjoying patronage and support from conservatives and xenophobes in the court down through the provincial administration to the gentry leadership in the countryside. The attacks on Chinese Christians and missionaries brought foreign pressure and the replacement of Shantung's Governor Yu-hsien with Yuan Shih-kai. In contrast to his predecessor's policies of pacification and absorption into the militia† Yuan, contrary to the court's instructions, sought to exterminate the Boxers. Meanwhile, in Chihli the movement flourished and extended its attacks to all symbols of foreign domination such as railways and telegraph lines. These events alarmed the diplomatic community, which in May 1899 strengthened the legation guards in Peking and summoned reinforcements. Shortly after, the Boxers prevented reinforcements from reaching the capital and events rapidly escalated towards war. The Boxers entered Peking on 13 June; the German minister von Ketteler was killed on 20 June, and the next day the court declared war on the foreign powers and adopted a policy of marshalling the Boxers together with the regular troops to besiege the foreign legations.

The government's declaration of war was not, however, accepted by the moderate provincial officials Li Hung-chang at Canton, Liu K'un-i at Nanking, Chang Chih-tung at Wuhan and Yuan Shih-k'ai in Shantung. This meant on the one hand that hostilities were localised in the northern provinces; on the other, the foreigners could see that providing the 'rebellion' were put down the repayment of debt would continue and the treaty system would remain intact. To ensure its suppression, the powers raised a force to relieve Tientsin on 14 July and one month later a force of about 18,000, comprising Japanese, Russian, British, American, French, Austrian and Italian troops, later to be joined by Germans, relieved Peking. The Empress fled to Sian and it was left to the veteran Li Hung-chang to salvage China's damaged foreign relations. As the allied forces swelled to 45,000 by late 1900, Li negotiated a settlement predicated on the mutually convenient assumption that the conflict had been a joint effort at suppressing an uprising. For the deaths of 231 foreigners, many more Chinese Christians and the cost of the allied intervention China agreed, under the Boxer Protocol, signed on 7 September 1901, to pay an indemnity of £67 million and to punish those involved. This did not include the Empress, since she was

---

* The slogan was *fu Ch'ing mieh yang*: 'Support the Ch'ing dynasty and exterminate the foreigner'.
† This resulted in the respectable designation *I ho t'uan*: 'righteous and harmonious militia'.

regarded as a victim of the uprising. The indemnity gave the powers more control over China's revenues. Russia received the largest share – about thirty per cent – and in spite of the terms of the settlement sought a separate agreement over the withdrawal of its troops which had occupied Manchuria 'to restore order'. Li Hung-chang, involved in the negotiations, died before they were concluded, and when agreement on a phased withdrawal was reached on 14 April 1902, it was more a result of foreign pressure on Russia than of Chinese diplomacy. Japan had been especially concerned at Russia's invasion of Manchuria, and the increasing rivalry between these two powers eventually led to the Russo–Japanese war of 1904.

The Boxer Rebellion was a brief, violent interlude in the process of reform as conservatives and reactionaries made common cause with the forces unleashed by a patriotic peasant uprising in an effort to repel foreign imperialism. In the aftermath, to stave off its collapse the dynasty embarked on institutional and social change reminiscent of that advocated in the abortive Reform Movement. Between 1901 and 1905 the most significant reforms included the abolition of the civil service examination system and its replacement by a modern school system and curriculum. The new system was to break the constricting influence of the old exams, so that Chinese education not only underwent a revolution in content and structure but, very quickly, in the type of student it produced. At this time numbers of students began to go to Japan to study. Reforms were also planned for the armed forces and with the deaths of Li Hung-chang (1901), Liu K'un-i (1902) and Jung Lu (1903), Yuan Shih-kai became the most influential official in the programme to reorganise the armed forces. This presaged not only military growth but better leadership too: officer candidates were to attend military schools and academies. An early example was Chiang Kai-shek, who at eighteen attended the Paoting military school in 1906 and a military academy in Japan in 1907.

Japan's influence was confirmed by the spectacular victory over Russia in 1905. Japan had invaded Chinese territory to conduct the war and while the outcome implied that in the long term Japan had replaced Russia as the power most likely to exploit a position of special advantage in China, the immediate implications were that Japan excelled militarily and that constitutional monarchy was superior as a polity to monarchy. The idea of constitutionalism rapidly gained currency, supported by intellectuals, officials and the exiled reformer Liang Ch'i-ch'ao. However, the ideas of gradualist reform and constitutional monarchy came under vigorous attack from proponents of a new ideology of republicanism, members of the T'ung Meng Hui (United

League) formed in Japan in 1905 by Sun Yat-sen. Unlike Liang, who was an intellectual, a member of the gentry *élite*, Sun was from peasant stock and had gone to Honolulu to join his brother at the age of thirteen. His revolutionary ideas, formed when the dynasty was approaching its nadir in the 1890s, reflect his unique educational background and experience. In Hawaii he had three years of Anglican schooling before returning to Hong Kong where, after two years at the Po Chi Medical School in Canton, he spent five years reading medicine. To this predominantly foreign influence was added the influence of overseas Chinese communities and Cantonese secret societies, to produce a new type of revolutionary. By 1905, when the constitutionalist movement was gathering momentum, Sun Yat-sen was already well known as a revolutionary, having staged two abortive small-scale uprisings in the Canton area through the Hsing Chung Hui (Revive China Society), his own secret society, and with the help of the local triads. He was also known in Britain as in 1896, having been detained at the Chinese Legation pending extradition, it fell to his old professor, James Cantlie, to mobilise British public opinion to secure his release.

In the event, although the court assented to constitutionalism, the reorganisation of 1906 was a sham. It merely expanded the old six boards into eleven 'modern-sounding' ministries and in so far as it increased the influence of Manchus it was retrogressive. But the movement would not be blocked. Under pressure from Liang's Cheng Wen She (Political Information Society) and many Constitution Protection Clubs the court adopted a nine-year programme leading to constitutional government, based on the Japanese precedent, in August 1908. However, it is doubtful whether even then the court was contemplating genuine constitutionalism. The Empress envisaged legislative, executive and judicial powers residing in the throne and a parliamentary assembly that would only consider issues, not decide them. When she died shortly after the promulgation of the programme, having survived Emperor Kuang-hsü by one day, giving rise to the view that she was implicated in his death, her three-year-old nephew became the Hsüan t'ung emperor with his father, Prince Chun, as regent. One of his first acts was to squeeze Yuan Shih-k'ai out of the government in revenge for Yuan's betrayal of the Kuang-hsü emperor in 1898. Turning his attention to constitutionalism, he authorised the establishment of provincial assemblies in 1909, but when the demands rose for the convening of parliament he baulked at the prospect, choosing to stall by telescoping the programme from nine years to six. That, together with his exercise of the throne's absolute control over appointments to consolidate Manchu domination of the cabinet in 1911, persuaded many reformers to throw in their lot with the revolutionaries.

From 1906 to 1911 there was a series of abortive risings culminating in the 'Canton Revolution' of 27 April 1911. Demoralised by their lack of success in Canton and the difficulty of raising funds the revolutionaries decided to concentrate their activities on Wuhan, since success there would give them more political leverage. A new rising was planned by two societies linked to the T'ung Meng Hui: the Kung Chin Hui (Common Advancement Society) and a branch of the Chen Wu Hsueh She (Military Study Society). The former was more prestigious but the latter more powerful as it was composed of army revolutionaries. T'ung Meng Hui leaders, Sung Chiao-jen and Huang Hsing, in the absence of Sun, who was abroad, were invited to lead the revolution. Planned for 19 October, the explosion of a bomb on 9 October in the revolutionary headquarters exposed the plot and compelled the army revolutionaries to seize power the next day. Fortuitously, with part of the garrison in Szechwan quelling riots over the nationalisation of the railways, they met with little resistance. Their success was followed by the fall of Hanyang and Hankow, and in a period of six weeks fifteen provinces seceded from the Ch'ing dynasty. Government counter-attacks produced little success, and after the fall of Shanghai and Nanking a provisional revolutionary government was set up pending Sun Yat-sen's return.

Sun, having sought support from Britain, returned to be inaugurated as provisional president on 1 January 1912. The revolutionaries realised, however, that the only person capable of forcing the abdication of the emperor and averting civil war was Yuan Shih-k'ai, who had meanwhile been made premier to lure him out of retirement. For this reason, Sun indicated his willingness to step down provided that Yuan pledged himself to republicanism. Yuan agreed and set about engineering the abdication, which was announced on 12 February, ending not only Ch'ing rule but also China's traditional system of government. With Yuan Shih-k'ai pledging his support for the new republic, he was formally inaugurated as president on 10 March and a provisional constitution promulgated on 11 March. Sun Yat-sen relinquished his duties and handed over responsibility to him on 1 April 1912.

5   1912–27: The Chinese Republic

The decline into warlordism

The Manchu dynasty fell because it was too weak to stand, not because it had been challenged by a closely organised revolutionary movement. Its main adversary, the Tung Meng Hui, now an open political party campaigning for democracy, had based its appeal on Sun Yat-sen's ideas for a republican revolution. Evolved over the years these were to be set out as the celebrated 'Three Principles of the People' (San Min Chu I): nationalism, democracy and people's livelihood. At the time nationalism meant pro-republicanism, anti-Manchu and anti-imperialism; democracy meant people's sovereignty and constitutional government; and the concept of people's livelihood included ideas of equalising land ownership and regulating capital to inhibit the enrichment of speculators and monopolists. When facing up to the challenge from Liang Ch'i ch'ao and the constitutional monarchists, the Tung Meng Hui had also promoted a three-stage programme comprising three years of military government followed by six years of tutelage under a provisional constitution culminating in full constitutional government under an elected president and parliament. Unfortunately this revolutionary philosophy was not matched by organisation, and the movement lacked training and discipline. Indeed, it is doubtful whether, besides Sun Yat-sen and the other leaders, its adherents had thought beyond the destructive stage of the revolution. The constructive work of the revolution, steps towards implementing Sun Yat-sen's revolutionary philosophy, would thus take many years.

Yuan Shih-k'ai suffered no such disability. From the start he single-mindedly began to reduce the influence of the revolutionaries in the government. The situation soon degenerated into a power struggle between the Tung Meng Hui, now merged with four splinter parties to form the Kuomintang or Nationalist Party, and Yuan Shih-k'ai, who had the support of the Republican, Unification and Democratic Parties, who later themselves merged to form the Progressive Party. The elections in December 1912 were won by the nationalists, who now stood firmly in the path of Yuan's ambitions. But Yuan intrigued and manoeuvred to overcome the opposition. In March the talented nationalist politician Sung Chiao-jen was assassinated; in April Yuan negotiated a massive £25 million reorganisation loan from a five-power consortium of Britain, France, Germany, Japan and Russia. He needed the money to finance military preparations: civil war was approaching. For their part the powers were merely acting out of self-interest: they sought to help a strong man usurp control in the new republic in order that he might repay the debt by acting as trustee for their privileges, loans and investments under the treaty system. The showdown came in the summer of 1913 in what is now referred to as the 'second revolution'. Yuan attempted to sack the nationalist military governors of Kiangsi, Kwangtung and Anhwei and this provoked declarations of independence from these provinces and from Kiangsu, Fukien, Hunan and Szechwan. But their gesture was in vain and within two months Yuan's well-equipped army had marched south to crush the opposition. The way was clear for him to fulfil his ambitions.

He now moved fast, brushing aside the constitution and parliament. Still opposed by the nationalists, he dissolved the party in 1914 and revoked the credentials of its parliamentarians. He became a dictator. By convening a constitutional conference to revise the 1912 provisional constitution he produced the Constitutional Compact of 1914 that assured him of lifelong tenure in the presidency and the right to nominate his successor. He was now but a step away from being emperor and it seemed that nobody in China could prevent it. But he feared foreign reaction, particularly that of Japan, as with the European powers heavily involved in the first world war that country now had much more freedom of action in east Asia.

Yuan's wish to further his ambitions actually coincided with Japan's desire to seek domination over China. Japan had in fact declared war on Germany to provide a pretext for taking over that country's sphere of interest in Shantung. In January 1915 she followed this by presenting Yuan with the infamous 'Twenty-one Demands',*

---

* The 'Twenty-one Demands' included the recognition of Japan's position in Shantung and of privileges in Manchuria and Inner Mongolia, the joint operation of certain iron and steel works in Hupeh and a colliery in Kiangsi, an undertaking not to lease any harbour, etc., to any third power, employment of Japanese political, financial and military advisers, together with many other economic privileges.

virtually all of which he agreed to accept, believing that as a *quid pro quo* this would cause Japan to acquiesce in his plan.

Confident of the outcome, Yuan now set about mobilising public opinion for a restoration of the monarchy. Besides exploiting an opinion by his American constitutional adviser Frank Goodnow, later president of the Johns Hopkins University, to the effect that China's tradition of autocracy would make constitutional monarchy more suitable as an institution on which to base the polity than a republic, Yuan now launched an open monarchical movement. Numerous petitions flooded in urging a change to constitutional monarchy, and after a 'ballot' in the provinces which was unanimously for a constitutional monarchy (on which count Yuan enjoyed even greater support than had Napoleon) and repeated requests that he should ascend the throne, Yuan 'reluctantly' accepted, worshipping heaven and earth at the Temple of Heaven, a prerogative of emperors, and choosing a reign title. The New Year 1916 was to be the start of his reign.

Yuan Shih-K'ai's monarchical dream was not, however, to come true. Before he could be enthroned, he was faced by fresh opposition from revolutionaries in Yunnan and Kweichow, from Sun Yat-sen in Japan, operating through the Chinese Revolutionary Party that had been organised from the old Nationalist Party, and a reluctance on the part of two of his generals to suppress the opposition. Serious though all this was, the deciding factor in Yuan's downfall was, ironically, the lack of Japanese support, of which he had been most confident. When Japan indicated that, as a result of its inability to keep the peace, his government had forfeited the right to represent all of China, it dealt him a mortal blow. One by one his henchmen abandoned him until even his right to the presidency was challenged. This complete reversal of his plans, turning the whole monarchical movement into a tragi-comedy, was too much for him. On 6 June 1916 Yuan Shih-k'ai died suddenly of uremia due to nervous prostration.

After this episode there was another attempt at restoring the monarchy. In the political manœuvring over the question as to whether China should declare war on Germany, an old Manchu supporter, Chang Hsun, occupied Peking and replaced the last Ch'ing emperor, P'u-yi, on the throne.* But this full-blown restoration lasted only two weeks and by this time the monarchical movement was discredited.

---

* His career is unique: emperor at the age of three in 1908, forced to abdicate in 1912, he was now restored to the throne. Within a few weeks he was deposed. In 1932 he was placed on the throne of Manchukuo by the Japanese only to be deposed in 1945. He was 're-educated' by the communists after 1949.

Yuan Shih-k'ai had, however, left a lasting legacy. China had lost its strong man. His régime had irreparably damaged the flimsy structure of the early Republic and his passing released centrifugal forces that plunged the country into a decade of warlordism.

From 1916 onwards parliament came increasingly under warlord domination. When this led to a north–south split in 1917 it gave Sun Yat-sen the opportunity to form a military government at Canton until that in turn was subordinated to southern militarists forcing Sun to retire to Shanghai and concentrate on reforming the Nationalist Party. At the same time the northern (Peiyang) clique itself split into An-Fu (Anhwei-Fukien) and Chihli factions. Further fragmentation occurred in the 1920s following the emergence of the Fengtien clique based on southern Manchuria and the appearance of a semi-independent militarist linked to one major clique or another in almost every province. China was now in the grip of politicians with private armies, undistinguished successors of the scholar-generals who had initiated the phenomenon of regional armies for the quelling of the Taipings. But the main difference now was that they were neither able to create a new order in China nor, on account of the progress towards modernisation, to effect change within tradition and bring about dynastic restoration. Controlling arsenals or ports through which arms could be imported, financed by irregular taxes levied in their own bailiwicks and, in the case of the main cliques, linked with foreign interests* in search of the strongest among the strong men, the warlords plunged China into chaos. In an effort to restore order, a federal system was proposed in the early 1920s, only to be rejected in favour of the centralised system lest provincial autonomy be further consolidated. But strong central government would elude China, as it did in 1911, until a leader emerged to link ideology and political organisation with military power.

The struggle for national reunification

This political crisis stimulated great intellectual ferment. Why had the Republic failed to produce strong enlightened leadership? Failure and political disarray led to a critical re-evaluation of China's entire cultural heritage. Leading intellectuals like Ch'en Tu-hsiu and Hu Shih, both of whom had studied abroad – Ch'en in Japan and France, Hu in the United States under Dewey – made Peking University a centre for what later came to be called the New Culture Movement. Born

---

* The Chihli clique was linked to Anglo-American interests, the An-Fu clique with Japanese interests; Japan also had links with the Fengtien clique.

towards the end of the nineteenth century and familiar with the cultures of East and West, these men subjected China's Confucian civilisation to withering criticism in the journals and discussions of the day, extolling the virtues of western civilisation. At the same time the cry went up for a literary renaissance in which a new written style based on the vernacular would make a new literature of protest accessible to the people. China's political predicament was the immediate reason for all this intellectual ferment but the range of topics under discussion, the media in which discussion was conducted, the many participants and the growing audience are all evidence of the changes that were being wrought in Chinese society. With the rural areas increasingly impoverished under the blight of warlordism and landlordism, urbanisation, particularly under foreign influence, was fostering new ideas and creating new classes. Besides the intellectuals and the modern-style students for whom traditional culture was the root cause of China's decay, the cities were now centres for increasing numbers of merchant entrepreneurs and modern factory workers who themselves had little cause to perpetuate traditional values.

In 1919 these new social classes were drawn together in a storm of patriotic indignation following the exposure at the Paris Peace Conference (which China attended, having entered the war in 1917) that German rights in Shantung were to be transferred to Japan. The collusion of the powers and the Peking government in this matter precipitated a wave of spontaneous protest. The most organised reaction came from Peking students, who staged a demonstration to commemorate the infamous Twenty-one Demands of 1915. Held on 4 May 1919, it ended in violence and severe punishment for offenders. But in the end the patriotic demonstrators triumphed. They attracted nation-wide support from merchants, who boycotted Japanese goods, from workers, who went on strike, and from public opinion generally. The cabinet was forced to resign and China refused to sign the Versailles Treaty. Marxist historians regard this manifestation of nationalism as a climactic point in the Chinese revolution, the culmination of the 'Old Democratic Revolution' (or bourgeois revolution) led by Sun Yat-sen. After 1919 China entered the period of the 'New Democratic Revolution' under the leadership of the Chinese Communist Party. 1919 is for this reason designated as the watershed between 'modern' history and 'contemporary' history.

The 4 May movement succeeded in spreading the existing intellectual and social revolution throughout China. New publications appeared, associations were formed, foreign scholars like Dewey, Tagore and Russell went on lecture tours as part of the New Culture Movement that had now entered a new phase. With the disillusionment that had surrounded the outcome of the Paris peace talks many intellectuals rejected the West and Japan as a source of inspiration and turned to Marxist socialism and the example of the Bolshevik revolution to seek guidance for China. This tendency was to some extent promoted by the excellent impression the Soviet Union had created in 1918 and 1919 by offering to surrender Russian privileges in Manchuria exacted under the unequal treaties. But the real appeal of Marxism lay in its providing a new and convincing scientific explanation for China's humiliation at the hands of western imperialism. At the same time, Leninism provided a new programme for action. By 1920 Ch'en Tu-hsiu and the Peking University librarian, Li Ta-chao, whose young assistant was a Hunanese student called Mao Tse-tung, were Marxist-Leninists. There were also converts among the worker-students who had gone to France, the most famous of whom was Chou En-lai, who had been jailed for his part in the 4 May demonstrations. With the help of a Comintern agent, Li and Ch'en established communist branches in Peking and Shanghai in 1920, and in July 1921 a meeting was held in Shanghai to found the Chinese Communist Party. Mao Tse-tung was one of the twelve delegates representing fifty-seven members.

The long-term impact of the Chinese Communist Party (CCP) provides the justification for the Marxist assessment of the pivotal role played by the 4 May movement. At the time, however, as we can see from the minute size of the infant Communist Party, the main events in the movement, the appeal of Marxist socialism and the lessons of the Bolshevik revolution were of greater immediate importance to the nationalists. This was recognised by the Comintern which, after its agent Maring had met Sun in Canton in 1922, realised that his party represented the mainstream of Chinese nationalism and advised that members of the Communist Party should join it as individuals while retaining their own party membership. Sun agreed to this in full knowledge of the risk from a block within, since he needed Soviet aid. Thus began an uneasy marriage of convenience between the two parties. With the help of Soviet political and military experts Sun reorganised the Party and created a party army. A young general, Chiang Kai-shek, was sent to the Soviet Union to study the military system and after three months returned to found the Whampoa Military Academy at Canton.

By 1925, despite the uneasiness of the alliance between the nationalists and the communists, a force had been welded together capable of reunifying China. But that task was not to be completed by Sun Yat-sen. In March 1925, during a visit to Peking to discuss the question of reunification, he fell ill and died. This deprived the alliance of a prestigous leader whose main quality was his ability to create unity by seeking common ground among people of disparate views. It is a measure of his achievement that in an atmosphere of increasing friction in Canton, preparations for national reunification could still go ahead. A national government was established in Canton in July 1925 to rival the warlord régime in Peking and a year later, after a localised pacification campaign, Chiang Kai-shek, as commander-in-chief of the National Revolutionary Army, launched the celebrated Northern Expedition. The early part of the campaign was an unqualified success. Within nine months southern China had been conquered, but then success was threatened as the alliance began to split at the seams. The main difficulty was the increasing unwillingness of the communists to participate in the alliance as individuals subject to nationalist leadership. As they began to operate more openly as a 'bloc within', collaboration between the two sides degenerated into conflict. Sun Yat-sen's unifying influence was much missed.

At the end of 1926, as Chiang was conducting his victorious campaign in east and south-east China, the Canton government moved north to Wuhan. There it came increasingly under the influence of the Soviet adviser, Borodin, and the left wing of the nationalists. However, as more territory was captured this trend was counterbalanced by an increase in the influence of the military, which was linked to the right wing of the movement. Matters came to a head when, having taken the vital financial and banking centres of Shanghai and Nanking, Chiang, with the support of local anti-communist elements, decided to eliminate the threat posed by the communists. Beginning on 12 April 1927, a full-scale purge was conducted in the principal urban centres, destroying the Chinese Communist Party's infrastructure. What had started as a split between two factions, Chiang's military linked to the right wing of the Nationalist Party on the one hand and the left wing of the party linked to the communists on the other, had now developed into antagonistic confrontation.

This confrontation was made irrevocable when Chiang, overriding all protests, including his dismissal as commander-in-chief, set up a rival government at Nanking on 18 April 1927. The Wuhan government responded by launching its own northern campaign as part of a strategy advocated by Borodin, the aim of which was to gather in more forces before dealing with Chiang. But this proved to be its undoing. Certain warlords hitherto relatively amenable to the policy of reunification, and upon whose support the Wuhan government had counted, now indicated their reluctance to co-operate with a communist-inspired régime. As a result, the nationalists in the Wuhan government, who had been harbouring doubts about the practicability of the new strategy, imposed restrictions on the communists, eventually excluding them from the Nationalist Party. This policy towards the communists hardened when their troops were involved in an uprising on 1 August at Nanchang, developing into a full-scale anti-communist purge.

With both wings of the Nationalist Party committed to an anti-communist policy, the way was now clear for a reconciliation between Wuhan and Nanking. Nanking became the seat of government and Chiang Kai-shek was formally reinstated as commander-in-chief to continue his northern conquest. By the beginning of 1929 Chiang had virtually completed the reunification of China after more than a decade of warlordism.

6 1927–37: The Nationalist Government at Nanking

The political union achieved by Chiang Kai-shek at the end of 1928 marks the beginning of the eventful decade of the Nanking government, a period that ended in Japan's all-out aggression against China in 1937. Three major issues dominate the history of this decade. The first is the quality of the reunification that the rapid advance of the Northern Expedition had brought about and the nature of the régime that the nationalists created to cope with the situation. The second is the attitude of the new régime to foreign powers, particularly Japan, whose aggression was to reach new heights even when viewed in the light of the modern history of China: Japan first engaged in a limited war over Manchuria ending in the creation of the puppet state of Manchukuo, before embarking on the unlimited war that was to cause the Nanking government to retreat to Chungking. The third is the state of civil war that existed between the nationalists and the communists from the time of the split in 1927 until the establishing of the united front against Japan at the end of 1936, together with the emergence from the intra-party struggle among the communists, of a definitive approach to revolution based on the 'unorthodox' tactics of Mao Tse-tung.

The unity achieved by the Northern Expedition had completed the first phase, the military stage, of Sun Yat-sen's original programme. China was poised to enter the second phase, a stage of political tutelage under the Nationalist Party that would last six years before the introduction of full constitutional government. No sooner had the government been set up under Chiang Kai-shek's presidency than it was put to the test. The question in 1928–9 was the demobilisation of warlord armies and placing the military under a single national command structure. For the warlords, most of whom had not actually been crushed by Chiang during his northern conquest but had merely acknowledged his pre-eminence as the strongest of the strong men and had reached an accommodation with him, this was tantamount to an invitation to sign their own death warrants. They proved unco-operative and offered nothing more than 'mutually balanced force reductions' to which proposals Chiang was, not surprisingly, equally intransigent.

This singular lack of success by the government in disarming the warlords underlines China's fragile unity at the time. It was a unity that would be unavoidably shattered between 1929 and 1936 by a series of costly separatist movements and rebellions, sometimes linked to intra-party struggles, whenever there was a conflict of interests. Chiang survived militarily with the help of the north-eastern warlord Chang Hsüeh-liang until the Japanese menace forced the protagonists to resolve their differences in the national interest. But in accepting the situation, that is to say by not attempting to mobilise the entire country on the basis of the upsurge in nationalism that existed in the urban areas in an effort to create greater unity, the government permitted the continued existence of semi-independent bases in much of China where resources were continually syphoned off for military and territorial aggrandisement at the expense of the population, especially the impoverished peasantry. Those areas still dominated by warlords contributed little to national revenue, nor did they benefit from it at the time when development was sorely needed. The corollary to this state of nominal union was that the pattern of Chiang's régime was warped from the start, concentrating on the urban areas and devoting increasing attention to military requirements.

The reluctance of the government to destroy warlordism and carry the national revolution through to the end reflects on the one hand the political and military realities of the period, and on the other the changes wrought in the Nationalist Party. Important realignments had taken place and the new concensus, influenced by Chiang's wealthy industrial and financial supporters, was for consolidation of gains before fresh revolutionary change. Between 1924 and 1929 the party became less revolutionary, as the proclamations of its congresses reveal. The first, in 1924, identified the party's enemies as the constitutional clique, the federalists, the compromisers and the business-dominated group. The second, in 1926, adopted a similar line but was distinctly more anti-imperialistic. But the third, in 1929, pointed to the 'agents of red imperialism' as the enemies of the party. Although these shifts represent pressure from collective opinion they parallel Chiang Kai-shek's own rise to power, and he cannot be dissociated from them. Year by year the Nationalist Party became less of a sharp weapon for revolution and more of a blunt instrument for restoring order.

Further evidence of the direction in which the party was now moving can be seen in the resumption in 1928 of the veneration of Confucius. In 1931 the sage's birthday was declared a national holiday. It was not that by now the nationalists had stopped discussing revolution: they had simply redefined it as part of a transformation in their ideology that was well advanced before the twin threats of communist-led internal rebellion and Japanese-provoked foreign war reappeared on the political horizon. When these threats did materialise, the nationalist response was, predictably, to model their policy on the Confucian T'ung Chih restoration. Confucian virtues were extolled, the great scholar-general Tseng Kuo-fan was held up for emulation. Even the *pao-chia* system of collective responsibility and the militia system for local security were revived. The gentry were rehabilitated and encouraged to resume their traditional functions. However, even if an all-out restoration policy had been implemented, incorporating agrarian economic restoration and improvements in local government and the administration of justice, it could not have guaranteed success. The monarchy had gone and China's ancient civilisation had already been irreparably eroded: twentieth-century China was vastly different from nineteenth-century China. The argument for Chinese studies to be used as a basis, borrowing only science and technology from the West, had long since been proved untenable. Most important of all was the fact that the communists, though at first enjoying less popular support than the Taipings, soon showed that with their revolutionary ideology they were qualitatively different as opponents.

As these shifts were occurring in the Nationalist Party, the communists were undergoing their own metamorphoses. After the break with the nationalists in 1927, they had themselves split into two movements. The Comintern-dominated Politburo, having gone to earth in Shanghai, organised strikes, sabotage and uprisings. The movement led by Mao Tse-tung, Chu Te and others was in the rural areas of Hunan and Kiangsi, where they were organising the peasants. Between 1927 and 1930 both movements were involved in the Moscow-inspired policy of fomenting urban uprisings, none of which proved successful. Taking place under the very noses of the nationalists, the activities under the auspices of the Politburo got more difficult and brought diminishing returns, precipitating serious squabbles within the party. Mao's activities, however, conducted among the peasants and well away from both nationalist centres of control and Politburo interference, met with increasing success. Besides organising soviets, practising guerrilla tactics and carrying out land reform, Mao and Chu repulsed two nationalist 'bandit-extermination' campaigns. They also survived a third, which had been curtailed by the Japanese invasion of Manchuria, by the time the First All-China Congress of Soviets was convened at Juichin on 7 November 1931. This was attended by members of the Politburo, now controlled by the so-called 'twenty-eight Bolsheviks', all returned students from Moscow, and the scene was set for a confrontation between the proponents of Moscow's unprofitable but orthodox tactics and Mao's realistic, successful but unorthodox approach.

The real issue at stake at this meeting was the need for the Comintern and the Politburo to take control of the rural movement and establish a Central Soviet government before, so to speak, 'the tail began to wag the dog'. This was achieved and while Mao was not out-manoeuvred, a fact that is borne out by his emerging as Chairman of the Council of People's Commissars of the Chinese Soviet Republic, his authority was obviously diluted and circumscribed in the new government hierarchy. At the same time, a Party Congress subjected his policies to severe criticism as part of a campaign that lasted right up to the Long March in 1934-5, wresting from him the power he exercised over the army. This was happening at an inopportune time: as the nationalists gathered strength for their fourth and fifth campaigns Mao had become more involved with political and economic work than military matters.

The fourth campaign ended in failure, partly because of the success of new communist tactics, which seemed to vindicate those who considered Mao's guerrilla activities obsolete. But the fifth campaign, launched after Chiang had signed a truce with the Japanese, finally succeeded in dislodging the communists. Said to have involved 700,000 soldiers, it was planned with the aid of German advisers and comprised military encirclement and economic strangulation. As the noose tightened, so the nationalists fortified their gains and carried out rural reconstruction. On 15 October 1934, after heavy losses, the communists were forced to break through the encirclement and retreat.

So began the Long March, which covered 5000 miles in about a year, an endurance test that was to end when the survivors reached an existing soviet in Shenshi province on China's north-western frontier at the end of 1935.

The statistics of this epic retreat are staggering. About 20,000 of the original 100,000 arrived in Shensi. They had achieved a mean daily stage of nearly twenty-four miles, crossing eighteen mountain ranges and twenty-four rivers along a route that took in twelve provinces and sixty-two towns. At the same time they encountered ten warlord armies, besides eluding the government forces sent against them. At the end of it all, Mao emerged at the head of the party having ousted the Moscow-dominated leadership at a conference convened in January 1935 at Tsunyi. Establishing his headquarters at Yenan in December 1936, he began to rebuild the Party machine from the survivors of the Long March in preparation for a period, lasting until 1945, in which class struggle would take second place to the needs of the war of resistance against Japan.

The growing threat from Japan throughout the period of the Nanking government had its origins in the success of the national revolution and the upsurge in Chinese nationalism of the 1920s. At the time, Japan's relations with China, in contradistinction to China's relations with the western powers, had been governed by less flexibility. None of China's adversaries had given much away at the Washington Conference* of 1921–2, which was only partly successful in providing a basis for stability in east Asia and for the restoration of China's sovereignty. Even so, increasing Chinese nationalism eventually compelled Britain and the United States to yield on a number of issues. Strikes, for example, organised by communist union leaders like Liu Shao-ch'i, spread to the Treaty Ports as the labour movement and the national revolution became integrated after the nationalist–communist alliance. Incidents like the anti-foreign demonstration in Shanghai on 30 May 1925, the clash at Canton between Whampoa cadets and Anglo–French forces on 23 June 1925, both of which ended in loss of life, and the Canton incident precipitating the crippling fifteen-month strike and boycott against Hong Kong, brought home to the westerners the need to make concessions before the rising tide of Chinese nationalism.

During Chiang Kai-shek's Northern Expedition the entry of Chinese armies into zones of foreign interest along the Yangtze was the cause of a succession of clashes. Foreign arrogance was sometimes matched by Chinese impetuosity, and brought a temporary return of gunboat diplomacy. However, the westerners were now keeping a 'lower profile', to avoid unnecessary provocation: missionaries were withdrawn from the interior and differences were settled in negotiations whose outcome favoured China. There were already signs of a community of interest between the nationalists under Chiang Kai-shek and foreign banking and business circles. Japan was an ominous exception to this trend. When Chiang Kai-shek resumed the Northern Expedition

---

* The Washington Conference was attended by Britain, the USA, France, Italy, Japan, China, Belgium, the Netherlands and Portugal. Japan agreed to give up wartime territorial gains but emerged in a dominant position as a naval power. The Nine-power Treaty did not provide for the invalidation of existing privileges, nor did it guarantee China's future independence.

in 1928, his troops were engaged north of the Yangtze as they made their way towards Tientsin by Japanese forces stationed in Shantung.

Once the Nanking government had been set up and the warlord in the north-east. Chang Hsüeh-liang, had integrated the provinces which had become Japan's sphere of interest into the new, fragile political union with Chiang Kai-shek, Japanese leaders, especially the militarists there, began to express concern. The new situation meant dealing with the Chinese foreign office in Nanking rather than with the local warlord. Their concern was heightened by the implications of more Chinese immigration into an area which, despite its status as part of China, was regarded as a solution to Japan's growing need for *lebensraum*. Together with China's attempts to isolate Japan's business interests there and the start of the world economic crisis, conditions became more and more conducive to Japanese militarism. One question remained unanswered. If Japan took steps to defend its interests, what would China's reaction be and would the other powers tolerate it? The answer came in 1929 with the Soviet Union's violent response to China's decision to take over railway rights exacted by the Czars in Manchuria. While denouncing imperialism, the Soviet Union found it necessary to 'defend' these rights by attacking Man chouli and Harbin. If Russia could get away with that, why should not Japan go one, two or perhaps several steps further?

Japan took the first step in 1931, when the Nanking government was enmeshed in civil strife caused by dissident nationalists, semi-independent warlords and communists, problems worsened by disastrous floods. In the evening of 18 September 1931 a bomb exploded, damaging the track of the Japanese-controlled South Manchuria Railway outside Mukden. A Japanese patrol guarding it claimed that after the explosion it was fired upon by Chinese troops and had to fire back in 'self-defence'. In the space of a few hours Mukden had fallen, and Japanese forces had begun a campaign that was to convert Japan's privileged position in Manchuria into outright occupation, coincidentally taking a path that would lead directly to the second world war. His government could not afford a foreign war, and being well aware that even if his forces made a stand in Manchuria the coast was fatally exposed to Japanese aggression anyway, Chiang Kai-shek chose to appeal to the League of Nations for help. He was not so naïve as to believe in the League's impartiality, but he considered that it offered at best a chance to cut his losses and at worst a chance to buy time.

Abroad, while there was sympathy for China, there was nevertheless doubt and indecision. In spite of having a national government, China seemed unable to govern herself and was threatened by bolshevism.

Japan might be a force for law and order. At the same time, the invasion of Manchuria was of more concern to the Soviet Union than the West. It could lead to an invasion of eastern Siberia and a conflict between Japan and the Soviet Union; and to investment opportunities the result of which could be the West's resumption of control over the balance of power in east Asia. Japan, predictably, turned a deaf ear to the League's and other nations' appeals for a halt to hostilities. In January 1932 a second front was opened in Shanghai and in March, before the arrival of an international commission of investigation, Japan created the puppet state of Manchukuo, whose chief executive was P'u Yi, the deposed Ch'ing emperor. In due course the League adopted the commission's report condemning Japan as the aggressor, but mere words in support of China were to no avail. Japan had already moved forces south into Jehol, and now responded by withdrawing from the League, and until the end of the second world war, developing China's north-east in the name of Manchukuo.

It soon emerged that Japan was not going to pause to digest Manchuria before embarking on further expansion. By May 1933, when the T'ang Ku truce was signed, Jehol had been incorporated into the puppet régime and the way was open for the political penetration and economic distruption of the five northern provinces of Hopei, Shansi, Suiyuan, Honan and Shantung. The aim was to prise this vast area away from the national government by fostering the idea that there existed a case for greater local autonomy. By now it was clear to the West, in particular Britain and the United States, that Japan's expansionism would not at present bring her into conflict with the Soviet Union, but that it would, if it continued unabated, threaten their own interests. The seeds of the anti-Japanese alliance between the United States, Britain and China from 1941–5 were now being sown. But before they could be harvested, patriotic indignation in China led to the conviction that the government had got its priorities wrong. Instead of squandering resources in an internecine war to exterminate the communists, now herded together in Shensi, the country should be united in a war of resistance against Japan.

Mounting popular pressure eventually crystallised into an incident that paved the way for a united front. In December 1936 the ineffectiveness of Chang Hsüeh-liang's troops against the communists in Shensi caused Chiang Kai-shek to fly to Sian to chivvy up both commanders and soldiers. In the event, he was faced with a mutiny by men whose main concern was for their homeland and who had been successfully won over by communist propaganda for a united front. Chiang was forcibly detained by Chang Hsüeh-liang, only being released after

Top: The emperor Pu Yi with Chiang Kai-shek in 1935.
Above: A pause for instruction at Yenan during the Long March.
Right: A suspected communist is searched by an armed picket in Shanghai in 1927. The finding of incriminating objects could result in death.

Above: The
terrible result of
Japanese outrages
in Nanking in 1936.
Right: Following
the Japanese
invasion, in 1937
the communists
entered into an
uneasy truce with
the Kuomintang to
repel the enemy.
Here, a section of
the communist
People's Liberation
Army is on duty at
the Great Wall.

Top: Villagers in the Honan region await government relief agents during the appalling famine of 1943.
Above left: The communists began their programme of reform in their 'base areas' in the north-west. Here peasants are celebrating the reduction of rents and interest rates in one of these areas.
Above right: An attack by the PLA on Chinchow, in the province of Liaoning, in 1946 during the civil war.
Left: The first PLA soldiers to arrive in Nanking are greeted with impassive stares.

Left, top to bottom: the extraordinary inflation of currency in 1948 resulted in queues such as this one in Shanghai, as people attempted to save their money.
Chairman Mao with Marshal Bulganin and Nikita Khrushchev during their visit to China in October 1954.
A mass meeting of Red Guards in 1967 during the Cultural Revolution.
Above: President Nixon, seen here at the Great Wall, visited China in February 1972, an indication of the greatly improved relations between China and the United States.

Facing page: Mao Tse-tung in the valley of the Yen Rian, Yenan, in 1946.

acing page: Top left: A shop on the Gao Kan
commune near Anshan. The
inscription is promoting the PLA as a
source of political guidance.
op right: Lunchtime at a kindergarten in Shanghai.
Bottom: Children hold the Red Flag
at a school in Canton.

Top: A worker's bedroom at Wuhsi.
Above left: Making embroidery in a
commune workshop, Kiangsu.
Above: Commune brigade leaders in
Kiangsu, 1973.

Top: Science students at the new
physics wing of Peking University.
The university has over 100,000
students.
Above: The Yangtze river bridge
in Wuhan. A road runs across the
top, a double-track railway
below
Left: Students help to build a road
with the members of a commune

the foundations of a united front had been laid. When Japan, as expected, escalated the 'limited war' in July and August 1937 into an unlimited war, another period of civil strife had ended and the second uneasy alliance between the nationalists and the communists had begun.

7 1937–49: China at war

To a major degree the anti-Japanese united front was an expression of popular sentiment for an end to internecine civil war and for a beginning to a patriotic war of resistance to expel Japan. Had he not been forced into it, Chiang Kai-shek would probably have pursued the policy of eradicating the communists before attempting to deal with the invaders. As late as 1941 he is reported to have said that the Japanese were 'a disease of the skin while the communists were a disease of the heart'. This echoed Prince Kung's 1861 evaluation of the twin menace from the foreign barbarians and the Taipings.* There were two reasons for his persistent reluctance to 'legalise' the communist movement by collaborating with it. Unlike the populace, he was aware that the communist shift in favour of a united front was in part a reflection of the basic shift that had taken place in Comintern strategy to cope with the upsurge in fascism and militarism: China's united front would slow up Japan's advance and take pressure off the Soviet Union. Important though that was as a ground for opposing a united front, it paled into insignificance when compared with the other ground for opposition, which was that the attacks on the depleted and hard-pressed communists would have to cease at the moment when victory seemed to be in sight.

In equating twentieth-century Japan with nineteenth-century European expansionism Chiang's thinking was obviously awry. But leaving considerations of patriotism aside for a moment, which is what the Chinese people refused to allow, the general strategy was sounder than it seems. Chiang knew that Japan and the West were on a collision course and that sooner or later there would be the world's most

---

* The rebels were a disease of the vitals, while the barbarians were an affliction of the limbs.

powerful country to fight the war for him. Meanwhile, why permit the communists to recover when his own government and party were to be pushed into what was for them a relative wilderness? It did not take long for the Japanese to prove that point. By 1938 his main forces had been swept out of the key political and economic areas of north, central and southern China to an area of relative security on the south-western periphery of the Japanese forces. The national government had, similarly, withdrawn beyond the Yangtze gorges to Chungking in Szechwan. In retreat his troops had fought at times heroically, and indifferently only when badly led. The Japanese troops were reported to have behaved with extreme callousness and brutality in the capture of Nanking on 12 December 1937, when approximately 100,000 civilians were massacred.

In succession, Japan established a puppet 'Provisional Government of China' at Peking in December 1937, and a puppet 'Reform Government' at Nanking in 1938. After the fall of Canton in the same year, Japan's plan was announced for a 'New Order in east Asia' that would supplant the existing treaty system and promote, or so it might be inferred, pan-Asianism and Sino–Japanese co-operation. It induced Wang Ching-wei, for long disgruntled as Chiang's number two, to defect to Nanking, where he became head of a 'Reorganised National Government'. In this period, Chiang's régime had been replaced in the cities and towns which formed its political and economic base by the Japanese occupation forces and their collaborators. They now had to regroup in much less familiar territory. Although much equipment had been salvaged and evacuated, manufacturing could only continue at a reduced level. In their new unfamiliar location, the nationalists were virtually cut off from the West, whence came much of their inspiration. They had a severely weakened manufacturing base and, since they relied heavily on customs duties, salt and commodity taxes, their sources of revenue were greatly diminished. As a party they were never close to the land and the peasants. The discrepancy between revenue and the cost of the war was to lead to deficit spending, the short-fall being met by note issue. This brought inflation and economic distress, ultimately laying the foundation for the great inflation that had such a damaging effect on the government after the war.

In contrast, the communists, now relieved of nationalist pressure, could build on their previous experience in the countryside. Where they were in total control in the north-west they could put their theories of moderate agrarian reform, now based largely on rent and interest reduction, into practice. They also trained large numbers of cadres and built up an infrastructure for mass organisations. Where possible, operations of the Red Army, reorganised first as the Eighth Route Army and later as the Eighteenth Route Army, and their New Fourth Army formed south of the Yangtze, were co-ordinated with those of the nationalist troops. In areas they only partly controlled – and these grew to include vast expanses of territory, the key points and communications of which would be controlled by Japanese forces – they conducted guerrilla warfare. The fact was that they were much better equipped, both politically and militarily, for operations requiring their men to exist among the peasants with what Mao Tse-tung has called a 'fish in water relationship'. In so doing they debilitated the enemy, tied down large numbers of his forces, and achieved much success in reorganising local government in the rural areas from which the existing leadership and administration had fled. What was to prove more important in the years to come was that by moving positively into the vacuum created by the withdrawal of the nationalists they succeeded in harnessing the persistent undercurrent of peasant unrest, which had manifested itself in the mid-nineteenth century rebellions and now in peasant nationalism, to their revolutionary cause.

While the communists flourished and took the offensive in the wartime environment, the nationalists fought a rearguard action both militarily and politically. In Yenan in 1942 the communists launched a movement to correct 'unorthodox tendencies' in the party. It succeeded in re-educating and disciplining new members, of which there were many, besides purging the party of the remaining influence of the 'orthodox', doctrinaire Soviet-trained leaders. The long-term impact of the 1942 'rectification movement' was the successful sinification of Marxism, the creative application of Marxism–Leninism to Chinese conditions and the evolution of the corpus of ideas that became identified with Maoism. By contrast, the nationalists had no such revitalising movement. Though they embarked on a number of developments after 1938, such as the training of a Youth Corps and the adoption of an 'Outline of Restoration and Reconstruction', they failed to invest the whole party with quite the same sense of conviction and single-mindedness.

In a situation where the nationalists had much to lose and the communists much to gain, Chiang manoeuvred assiduously to minimise their influence in the alliance. Mao had assessed that if China won the war the nationalists would be exhausted and China would be ripe for revolution; if China suffered a military defeat the country would be divided between the Japanese in Manchuria and north China, the nationalists in the south-west and the communists in the north-west; if China were completely subjugated then the nationalists would be completely subjugated too, leaving only the communists, who would survive by going underground. On the horns of a dilemma, Chiang attempted both to limit the activities of the communists and to preserve intact his own military superiority. This policy brought frequent clashes between the nationalist and communist forces, the most serious of which was the attack in January 1941 on the New Fourth Army by the government Fortieth Division. Politically, this almost wrecked the alliance.

This policy eventually also soured relations with the United States. Before the attack on Pearl Harbor in 1941 China had received massive support from the Soviet Union. With the entry of the United States into the war and German pressure on the Soviet Union, American aid built up to US\$500 million in credits between 1942–5 and a total of US\$1.54 billion in Lend Lease. Up to 1943 the Roosevelt administration had taken the nationalist government on its own evaluation, but from then on criticism by Chiang's American chief of staff, General Stilwell, of its refusal to engage the Japanese, besides creating acrimonious relations in Chungking, sowed doubts in the minds of the American leaders. Two issues were particularly influential in these beginnings of American disillusionment with Chiang. The first bone of contention was that by February 1944 Chiang had deployed 500,000 troops against the communists in north-west China at the expense of the effort against the Japanese. The second was that in April 1944 the Japanese, with sixteen divisions, launched – and by September had successfully completed – Operation Ichi-Go, in the face of the overwhelming numerical superiority of nationalist troops. Japan had swept through central and east China, overrunning allied airfields and valuable equipment that had had to be destroyed. Particularly galling had been Chungking's failure to reinforce General Hsueh Yueh in his forty-day stand at Hengyang in southern Hunan.

The differences between General Stilwell and Chiang brought General Hurley to China in 1944, first as President Roosevelt's representative and later as American ambassador. Stilwell was replaced by General Wedemeyer, who proved less abrasive, while Hurley endeavoured 'to unify all the military forces in China for the purpose of defeating Japan'. But it soon became clear that neither was Chiang Kai-shek receptive to the concept of coalition government on which Hurley, having consulted Mao Tse-tung, pinned his hopes, nor was the defeat of Japan to be achieved in the China war-zone. With an eye to the post-war period the United States strove to persuade Chiang to settle his differences with the communists and to broaden his government, but the more it did so the more Chiang resorted to buttressing

197

his own position. In the end those endeavours were overtaken by developments elsewhere.

The impending defeat of Germany focused allied attention on Japan, and at Yalta in February 1945 terms were agreed, in the absence of Chiang Kai-shek yet affecting China's sovereignty, for the entry of the Soviet Union into the Pacific war. Notwithstanding the diplomatic horse-trading that occurred at Yalta, China was expected and encouraged to negotiate a treaty with the Soviet Union on the basis of the Yalta Pact. Ironically, contrary to all estimates at the time of the Yalta meeting, Japan's surrender could in the event have been achieved without the Soviet Union's invasion of Manchuria: the atom bombs dropped on Hiroshima and Nagasaki on 6 and 9 August forced Japan's unconditional surrender on 14 August 1945. On the same day, China signed the treaty with the Soviet Union, which had advanced speedily into the north-east on 8 August.

With the end of the war in sight, both nationalists and communists began to make dispositions to receive the surrender of Japanese troops. Located in the 'liberated areas' in north, south and central China, the communists were better placed to capitalise on the situation and their forces went on the offensive. On 11 August Lin Piao's troops entered Manchuria, where they acquired quantities of Japanese weapons. With his forces at a geographical disadvantage, Chiang appealed on the one hand that the Japanese should not surrender to the communists or permit passage to troops other than his, and on the other hand approached the United States for air and sea transport to facilitate the strategic redeployment of his forces. The United States quickly complied, putting in 53,000 marines to secure key communications and other centres in north China.

With the war over, attention now turned to the peace. As the nationalists received the surrender of Japanese forces in China, the American ambassador, Patrick Hurley, prepared to bring Mao Tse-tung and Chiang Kai-shek to the conference table to avert another civil war.

Civil war and the collapse of the nationalists

Chiang Kai-shek approached the Chungking negotiations as a victorious national leader. The Japanese had been beaten and he had been vindicated. At the same time, he had achieved for China a distinguished status in world affairs. Under his leadership during 1943, China had persuaded the United States and Britain to renounce the unequal treaties, had become one of the 'Big Four' powers prosecuting the war, and at the Cairo Conference had secured the future restoration of all Chinese territories lost to Japan once that country's unconditional surrender had been forced. Even the outcome of the Yalta Pact, the Sino–Soviet treaty of 1945, was looked upon with some satisfaction. While it gave the Soviet Union temporary railway and harbour facilities, it secured recognition of China's sovereignty over Manchuria and Sinkiang and the right to hold a plebiscite in Mongolia to determine its future. With these achievements behind him and the conviction that he was negotiating from strength, Chiang was in no mood to compromise over such questions as troop reductions, constitutional government and areas of influence. Neither was Mao Tse-tung, and after weeks of fruitless discussion he returned to Yenan.

The United States made a second initiative in November 1945, when it replaced Ambassador Hurley with General Marshall, whose instructions pledged American support for the nationalists provided such support did not go towards the civil war. Marshall's mediation attempts appeared to bring success when, in early 1946, a ceasefire was arranged, a Political Consultative Conference convened to consider constitutional matters, and agreement reached on the formation of a national army. However, no sooner had he returned to the United States when, in April 1946, fighting resumed. After initial setbacks in Manchuria, where the nationalists faced communist troops who had taken up positions when the Soviet troops were withdrawn, Chiang won a series of victories from July to September 1946. His appetite whetted for outright conquest, Chiang now turned a deaf ear to Marshall's plea for a ceasefire and, after the communists had accused the United States of actually supporting the nationalists while pretending to mediate, Marshall returned to the United States a disillusioned man.

Encouraged by the military success, the high point of which was the capture of Yenan in March 1947, the nationalists went ahead with establishing constitutional government. The National Assembly was convened in December 1946, approved a constitution and proceeded with the election of a new National Assembly in November 1947 which, when convened in March and April 1948, elected Chiang as President of the Republic. This ended the period of political tutelage under the Nationalist Party and inaugurated the final stage of Sun Yat-sen's plan. Ironically, as the nationalists took these steps towards constitutional government, their military campaign began to falter. Towards the end of 1947 the communists had gone over to the offensive and achieved successes in north China. But the decisive battle was to be fought in Manchuria in 1948.

The Manchurian campaign was executed by Lin Piao's army against crack nationalist troops committed to an untenable position. A third of a million men were forced to surrender and the communists had, as it turned out, inflicted a blow in terms both of material and of morale from which the nationalist troops would never recover. The remainder of 1948 was taken up with the defeat and, as time wore on, the defection of substantial units of the nationalist army. The extent of this military *débâcle* is staggering: from September 1948 to January 1949 the nationalists lost one and a half million troops.

These losses brought demands for Chiang's resignation, which he tendered on 21 January 1949. His successor, Li Tsung-jen, attempted to stave off by negotiation the impending communist assault across the Yangtze into southern China. But Mao Tse-tung was in no mood for compromise. Nanking was taken in April and Shanghai in May, forcing the government to withdraw to Canton and from there to Chungking. Finally, the nationalist political and military establishment, together with over two million mainland refugees, withdrew to Taiwan, which had already been prepared as their final military bastion. Mao Tse-tung celebrated the nationalist demise on the mainland before their departure, when he proclaimed the establishment of the People's Republic of China on 1 October 1949.

In retrospect, the turnabout in nationalist fortunes is not difficult to explain. The Nationalist Party controlled the government and was held responsible by the people for the state of the country, regardless of the extent of their control. Its history since 1927 shows a tendency to neglect economic considerations and a belief that political and military power, in the final analysis, decide everything. That may be so, as indeed Mao's success proved, but it was clearly the case with the communists that they based their initial appeal on people's livelihood as well. Had the nationalists implemented the third of Sun Yat-sen's principles of the people, history might have been different. Instead, they exposed their supporters to ruinous inflation in which prices rose thirty per cent per month during 1945–8. While the whole of China suffered under this economic mismanagement, the worst impact was felt in the urban areas and particularly among China's emerging middle class, among whose numbers were many nationalist supporters. From the time the government lost their support its fate was sealed. With the country in disorder, many now transferred their support to the communists, whose wartime record had won much admiration. Theirs would be the patriotic task of building a new China.

8   The Chinese People's Republic

The legacy of two wars

When the Chinese communists came to power in 1949 they were faced with the problem of transforming 540 million people, over ninety per cent of whom were peasants, into citizens of a modern socialist state. In reality, as the history of the ensuing two decades shows, the primary problem could be broken into two separate interrelated secondary problems: how best to create a modern socialist state and, at the same time, how permanently to win over to socialism the minds of its citizens.

The scope of the task that lay in front of them in 1949 can be ascertained with a fair degree of accuracy by examining the political, social and economic legacies of nearly two decades of civil strife and war. First, from the aspect of politics, the communists had triumphed on a national scale in the train of, and to some extent as a result of, the successful waging of a patriotic war of resistance against Japanese imperialism. It is important to take into consideration, therefore, that many of their supporters were motivated by nationalism and patriotism rather than by principles learnt from reading Marx and Lenin. Party membership on VJ Day was 1.21 million and, while it was plainly only a fraction of the organised support the communists enjoyed, the latter in relation to the entire population was itself perhaps an even less significant fraction. Between the end of the Pacific War and their accession to power in 1949, party membership increased to 4.5 million and the ranks of supporters had been swelled by many who had become disaffected when the nationalist government failed to control the inflation that increasingly gripped China during this period. Even so, strictly speaking, the majority of the supporters were first and foremost opposed to continued nationalist misrule, rather than opting for a change that would usher in socialism.

While the motivation of the new government's supporters was a main political consideration for its leaders, they had also to cope with the practical questions posed by the sudden collapse of the nationalists. This had brought about an extension of the territory administered by the communists from the so-called 'old' liberated areas, consisting of about one-third of the area, predominantly rural regions, to the entire country, creating severe administrative and personnel problems. The 'new' liberated areas contained most of the population and the vast majority of the vital urban complexes which formed the mainstay of China's industrialisation. The communists had experience in governing rural areas where, as a result of the skilful execution of broad popular reforms, such as land redistribution, they enjoyed wide support. They now inherited an area, part of which had suffered disintegration and decline over a long period, the scope and nature of whose problems were unknown to them in contrast to their grasp of rural problems.

The social aspects of the new government's inheritance were no less daunting. In the rural areas yet to be reformed were landlords, remnants of the old gentry, who had exercised leadership in the villages by virtue of status, land ownership and access to power. In the urban areas, many of which were like great residential slums, the withdrawal of the nationalists had weakened the existing formal urban government based on bureaucratic administration and police control, compounding the chaos that reigned over food supplies and inflation. There was much hardship and the lack of formal administration had provided the opportunity for secret societies and other criminal elements to gain hegemony.

While economic aspects of the legacy presented immediate challenges in the form of the dislocation of communications, inflation, speculation, hoarding and corruption, it was clear that the inherited economy, even if it was made to function again, would not provide the base for the creation of a strong socialist state for the future. In fact the communists had inherited not a badly damaged integrated economy but three separate economies, each of which had suffered in the war period. These were a traditional, essentially rural economy comprising most of the country, the advanced industrialised economy in the north-eastern provinces (Manchuria) and the modern urban commercial economy in the Treaty Ports located on the maritime frontier.

The rural economy supported a high-density farm population by intensive land use. Traditional conservation and irrigation practices produced high yields per acre but low yields per worker. Farms were small and the peasants were kept at a bare margin of subsidence by a combination of landlordism, interest rates, taxes, natural disasters and

202

customary ceremonial obligations such as weddings and funerals. In these circumstances those who accumulated capital, notably landlords and usurers, tended to use it to buy more land or to channel it back as credit for financing peasant consumption rather than for financing increased production, thereby creating a circular flow pattern that inhibited the integration of the rural, industrial and commercial sectors of the economy.

The advanced industrial economy had been created in Manchuria by the Japanese between 1931 and 1943. There they had taken advantage of a sparsely populated region with rich forest, land and mineral resources to create a heavy industry base that accounted in 1943 for a third of China's railways and forty per cent of its coal, seventy per cent of its cement, eighty-five per cent of its pig iron and over ninety per cent of its steel production. The Treaty Ports had been the vehicles for and the product of the expansion of western trade on the China coast. Over the years these had developed into modern commercial and industrial complexes. The exemplar was Shanghai which had sophisticated shipping, banking, godown and public services, together with cotton textiles, flour milling, cigarette and match factories. All three economies inherited in 1949, owing to factors of separate development and the existence of different institutions, had still to be fully integrated before they could be transformed into the economic base of a modern socialist state.

The new democracy 1949–53

It was against this political, social and economic background that the new régime began to consolidate its newly-won power. As has already been shown, according to the Chinese communist scheme for periodising the modern history of China, 1949 marks the culmination of the 'New Democratic Revolution' that characterised the period of 'contemporary history' beginning with the 4 May movement in 1919. With their victory the Chinese communists had succeeded where the bourgeois revolutionaries had failed in ending China's semi-feudal, semi-colonial society. China was entering the period of 'current history' or the 'epoch of the People's Republic of China' when it would undergo the transition from semi-colonialism and semi-feudalism to socialism.

A blueprint for such a transition already existed in Mao Tse-tung's major theoretical work originally published in 1940, entitled *On New Democracy*. Together with *On Coalition Government* it had been advanced at the 7th National Congress of the Chinese Communist Party in

April 1945 as a plan for China's future after the defeat of Japan. (Chiang Kai-shek, it will be recalled, had already advanced his blueprint in 1943 in the euphoria following both the abrogation by the United Kingdom and the United States governments of the unequal treaties from which China had suffered for a century, and the Casablanca Conference at which both Roosevelt and Churchill resolved to seek nothing less than Japan's unconditional surrender.) But the situation in 1949 was very different from that in 1945: the defeat of Chiang Kai-shek meant that there was no longer the need to provide for a transitional period from nationalist 'tutelage' to Mao's New Democracy. Accordingly, the announced policy for the first few years amounted to a programme for implementing Mao's original idea of New Democracy.

In his article *On People's Democratic Dictatorship*, published on 1 July 1949, he advocated that China should be governed by a democratic coalition of four classes, namely the proletariat, the peasantry, the petty bourgeoisie and the national bourgeoisie, led by the Communist Party. This coalition would at the same time be a dictatorship directed against counter-revolutionaries, reactionary classes and enemies of the people. A significant aspect of the policy advocated by Mao Tse-tung was its political gradualism. These tactics differed from those propagated by Moscow: the Chinese, unlike the Russians, sought the co-operation of the national bourgeoisie and demonstrated this by even including them not only among the 'people' but also among the 'dictators'. For this reason the Chinese were regarded as 'rightists' by the Russians. But there was method in Mao's tactics. As we shall see, he wished to avoid unnecessary sacrifices as he worked to consolidate and centralise power. The united front envisaged in *On the People's Democratic Dictatorship*, far from perpetuating a diffusion of power, was a transitional measure that was aimed at a greater centralisation of control by the party.

Mao Tse-tung's blueprint for the new state system and political structure became a reality with the formal establishing of the régime by a mandate of the Chinese People's Political Consultative Conference (CPPCC). Preparations for this constituent assembly had been in hand since June 1949. It was in reality an assembly, convened under the aegis of the Communist Party, composed of its own delegates together with those of other minor parties that could co-exist with the CCP, such as the KMT Revolutionary Committee, the Democratic League, the Chih-kung tang and so on, mass organisations, occupational groups, national minorities, the armed forces, regional administrative units, overseas Chinese and specially invited individuals. Altogether 622 delegates were at its first session on 21 September 1949, of whom 510 represented 45 different parties, classes, professions and national minority groups. It adjourned on 30 September 1949, having adopted the Organic Law of the Central People's Government and a Common Programme, which together constituted a detailed statement of the government structure, the current philosophy, programme and aims of the régime.

The CPPCC remained China's supreme legislative body until the holding of national elections and the convening of a National People's Congress in 1954. In the interim, under the Organic Law the supreme organ of state was the Central People's Government Council, with executive, legislative and judicial powers, whose Chairman was Mao Tse-tung. When not in session, the powers of the Government Council were delegated to the State Administrative Council, whose premier was Chou En-lai. Subordinated to the State Administrative Council were four major committees, comprising political and legal affairs, finance and economics, culture and education and people's supervision, which in turn directed the thirty various ministries, commissions and boards. Completing the major organs of central government were the Revolutionary Military Council, the Supreme Court and Procuracy, each on a par with the State Administrative Council. The entire political structure of the nation was, until 1953, on a four-tier basis: central government, six great administrative areas (each enjoying jurisdiction over several provinces) provincial and county administrations. Paradoxically, in 1953 the concept of the great administrative area, originally conceived as an aid to consolidating the centre's hold on the provinces, was abolished on account of the risk of its encouraging centrifugal tendencies.

With Mao Tse-tung's views on the theory and practice of statecraft written into the Organic Law and Common Programme, the new united front or coalition government set about the tasks of economic, social and political reform that were a prerequisite to the consolidation of power. In his report on 6 June 1950 to the National Committee of the CPPCC, Mao Tse-tung defined the short-term economic objectives of the new régime. It was proposed to achieve in about three years a fundamental turn for the better in the war-damaged and shrunken economy. This aim comprised (1) extending and consolidating state control over the economy; (2) restoring fiscal and financial stability; (3) restoring productive capacity and output and (4) preparations for long-term planning.

The first requirement was to extend and consolidate state control over all sectors of the economy. The Common Programme provided the bourgeoisie with the prospect of maintaining, at least temporarily, a sector of privately owned industry. In the event, private enterprise was permitted to continue but production and commerce were brought progressively under state control by means of controlling credit and raw materials and by the state monopoly of key commodities. For the peasants there had been the prospect of maintaining for the time being private property in land. The government now turned its attention to establishing complete control of the surplus product of the land. Land reform, in which the communists had much experience and success prior to their victory, was begun in mid-1950 and completed in the main by early 1953. Under the provisions of the Land Reform Law of 1950 some 700 million *mou* (6 *mou* = 1 acre) were redistributed to 300 million peasants, benefiting labourers and poor peasants at the expense of the landlords and rich peasants. The so-called middle peasants (each category being carefully defined on the basis of its extent of ownership or lack of it, and of the means of production) were least affected.

I have already referred to the plight of the poorer classes of peasantry, and it would be remiss not to stress the results of the land reform for these immediate beneficiaries. It is also important not to lose sight of the implications of the successful implementation of land reform for the régime in its drive for a fundamental turn for the better in the economy. For the peasant it meant that with the new agricultural tax in kind representing between eighteen and twenty-seven per cent of his yield, depending on the locality, he retained a far greater share of the produce. For the government, it meant the certainty of control over the surplus product of the land and of the support of the majority of the peasantry and of the peasant associations which had played a large part in the movement. For both it was the death knell for the landlord-cum-tax-collector-cum-usurer class that not only had kept the bulk of the peasantry at bare subsistence level but which also hitherto had constituted a virtually insurmountable barrier to strong central government.

Before economic recovery could be ensured it was clear that the government had to find a comprehensive solution to the existing fiscal and financial instability. In early 1950 the policy incorporated measures for the curtailment of government expenditure, a reorganisation of the tax system that increased urban taxation, a greater degree of fiscal management in the hands of the central government by reducing local government functions and the operation of a tight deflationary credit policy by the People's Bank. At the same time more revenue was raised and liquid purchasing power was mopped up through extraordinary levies and campaigns associated with the Korean War. But despite all these efforts, focused on a drastic reduction in the amount of money in circulation, to achieve price and wage stabilisation, inflation was not finally defeated until the flight of money into goods was discouraged by guaranteeing purchasing power in certain transactions. The actual measure devised for this purpose was the expression of wages, bank deposits and some government payments and bond issues in terms of commodity units linked to fixed quantities of daily necessities. The effect was to protect the purchasing power of wages, savings, etc., as prices rose. The overall results of this comprehensive set of fiscal and financial measures was the conquering of inflation and an increase in savings and bank deposits by mid-1950.

The measures for dominating the economy and for achieving fiscal and financial stability prepared the way for a recovery in economic capacity and production. In 1949 industrial production indices reflected the continued shortage of plant in Manchuria,* depreciation and obsolescence as well as the removal of some facilities to Hong Kong and Taiwan, raw material shortages and the dislocation of internal trade and transport, not to mention the demoralising effect of all this on the work force. However, once communications were restored and expanded, and the economic measures outlined above had begun to bite, the national economy began to show signs of a remarkable recovery. To illustrate this, 1952 coal and iron production had nearly reached pre-1949 peaks, while steel exceeded that level by thirty per cent; at the same time China's railways had been fully restored and priority was being given to the laying of new track. In other words, in the space of three years the new Chinese government had restored agricultural and industrial production and had rehabilitated and expanded the transport network. The success of the entire economic effort so far was in no small way due to the public confidence enjoyed by the government. The national economic emergency had been successfully overcome and the task that now faced China's planners, preparations for the first five-year plan, necessitated a shift of emphasis to long-range planning.

The success of these short-term emergency economic measures between 1949 and 1953 can be attributed as much to the political and social reforms that accompanied them as to their own intrinsic content. Clearly, land reform was itself a multi-functional reform measure: besides land redistribution it began a long process of breaking down existing structures of social organisation and replacing them with new institutions centred around the Chinese Communist Party. This

---

* The Russians had dismantled much of the plant and removed it in 1945.

process was to be extended across the country as other reforms affected other sectors. Interestingly, as we shall see, these political and social reforms also included a distinctive feature of Chinese communism, which one may suggest is inherited from the Confucian tradition, that upheld self-cultivation and the idea of the moral improvability of human nature.

A major social reform carried out in this period was achieved under the Marriage Law of 1950. The direct result of the new law was to give full equality to women in marriage, divorce and ownership of property. At the same time, it heralded a pattern of family life that would conform to the emerging social structure in which modes of production in agriculture, industry and commerce would cut across traditional family barriers. Patriarchal and clan loyalties had survived the war; the new law, in conjunction with land reform and the education system, hastened the transference of the individual's allegiance within the new conjugal family unit to the state. Instead of a comprehensive list of obligations and services provided on a particularistic basis through kinship ties, adult members of conjugal families now became increasingly aware of the penetration of administration, government and party down to the grass roots of Chinese society.

The key link in the implementation of social and political reforms was the party. Its members increased from 4.5 million in 1949 to 6.6 million at the end of 1953. Accompanying the growth in party membership was a parallel upsurge in the membership of popular or mass organisations. Examples like the All-China Federation of Trade Unions (13 million members in 1956), the Young Communist League – the New Democratic Youth League up to 1954 – (25 million in 1959), the Young Pioneers (60 million members in 1960) and the All-China Federation of Democratic Women (80 million members in 1954) underline the extent to which the Chinese, once described by Sun Yat-sen as a pile of loose sand, were now organised. Led by party members from within and operating on the principle of democratic centralism from basic levels, these mass organisations cut across the territorial boundaries of formal government to mobilise the people on the basis of professional or social functions. They were not only essential in putting over the government policies, in indoctrinating and propagandising but also in keeping the leadership in close contact with the people through several channels. In this respect they were a vital link in the application of the 'mass line' which necessitated a constant flow of information from the people to the government and back to the people.

Examples of the ways in which the population could now be mobilised by the government can be seen in the campaigns organised in

1951 and 1952. The Korean War gave rise to the 'Resist America, aid Korea' and 'Suppress counter-revolutionaries' campaigns. The 'Three Anti' (San-fan) movement in 1951 against corruption, waste and bureaucratism was launched to bring the enlarged bureaucracy under stricter central control. The 'Five-Anti' (Wu-fan) movement in 1952 was against bribery, tax-evasion, theft of government property, use of bad material and insufficient labour in construction, and theft of government economic information. It subjected all urban trade and industry to close scrutiny and irreparably weakened the position of the bourgeoisie in the new society.

Like land reform, these campaigns had results beyond their immediate aims. They popularised the practice of large political gatherings, participation in 'struggle' sessions and self-criticism, and introduced on a nationwide basis the ideas of indoctrination and moral transformation. Each was closely co-ordinated and state control of the mass media was exploited to the full. In the land reform and 'resist America, aid Korea' campaigns, for instance, the All-China Association of Literary Workers, membership of which was a prerequisite for professional status, organised its members to go to the rural areas and factories to overcome the tendency to write of their individual reactions to situations and to gain experience in presenting the collective viewpoint. However, perhaps the most important point to make about the development and role of the mass organisations is that they established a pattern in these early years of the People's Republic for what has come to be recognised as a unique characteristic of Chinese government: the mass mobilisation of large sections of the population, either for purposes of rectification, as with the most recent massive Cultural Revolution in 1966, or for the purpose of production, as with the Great Leap Forward in 1958.

While these social and political reforms underline a uniquely Chinese approach to the situation inherited in 1949, the adopted economic strategy was to reflect more and more the influence of the Soviet Union. Three factors interacted to draw China and the Soviet Union closer together: the Chinese were motivated by considerations of geopolitics; the Russians wished in any event to pull China into their orbit; while the Americans, it seems, obstinately refused to face facts and recognise what by now was the government of the overwhelming majority of Chinese. In these circumstances it came as no surprise when, on 1 July 1949, Mao Tse-tung announced that China would 'lean to one side in world affairs', and his eight-week visit to Moscow from December 1949 culminated in the signing, on 14 February 1950 of the thirty-year Treaty of Friendship, Alliance and Mutual Assistance. The alliance brought some immediate economic and technical assistance for China's reconstruction, but arguably its major contribution lay in the protection it gave China during the essential period of consolidation.

It is not known to what degree the alliance was purely defensive, or indeed whether there was any consequential relationship between it and the outbreak of the Korean War in June 1950. On balance China was much less preoccupied with Korea than she was with Taiwan, whose conquest seemed imminent. It seems, therefore, that Stalin was guilty of either gross miscalculation or consummate Machiavellianism, the former being more likely than the latter. In the event, instead of turning a blind eye to the demise of South Korea, President Truman sent in troops and saw fit to guard the Formosan Straits to boot, pending arrangements for the formal involvement of the United Nations. The military outcome of the war was deadlock; its political outcome was to have far-reaching implications. Once China perceived a threat to the sensitive Manchurian industrial complex as UN forces pushed over into North Korea and on towards the Sino–Korean frontier, Chinese troops were committed and bore the brunt of the fighting between November 1950 and July 1951. This, and the American action over Taiwan, eliminated any possibility of Sino–American accord and laid the foundation for what, until the Nixon visit to China in 1972, have been two decades of mutually antagonistic relations. At the same time, China's war effort was predicated on immense Russian military aid to Chinese forces that fought a 'conventional' rather than a 'guerrilla' type war. By the time the Armistice was finally signed in 1953, China's entire military philosophy had probably moved much closer to the Soviet ideal than had hitherto been the case.

The transition to socialism 1953–7

The formal conclusion of the Korean War, an agreement with the Russians over the delivery of equipment and capital goods, and the rehabilitation of China's domestic economy created the preconditions for long-term planning for socialism. In late 1952 the government had announced that the first five-year plan would begin in 1953, but a detailed version of the plan was not released until 1955. When the plan was made public it revealed that the priority was to be given to heavy industry: 694 above-norm industrial construction projects were to be completed, at the core of which were 156 to be designed with Soviet aid. At the same time, semi-socialist agricultural producers' co-operatives and handicraft co-operatives were to be organised, and most of capitalist industry and commerce was to be incorporated into forms of state capitalism. The plan bore the hallmark of the Soviet strategy for economic development. Of the total capital outlay 58.2 per cent was voted for industrial construction, while only 7.6 per cent went to agriculture, forestry and water conservancy. What the terms of the plan revealed in 1955 was that China aimed at rapid industrialisation by domestic capital accumulation, and that domestic capital accumulation was to be achieved through the collectivisation of agriculture. What it did not reveal was the dilemma in which Chinese planners found themselves between 1953 and 1955.

At the outset China had been committed to a cautious policy of agricultural reform. The stress was on the development of permanent mutual aid teams* and towards the end of 1957, to a limited extent, semi-socialistic co-operatives.† It rapidly became apparent that agricultural institutions as presently organised were unable to produce the surpluses now needed to promote the required industrial progress. There was talk of the 'contradiction' between agricultural and industrial growth. Ironically, it was the re-emergence of a wealthy farmer class who put self-interest before national interest *after* land reform, plus the continued existence of inefficiently managed, fragmented land holdings, that together were responsible for this contradiction. Eventually, it was the belief that increased socialisation and increased agricultural production operated in direct ratio that ultimately brought about the decision to accelerate the whole process of the socialist transformation of agriculture.

This belief was voiced on 31 July 1955 by Mao Tse-tung in a speech to provincial party secretaries, when he overturned all previous decisions about co-operativisation and launched the country on the path to rapid collectivisation. The speech is significant for two reasons. Firstly, the subsequent achievements of the movement it launched even exceeded Mao's proposals. Whereas he envisaged complete co-operativisation by the end of 1957, in the event, by the spring of 1958 99.7 per cent of all peasant households had been collectivised.‡ Secondly, it marked a

---

* The mutual aid team envisaged simply the pooling of labour, implements and so on of up to eight households. The ownership of resources was mainly private, as was the distribution system.
† The semi-socialist agricultural producers' co-operative comprised a number of teams (up to forty households) pooling privately owned land, etc. for central management. The distribution system was based on the amount of work contributed.
‡ The Collective or Advanced Stage Agricultural Producers' Co-operative incorporated approximately 300 households and had a three-tiered management comprising the collective, the production brigade and the production team. In it all major factors of production were publicly owned (with the exception of a small private plot) and the distribution system, while resembling that in the co-operative according to which work contributed was the main criterion, differed in that rent for land was no longer payable.

watershed in the history of the Chinese People's Republic, since from then on China progressively abandoned the main features of the model based on the Soviet strategy of economic development and under Mao Tse-tung's leadership struck out on its own path towards socialism. For these reasons, the socialist transformation of agriculture dominates the history of this period. Yet it was the nationalisation of industry and commerce, not to mention the achievements of the plan, that made the greatest tangible contribution to China's modernisation and subsequent great power status.

In industry, nationalisation involved an expansion from a substantial existing state sector. By 1953 the state had comprehensive control, and the only gaps were as regards actual ownership and control over the distribution of profits. These 'gaps' involved about half of light industry and most of the retail trade and handicrafts. The problem was essentially how to convert control into ownership. The answer was found in a new mass organisation (for the bourgeoisie) called the All-China Federation of Industry and Commerce, formed in 1953 to encourage and persuade businessmen to join the state sector. This organisation, invoking the slogan that private enterprise should be 'used, restricted and transformed', was largely responsible for the transformation by the end of 1956 of the remaining private industrial concerns and the retail trade into joint state-private enterprises. At the same time, handicraftsmen were organised into co-operatives while small traders and peddlers were brought under the aegis of state shops. Under the arrangements for joint ownership the former managers normally became state employees and the former shareholders received an annual fixed share of the profits, which were now devoted on a much larger scale to reinvestment.

China had meanwhile also gone through a phase of political development. A sign that the party (whose membership grew from 6.6 to 12.7 million between 1953 and 1957) had achieved total control down to the lowest units of social organisation was the holding of elections in 1954 for the National People's Congress. This new supreme organ of state approved the Constitution at its first session in September that year. With a new state structure and socialist transformation proceeding apace the only important causes for concern remained the questionable loyalty of the intellectuals in the new socialist climate and the quality of the expanding cadre force. These two groups, though minute in relation to the total population, were essential to its socialist well-being. The former were predominantly western-trained and possessed invaluable expertise; the latter were young and inexperienced, yet held the key to the successful transition to socialism.

To cope with the intellectuals the party launched a drive to suppress 'rightist conservatism' in the spring of 1956 and, apparently satisfied with the spiritual transformation of this group, then invited their views* on the cadres and the bureaucracy. By the spring of 1957, by which time the world had witnessed the Hungarian uprising, the leadership was seriously disturbed, on the one hand at the political disaffection shown by the intellectuals and on the other at the shortcomings of the party's work style, manifest, in the collectivisation drive in particular, in the form of 'commandism' that led to friction between young, over-enthusiastic, and older, more experienced cadres. This was not a major crisis but it was an important problem. To resolve it, a big campaign† was launched to send intellectuals, cadres and urban employees to the countryside for periods of reform alongside the peasants, where they would also be able to contribute to agricultural production.

Over the same period China pursued an active foreign policy. The Korean war had, on balance, been counter-productive in purely objective terms, though arguably the performance of Chinese troops inspired a national pride that ought not to be entirely discounted, in view of China's reaction to the humiliations of the nineteenth century. A key-note for a new role, however, was struck when, having helped the Vietminh at Dien Bien Phu, China was invited to participate in the Geneva Conference of 1954. There, the negotiating skills of Chou En-lai were revealed to the world when a settlement to the Indo-China dispute was reached. In negotiations at about the same time with India and Burma he was instrumental in the formulation of the 'five principles of peaceful co-existence'.‡ This conciliatory period culminated in the Bandung Conference of 1955, attended by twenty-nine Afro–Asian States at which China, excluded from the UN, gave a clear signal about her views of her place in the world, particularly to the two super-powers, the United States and the Soviet Union. This conciliatory phase was matched by the United States taking steps to 'contain' China, beginning with the South-East Asia Treaty Organisation (SEATO) in 1954 and separate pacts with South Korea (1953) and Taiwan (1954). Eventually, China's concern over the refurbishing of the nationalists on Taiwan by the United States crystallised, in late 1957 during Mao's visit to Moscow, in the emergence of a new 'hard line' policy.§ What Mao was

---

* The campaign took its title from the classical slogan 'Let a hundred flowers bloom together, let the hundred schools of thought contend'.
† The *Hsia fang* or campaign for 'downward transfer'.
‡ (1) Mutual respect for sovereignty and territorial integrity; (2) mutual non-aggression; (3) non-interference in each other's internal affairs; (4) equality and mutual benefit; and (5) peaceful co-existence.
§ Called the east-wind line: after Sputnik, Mao stated that 'the east wind prevailed over the west wind', underlining the technological superiority then enjoyed by the Soviet Union.

213

really seeking was a willingness on the part of the Soviet Union to risk a new belligerency in East–West relations now that it had demonstrated with Sputnik its lead in rocketry, presumably to enable on the one hand the Taiwan question to be resolved and, on the other, a more forceful approach to be taken in the international arena.

From Great Leap Forward to Cultural Revolution

By the end of 1957 China's image reflected the stability of her domestic institutions, a modernising economy whose industrial growth was the most rapid in Asia and, in general, a pragmatic foreign policy. At first glance, one could conclude that much of this was due to the beneficial effects of the Sino–Soviet alliance and to the universal applicability of the Soviet model. But at the close of the period Mao's policies demonstrated more and more clearly China's search for a Chinese way to socialism. The main signs came in the crucial agricultural sector where, departing from Leninist practice, collectivisation had preceded mechanisation. That would have been an academic point had it not been accompanied by an overall shift away from technical and objective factors and in the direction of a distinct preference for relying more on human and subjective factors in such tasks as modernising the economy, changing the material basis of society and moulding men's minds. This tendency, as we have seen, has always played a significant part in the Chinese 'revolution' particularly when the communists were fighting for survival in Chingkangshan, re-establishing their influence in Yenan and fighting to seize power. But it had been partially eclipsed in the early period of the People's Republic when, despite the unique features of China's polity and the methods for social and psychological control, the Soviet model was in the ascendant. Now, China was asserting the validity of its own approach to socialism before a world audience and in so doing compounding the differences that existed with the Soviet Union. The issues that were to divide the two countries and ultimately the Chinese Communist Party were crystallising.

Against this background a new development strategy, entitled the Great Leap Forward, emerged. The economic rationale for this was that there existed a large pool of seasonally underemployed labour that could be put to work locally to boost production without any increase in consumption. An agro-industrial proletariat would come forward to work on labour-intensive projects including water control and conservation, coal extraction, power generation, back-yard iron and steel furnaces, fertiliser plants and so on. The extra cost would be minimal, since the underemployed were consumers whether or not they worked.

More important was that a small-scale labour-intensive industrial sector would permit the parallel operation of a large-scale capital-intensive industrial sector: hence the epithet 'walking on two legs'.

The essential corollary was that the rural sector would in future satisfy much of its consumption needs, thus overcoming one cause of stagnation, and continue to produce surpluses to finance the capital-intensive heavy producer goods sector whose own surpluses would be reinvested. To achieve all this China embarked on yet another institutional change in agriculture, the reorganisation of the 740,000 collectives into People's Communes. Unlike the collectives, which were agricultural units, the communes were multi-functional. They incorporated between 5000 and 8000 peasant households and had a tiered structure that included large brigades, brigades and teams. The scope of their activities covered local government (they were merged with the *hsiang*), agriculture, industry, education and defence. Finally, all the means of production were communised and while the bulk of the distribution was still according to work done, there was for the first time a 'communist' element of free food supply in the newly-created messhalls.

In the event, the Great Leap Forward failed to produce the expected results. For example, on the basis of claims that food grain and cotton production in 1958 had reached 375 and 3.35 million tons, up 102 per cent and 104 per cent respectively on 1957 figures, targets were set for 1959 of 525 and 5 million tons. This euphoria was halted in August 1959, when Chou En-lai reported that in fact the figures for 1958 had been 250 and 2.1 million tons. As for steel turned out by the back-yard blast furnaces, much could not meet industrial requirements. At the same time it became clear that the peasants were not happy with the greater centralisation of planning resources and distribution, the loss of the private plot and the public messhalls, all of which, conceivably, combined to reduce incentive. Much more damaging, however, were, as meteorologists can verify, the natural disasters that struck China in 1959 (the worst for a decade) and 1960 (the worst for a century). This concatenation of circumstances reduced China between 1959 and 1961 to a situation in which the struggle was no longer for record production but one in which the aim had to be to overcome food shortages.

These events had been accompanied by important political developments epitomised by the slogan 'politics takes command'. At the start, the economic rationale was associated with a political approach that stressed the need for the decentralisation of economic management (counterbalanced, it should be noted, by greater centralisation at the basic level with the formation of communes), and greater reliance on local cadres and the masses. This was not surprising, in view of the general amenability of the peasants during socialist transformation, as contrasted with the hostility and ideological unreliability of the intellectuals and professionals revealed by the 'one hundred flowers' campaign. This was a time when it was necessary to be both 'red and expert'; the failure by many experts to pass that test reinforced the idea of placing more stress on political reliability at the expense of technical competence. Undoubtedly these decisions all contributed to the failure of the Great Leap Forward to achieve the expected results. But even more damaging at this time was the decision by the Soviet Union in 1960 to withdraw her technicians and blueprints from China. This decision, while it obviously took into account the deterioration in relations over a fairly lengthy period, in which destalinisation, the refusal to supply China with atomic weapons and the Soviet Union's changing attitude to the western world, had become new sources of friction, undoubtedly reflected Khrushchev's contempt for, and displeasure at, the Great Leap Forward. Looking back, however, it was the effect of this period on China's internal politics that remains most significant. The evidence suggests that not a few leaders remonstrated with Mao Tse-tung on its content and method. Among them was Peng Teh-huai, the Defence Minister, who was replaced by Lin Piao. Arguments deployed suggested a preference for a developmental model not so far removed from that of the Soviet Union, and their fruitlessness must have exacerbated existing divisions within the party. It was only when real crisis struck with two years of natural calamities that the Great Leap Forward was finally abandoned.

As soon as the seriousness of the economic situation was realised, China began to retreat from the commune system as originally conceived. In practice, this involved a reversion to planning and distribution at levels closer to the production point by utilising the large brigade and brigade organisation, which corresponded in size to the former collective and co-operative, while retaining the concept of the commune. At the same time, peasant incentive was further restored by the reintroduction of the private plot and permission to trade in its produce at rural trade fairs. At first it looked like a retreat in order, once conditions had improved, to advance along the same lines. However, once the overall strategy had been elaborated by Chou En-lai at the National People's Congress in 1962, it was clear that the new policy was a permanent shift and was qualitatively different from its predecessor.

The new policy was focused on agricultural recovery and development, and it envisaged a much more balanced growth in agriculture and industry. 'Agriculture as the foundation and industry as the leading factor', an epithet not without its ambiguities, was one description;

216

another, the 'building of an independent comprehensive and modern economic system within not too long a historical period', was more explicit over the break with the Great Leap policy. In practice, relative to the previous pattern, agriculture and the consumer goods industries now enjoyed more investment at the expense of the producer goods industry. The approach to the latter was in any case much more selective and led to a growth in significant branches like fertilisers, man-made fibres, specialist mining and iron and steel production. At the same time more attention was paid to quality and efficient management.

The attitude of some Chinese leaders in this period was that economic recovery must take first priority. A comment on economic method attributed to Teng Hsiao-p'ing, then head of the secretariat of the Chinese Communist Party Central Committee and a member of the Politburo, was that 'so long as cats, black or white, catch mice they are good cats'. Teng, who lost his job a few years later in the Cultural Revolution, was obviously not alone in so thinking and, pending economic recovery, the economic argument was difficult to refute. By the time recovery was a reality the enforced period of liberalisation had made respectable once more the role of material incentives, expertise and professionalism in the national economy. These developments had been accompanied and to some extent furthered by the publication of articles in the Peking press that criticised Mao Tse-tung* and his policies by means of sarcasm, innuendo, and historical analogy or illusion. This suggests nothing less than a co-ordinated threat to his personal authority.

These developments cannot but have demoralised the party and exacerbated still further its divisions. Worse still, the Sino–Soviet dispute had become public in 1960 and in 1963 escalated beyond the stage of mutual recriminations over the revision of theory, dogmatism and the spiritual ossification of Marxism. Dialogue was replaced by statements of position directed more at supporters than at adversaries. For China, the Nuclear Test Ban Treaty of 1963 was both symbol and proof of Soviet–American collusion to achieve world hegemony. If it was proof of *their* collusion and common interest as two developed powers, it was equally proof of the common interests of all the underdeveloped world. China's message was clear: just as the major contradiction in world politics was no longer between imperialism and socialism but

* For example, Teng T'o, then secretary of the Peking Municipal Party Committee, published an article in the *Peking Evening News* of 15 June 1961 comparing the Great Leap to building a castle in the air. Another article, in the journal *Front Line*, to which he also contributed, examined the symptoms of amnesia and pointedly suggested that sufferers should rest, stop talking or doing things to avoid disaster.

between imperialism and the national liberation movements of the underdeveloped nations, so the epicentre of world revolution had shifted. This view was articulated as China sought to champion the cause of the Afro–Asian bloc to gain its members' commitment to anti-Americanism and anti-Sovietism in the period approaching the abortive second Bandung Conference in 1965. Its exemplar became the Vietnam war. Significantly, its non-violent aspect can be clearly identified in China's policy towards the third world since the Cultural Revolution. Indeed, China's membership of the United Nations was due to support from third-world countries.

At this time, it seemed that the Sino–Soviet dispute was the major preoccupation of China's leaders. Looking back, one could link this dispute and China's relations with the United States over Vietnam as major causal factors of the Cultural Revolution. But on balance, while they were obviously important considerations, they were symptoms rather than causes of issues arising within China. In fact, China's political life was more and more dominated by internal events up to the launching of the Cultural Revolution. For example, in 1962, once the economic recovery was well under way, Mao Tse-tung warned of the dangers of revolutionary degeneration. In 1963 he launched the Socialist Education Campaign, whose aim was to prevent the Soviet Union's present from becoming China's future. During the great polemics of 1963–4 Mao revealed his concern over the need for revolutionary successors. Finally, in 1964, on the eve of the Cultural Revolution, he launched the campaign to learn from the People's Liberation Army, which under Lin Piao's leadership had already undergone training to strengthen its ideological resolve and which was currently manning strategically-placed offices in branches of commerce and industry. In retrospect it is clear from the rapid succession of campaigns that Mao Tse-tung considered that there was an urgent need for moral regeneration following the period of economic recovery. When it did not come, it was inevitable that blame should be laid at the door of the Chinese Communist Party.

These internal events from 1962 onwards show clearly the inevitability of collision between opposing groups in China's leadership as long as each stuck to its course. Mao Tse-tung and his supporters were intent on creating an ideological and political climate that would permit a reversal of the across-the-board liberalisation of the early 1960s. The Socialist Education Campaign was conceived in the autumn of 1962 and launched in 1963. It sought to deal with the apathy, disillusionment, dissatisfaction and cynicism that had set in during the three bitter years from 1959 to 1961. 'Man was to be educated anew and the revolutionary ranks were to be reorganised.' At the Tenth Plenum of the Central Committee in September 1962, Mao warned (*inter alia*) of intellectual dissidence, the need to carry out class education for youth to cultivate loyal revolutionary successors and the need to re-establish socialist collective controls over the economy by putting an end to individual economy. The initial focus of the campaign was on the elimination of 'harmful bourgeois influence and unhealthy phenomena in literature and the arts', but in the year that followed the Plenum the campaign concentrated on stamping out the 'spontaneous tendency to capitalism' in the countryside. In effect, this incorporated a rectification of rural cadres who were held to be responsible by subjecting them to a 'five-antis' campaign.

The problem, presented by the need to produce reliable revolutionary successors, was tackled by launching a propaganda campaign designed to promote ideological and moral substitutes for material incentives in the motivation of youth. The central figure in this campaign was Lei Feng, a young soldier from a poor background who had died in 1962 at the age of twenty in the course of his duty. He was chosen for his devotion to duty and his diligent study of Mao's works, a young martyr – the first of a number at this time, all of whom kept diaries paraphrasing and amplifying Mao's thoughts – whose example was held up to young people for emulation. As the Socialist Education Campaign and the publicity associated with Lei Feng unfolded, a new campaign was inaugurated in the urban areas that directed social, political and economic organisations to study and emulate the People's Liberation Army. By this means it was hoped to improve the reliability and efficiency of party cadres in the urban areas. Later, a political commissar system, modelled on that of the PLA, was set up throughout the economy and government, and by 1965 this new political network had been staffed by most of the 200,000 ex-PLA officers and men at work in the trade and finance sector.

The expanding role played by the armed forces in these campaigns is a tribute to the skill with which Lin Piao had built up their morale and discipline since taking over from Peng Teh-huai in 1959. At that time the officer corps was divided over the question of whether China should have an '*armée de metier*' equipped with advanced (Soviet) weapons for conventional warfare or an army equipped for guerrilla campaigns. The soldiers' morale had been depressed by the adverse effects of economic difficulties on their families in the villages. The launching of campaigns to 'learn from Lei Feng' and to 'learn from the PLA' culminated Lin Piao's efforts to restore morale and claim the total allegiance of the armed forces for Mao Tse-tung. Moreover, the elevation of the PLA to the position of a model at once placed it in an unassailable position, as the Cultural Revolution was to prove, and constituted the clearest possible indication of Mao Tse-tung's misgivings about the party.

The evidence concerning the progress of these campaigns in the early 1960s suggests that, while Mao strove to create the preconditions for a move away from liberalism back to orthodoxy, a significant section of the party leadership, though it conceded the need to restrict capitalist tendencies, did not envisage a revival of earlier policies at a time when the downward spiral in the economy had only just been reversed. That Mao's policy could be retarded is consistent with the diminution in his personal authority that had taken place as a result of the 1959–61 *débâcle*, the blame for which his opponents sought to lay at his door. Up to 1958 he had continued to exert great personal influence, despite having to contend with a new collective leadership after a party reorganisation in 1956. But the retreat from the commune system in late 1958 had strengthened the hand of the collective leadership at his expense, particularly in the case of Liu Shao-Ch'i and Teng Hsiao-p'ing, who were both less idealistic and more pragmatic than Mao. In parallel to his diminished authority as Chairman of the Party's Central Committee *vis-à-vis* his four vice-chairmen and the party secretary-general, Mao relinquished the post of head of state (Chairman of the Chinese People's Republic), at the same time as the amendments to the policy on communes were adopted at the end of 1959. It was subsequently reported that he claimed he was eased out of that position and was extremely discontented at the decision.

The circumstances suggest that by 1964 Mao Tse-tung, supported by Lin Piao and the PLA, was already set on a collision course with a substantial section of the party leadership. In that year Mao intensified his efforts. Firstly, he sharpened the attack on the intellectuals, charging P'eng Chen with the task of purging the party of intellectual dissidents by sifting their recent literary and artistic work. Secondly, he set out criteria for the selection and training of 'successors to the revolution', which by virtue of the requirement that they should gain combat experience in class struggle and prevent bad elements from usurping party and government jobs, heralded the development of the Red Guard movement. Thirdly, the Socialist Education Campaign was metamorphosed into a new rural rectification campaign called the 'four clean-ups', to be administered by work teams against lax, apathetic and corrupt cadres in the villages. Finally, steps were taken to complete the new political network throughout the government and the economy staffed by former members of the armed forces. These

220

measures did not, however, achieve the results Mao was seeking, as suggested by the evidence of a conference convened in January 1965 to consider 'mistakes' (later identified as opposition to Mao thought), committed in the Socialist Education Movement.

The urgency of these moves must be related to the overall situation in China. At the end of 1964 the third National People's Congress was held in an atmosphere of optimism. Economic recovery was certain and attention was already turning to the third five-year plan, due to start in 1966; there was even speculation as to the possibility of another 'Leap'. At the same time, China conducted her first nuclear test. In the light of these developments it is not surprising that Mao, who held that the cultural establishment was fostering élitist trends, eroding the mass line and encouraging the growth of revisionism, should press for an extension of the current cultural rectification movement. So far, the established propaganda apparatus under Lu Ting-yi and Chou Yang had presided over efforts to replace the traditional drama with revolutionary dramas on contemporary themes, a move in which Chiang Ch'ing, Mao's wife, was playing an important part; while it had clearly adopted a stricter attitude towards culture, it had evidently baulked at the prospect of a cultural revolution. This idea was postulated by Mao Tse-tung at the September 1965 meeting of the Central Committee, only to be turned down on the grounds that it was too divisive. From then on Mao knew that he would have to conduct the purge he wanted through other channels and by other means.

The Cultural Revolution and beyond

Opposition to the idea of a major campaign that would destroy the equilibrium so recently achieved compelled Mao to launch it from Shanghai rather than Peking. On his instructions, the editor of the *Liberation Army Daily*, Yao Wen-yuan, published a critique of Wu Han's historical drama, *Hai Jui's Dismissal*, on 10 November 1965 in the Wen Hui Pao. The play, written in 1959, was about an upright official of the Ming dynasty who was wrongfully dismissed by his emperor. The article revealed that Mao and his supporters had interpreted the play, quite correctly, as being a comment on the current situation rather than history. It had been taken as championing the cause of Peng Teh-huai, the former Minister of Defence, who had been sacked for opposing the leadership over the Great Leap and the communes. The campaign in which the critique was the opening burst lasted for about six months, during which time a number of other literary figures were attacked. It was significant from the start that these events were qualitatively distinct from criticisms levelled in the past in that there was a preoccupation with the political content of the work under scrutiny, quite apart from the substantive moral issues involved.

At the same time, another thrust was directed at the educational system, long regarded as a breeding ground for dissidence. Particular attention was paid to the universities. In Peking work teams were sent in to 'administer' the campaign and it was later revealed that these were working on behalf of the opposition, notably Liu and Teng, siding with the majority against the revolutionary left, attempting to reduce the humiliation heaped on teachers and generally seeking to contain and divert the movement just as they had in the Socialist Education Campaign. This period saw the birth of the first Red Guard organisation in a middle school attached to Tsinghua University. These two thrusts, the literary attacks with serious political overtones and the attacks on the educational system, yielded major results between April and July. In that period. Mao won the struggle for Peking by ousting its Municipal Party Committee with the influential political figure P'eng Chen (ranked eighth in the national hierarchy and often referred to as a possible successor to Mao), and took a firm hold on the Party's cultural and propaganda apparatus. And he suspended entry to schools and universities pending reorganisation. The solidarity in the ranks of the opposition was now broken, and the way was open for a major onslaught on the Communist Party apparatus that had for years been frustrating his attempts to achieve an all-round moral regeneration.

Mao now returned to Peking and at an enlarged Plenum of the Central Committee, meeting from 1 to 12 August 1966, got a majority for the second phase of the campaign. The threefold objective was to be the overthrow of 'all in authority taking the capitalist road, the repudiation of bourgeois academic authorities and the ideology of the bourgeoisie and the transformation of all parts of the "super-structure" that did not correspond to the socialist economic base.' These tasks were to be carried out by revolutionary young people. The stage was now set for the mass meetings of the Red Guards from all over China that took place in the autumn, and the period of havoc in which any identifiable aspect of bourgeois life was attacked. While these events attracted most of the attention outside China, the real strategy for the campaign was being finalised. The main target was the party apparatus.

The visits to Peking by up to eleven million Red Guards at this time were an integral step in the formation of that extra-party force for the onslaught on the party. These young people learnt from what they saw of the attack in and around Peking and in due course applied their

222

knowledge in their home areas. The visits gave the leadership (and by now it was clear who was for Mao – Lin Piao, Chou En-lai, Chen Po-ta, Kang Sheng and Chiang Ch'ing) time to organise a hierarchy of control through the Cultural Revolution Group of the Central Committee at the top, down to an expanding network of cultural revolution groups at local level. They also presented the opportunity to convey decisions to the Red Guards directly, circumventing conventional channels that would have given dissidents prior knowledge of tactics. However, the more the attack was pressed home the more the party apparatus organised its defence by means of forming its own Red Guard groups, using workers, peasants and soldiers and sometimes attempting to 'outflank the revolutionaries to the left'. This set the scene for the pattern of large-scale violence that persisted in China during the combat period of the Cultural Revolution in 1967 and 1968.

The increasing role of the armed forces, which had already assumed responsibility for co-ordinating Red Guard activities at the beginning of 1967, together with the emergence of a new administrative institution, the *Revolutionary Committee*, wherever the local party apparatus had been overthrown, were the main developments in this period. Looking back, it seems likely that the propaganda through the media and the wall-poster campaign were intended to intimidate opponents in a general softening-up process, to be followed by a struggle for power destined to end with the overthrow of the old administrative and party institutions and the establishment of Revolutionary Committees. It took the best part of two years for the Maoists to achieve complete control, and for a long time a map of China representing provinces under their control looked like a patchwork quilt. At times it seemed that the country was on the brink of civil war, but events have shown that the army was always there to hold the ring and see the revolutionaries through to victory. But there were instances when local commanders were clearly perplexed and unhappy about the – at times ultra-leftist – course being taken, and the implications it had for the PLA itself. The composition of the new institutions of power, the revolutionary committees, is a clear indication of the degree to which PLA support was essential. These were a three-way alliance of party officials supporting Mao Tse-tung, representatives of the Red Guards, Revolutionary Rebels and other mass organisations, together with those of the local army garrison.

The combat period of the Cultural Revolution ended with the establishment of the last two provincial-level revolutionary committees, Sinkiang and Tibet, in September 1968 and soon after, in October, the severely purged Party Central Committee met and, together with other supporters, gave *ex post facto* approval to the events of the past two years, including the overthrow of Liu Shao-ch'i as head of state (which in fact, legally, required the approval of the National People's Congress). The emphasis was now on consolidation, re-establishing order, rebuilding the party and purifying the ranks through a nationwide movement for struggle, criticism and transformation. A major concern was what to do with the Red Guards, which was dealt with by launching a great movement to despatch young people to the remote, under-populated borderlands and the rural areas where they would 'put down roots'. Millions of China's youth were so despatched for varying periods. As for cadres who had committed mistakes, they were sent to rural cadre schools for reform through labour. This massive 'Hsia Fang' or downward transfer movement was soon extended to urban dwellers not engaged in manual labour, all of whom were required to spend a short period in the countryside. At the same time, order was restored to the education system by sending in 'Mao thought propaganda teams' whose work produced a consensus for new teaching programmes and management systems, the general purport of which was shorter courses that would be more politically and vocationally orientated, and closer links with factories and communes. Selection was to be based on political criteria. But it was evident that the major preoccupation was the need to rebuild the party, and it was announced that a Party Congress would be convened in the new year.

This, held in April 1969, ushered in a new phase in China's modern history, during which the effort has been focused on the task of rebuilding the party and restoring to it the authority vested in the armed forces during the combat period of the Cultural Revolution and, simultaneously, improving China's damaged diplomatic relations. The magnitude of the first task can be seen by looking at the details of the Congress. Lin Piao. Minister of Defence. was written in to the new Party Rules as Mao's successor, and the great influence of the armed forces on the revolutionary committees was now matched by similar power at the party centre, where about forty per cent of the leaders were serving military men.

The difficulties in foreign relations had arisen as a result of the maltreatment of foreign diplomats in China – as, for example, the burning of the British mission in 1967 – when the Foreign Ministry was briefly controlled by ultra-leftists who were subsequently purged for their actions, and the behaviour of Chinese diplomats abroad. But these difficulties, as events have proved, were insignificant in relation to the low ebb that had been reached in China's relations with the Soviet Union, the United States and to a lesser extent with Japan. The border clashes that occurred in early 1969 signalled a new threat to China, particularly when viewed in the light of the Soviet invasion of Czechoslovakia and the Brezhnev doctrine of 'limited sovereignty', and it would have been surprising had they not had a telling effect on China's future calculations. As for Sino–American relations, the war in Vietnam had been perceived not merely as an act of imperialist aggression but also as a threat to China itself. At the same time as China confronted the two super-powers, Japan was emerging as a major power with a challenge in Asia that, for China, had all the overtones of pre-war militarism and imperialism.

Rebuilding the Chinese Communist Party and reorganising and restaffing the government and party machines has taken much longer than anticipated. A major milestone was reached in September 1971, soon after the fiftieth anniversary of the party, when it was announced that the rebuilding of the party had been completed at provincial level. The task was now to consolidate control over the Communist Youth League and other mass organisations. An interesting reflection of the disunity and generational stratification to which the Red Guards had contributed, as well as the urgent need to rely on the experience of former cadres as the party took over from the army, could be seen in the new formula advocated for party rebuilding. In place of the three-way or triple alliance between the army, cadres and revolutionary masses, there appeared the 'three-in-one combination of old, middle-aged and young people at all levels of party leading groups'. According to reports this means 'the inclusion in these bodies of both proletarian revolutionaries of the older generation and fine party members who are middle-aged or are of the younger generation and the inclusion of new blood from workers, peasants and cadres at the grassroots level.'

At this stage it appeared that the convening of the National People's Congress and the adoption of a new Constitution were imminent. However, this progress was interrupted, and to some extent the achievements in reconstruction so far were placed in question, by the exposure of the Lin Piao plot against Mao in September 1971. Clearly no one issue precipitated this crisis. On the available evidence, it had been brewing for at least a year and must be viewed against a background of both internal and external developments. As far as the former are concerned, the pressure on the army to yield authority to the party at a time when senior cadres overthrown in the Cultural Revolution were being rehabilitated was a significant development. Since Lin Piao had a hand in the demise of not a few senior cadres it is unlikely that he would have felt sympathy for that policy even if, in the unlikely event, he was ready to acquiesce in the ideal of the party controlling the gun.

Lin Piao's plot must also be considered in the light of developments in China's foreign relations. From 1969 onwards diplomatic initiatives had been taken, first to restore all China's damaged links with the exception of that with the Soviet Union, whom China sought to isolate by driving a wedge between that country and its satellites. The main thrust, however, was towards third-world underdeveloped nations, for many of whom China not only had ideological or developmental appeal but also the means and the will to give aid, either through loans or through experts or, as in the case of Zambia and Tanzania in regard to the Tanzam railway, both. This 'third-world' policy was a practical application of Mao's contention that the major contradiction in the world was between the underdeveloped nations and imperialism, and its implementation earned for China the votes that secured the ousting of Taiwan from the United Nations and the restoration of the China seat to the People's Republic in October 1971.

While successfully applying this policy, however, China had to take heed of the situation in which hostility was a common characteristic in her relations with the Soviet Union, the United States and Japan. This led to the decision to seek a *rapprochement* with the United States. There is no evidence to suggest that the conciliatory third world policy produced disagreement among China's leaders. However, that cannot be said with certainty about the move to improve relations with the United States in preference to the Soviet Union. Judging by the official report on the Lin Piao plot, according to which he was killed in a plane crash while fleeing to the Soviet Union, he would have preferred, in the event of a choice being necessary, Sino–Soviet rather than Sino–American *rapprochement*.

The future will determine the wisdom of the choice that has been made. For the present, China under Mao Tse-tung's leadership has regained the strength, status and prestige lost in the nineteenth and early twentieth centuries. President Nixon's visit, closely followed by that of Japan's premier Tanaka in 1972, has led to the structuring of a new east Asian system of international relations in which China will be dominant for the first time since British gunfire knocked down the outward manifestations of the old 'tribute system' in the 1840s. Even more reminiscent of the past is the present preoccupation with the Inner Asian frontier which, with the international recognition for China's sovereignty over Taiwan and the settlement of the Vietnam war, can now receive undivided attention. Farther afield than east Asia, China has split the zones of influence of the two super-powers by fostering mutually beneficial relations with developed countries in Europe and

Latin America while forming and leading her own coalition of developing countries in the United Nations.

If the consequences of the decision to seek better relations with the United States dispel any lingering doubts about China's future place in the modern world, what course, meanwhile, will China's internal development take? Mao Tse-tung's Chinese 'way' to socialism has emphasised, in the years following the abandoning of the Soviet model, the need to give priority to the transformation of society and the psychological transformation or moral regeneration of its members rather than just adhering to strict economic and technical rationality, lest the latter promote new forces and class divisions that could subvert the revolution. Coming so soon after the Cultural Revolution, in which that formula was applied with great severity, it is not surprising that among the leaders there should be those who question a policy that has, as a main element, reaching a *modus vivendi* with a former enemy whose social system is the antithesis of China's. Not only could it be argued that this is to risk foregoing even the remote chance of reuniting the socialist countries but, more forcibly, that it is inevitably to risk exposing China to the two most potent capitalistic economies in the world, those of the United States and Japan.

These are the contrasting views, the contradictions inherent in the present policy. For Mao Tse-tung and Chou En-lai, whose brainchild it is and who will have weighed it carefully against the implications of another period of history in isolation, China has accumulated the strength from socialism and from her people the resolve to meet the challenge.

Part Five

China in the world today

It seems to be China's fate always to attract excessive praise or blame.
It has been so in the past, and in our own century as well. In the 1950s,
many people in the West saw her as the menacing giant about to awaken
and devour the world. At the other extreme, there are now people who
believe they have found ready-made answers to the problems of advanced industrial societies in what they choose to call Maoism, a system
of ideas developed to suit the needs of an underdeveloped, mainly
agrarian, revolutionary society.

Apologia and prettification do China no more good than detraction
or scare-mongering. What China badly needs is accurate description.
Happily, this is becoming more and more feasible, with the gradual
opening of the country to more independent observers from the outside
world.

China's leaders describe the present political situation there as a
dictatorship of the proletariat. The word dictatorship does not serve
China's image well in the West, where it arouses the ideas of police
state and arbitrary terror. What the phrase really means when applied
to China is strong, centralised guidance by leaders who regard themselves as representing the aspirations of the workers and peasants.
Many students of Chinese history point out that the better periods of
dynastic rule could have been described in the same terms. But this
comparison would be rejected by the present leaders, as disguising the
feudal and oppressive nature of the former imperial system.

China's leaders appear to have several clear priorities in their
strategy of government. They aim at defending the sovereignty and
territory of the People's Republic established in 1949; at preventing
revision or overthrow of what they regard as true Marxism; at moving
the economy steadily ahead through the development of agriculture,
industry and technology; at maintaining social discipline and public

morality; and at enhancing China's prestige and authority in the community of nations.

It is worth noting that nothing the Chinese leaders say or do at present indicates that they aim at spreading their own system of government or bringing other nations under their sway by force or guile. They support the struggle of colonial peoples for independence, where such a struggle exists; and they believe, as Marxists, that revolution will eventually come to the capitalist world. But subversion and infiltration of other established governments are not among their present methods.

The People's Republic is the organ of state set up by the Chinese Communist Party to guide China through socialism towards the more remote goal of communism – an economic condition in which there will theoretically be enough of everything for everyone, and organs of state will become unnecessary. That is the theory.

The People's Republic has largely inherited the territory ruled by the last imperial dynasty, with the exception of Outer Mongolia, which has been dominated by the Soviet Union since the early 1920s. China's leaders also accuse the Soviet Union of illegally occupying areas of Chinese territory over and above those ceded by the 'unequal treaties' of the nineteenth century. Areas of the Sino-Indian frontier still remain to be settled. The island of Taiwan is, in 1973, still under the rule of the Chinese Nationalists led by Chiang Kai-shek, but it is a cornerstone of Peking's policy that Taiwan remains a part of China and must be brought fully into the political structure of the People's Republic. Hong Kong, ruled by Britain, and Macao, ruled by Portugal, are also regarded by China as parts of her own territory, and there is little doubt that at some time in the future they will revert. But the Chinese leaders have said that they and they alone will choose the appropriate moment for this. In Tibet, China has established the authority of the People's Republic over the resistance of those who preferred the former rule by Buddhist lamas.

This large and variegated country – with a population estimated, in the absence of a recent census, at between 750 and 850 millions – obviously presents great problems of defence. Throughout the 1950s and most of the 1960s, Peking saw the chief threat to its territory and sovereignty as coming from the United States. Now the Soviet Union is considered to be the main threat. Peking's quarrel with Moscow is not just a war of words. Troops and supplies have been built up on both sides of the border as each has begun to worry about the possibility of an irrational or cynical attack by the other. The Chinese talk of a force of more than one million Soviet servicemen on their northern and north-western borders.

230

Anti-Chinese feeling runs deeper in the Soviet Union than anti-Russian feeling in China. A Moscow taxi-driver may launch into a torrent of abuse when asked what he thinks about the Chinese, whom he has been encouraged to fear and despise by his press. A Peking taxi-driver will say, as she has been taught to: 'The Soviet people are good. We are grateful for the aid they gave us in the past. Only their present leaders are bad.' The Chinese doctrinal position is that things went wrong in the Soviet Union after Stalin's death.

Despite all the danger signals, most people refuse to believe that China and the Soviet Union could ever fight a major war with each other, though both the potential parties have frequently given warning of such a possibility. China's nuclear strength is tiny compared to that of the Soviet Union, but it seems unthinkable that the latter could ever make a nuclear attack on a Chinese population centre without a first strike by the Chinese. And the Chinese proclaim that they will never be the first to use nuclear weapons. Russian nuclear attacks on China would destroy for ever Moscow's claim to be the champion of the rights of weak nations, especially since China has now lived down the irritation and incredulity which were aroused internationally by the Red Guards' treatment of foreigners during the Cultural Revolution. China has become a popular and respected nation, and with every passing month it seems less feasible that the USSR could attack her. The presence of an American mission in Peking, fulfilling all but the most formal functions of an embassy, makes the idea seem even more remote.

Yet the Chinese themselves have gone ahead with an active programme of building large underground shelters in cities and even in rural areas to protect themselves against nuclear attack. A more plausible threat seems to be that a conventional war might break out on the border, touched off by some territorial dispute, and prove impossible to bring under control. Such a war would have damaging effects on the strained economies of both sides, and its possible development and consequences would be impossible to predict.

China's bad relations with the USSR cannot be separated from Mao Tse-tung's struggle to impose what he has regarded as the correct political line in the country's internal affairs. The main individual target of Red Guard denunciations in the Cultural Revolution was the former head of state, Liu Shao-chi, who was accused of revisionism and attempting to restore capitalism.

What is revisionism? In economic terms, it means the application of more and more material incentives to the running of a socialist economy, to the point where it becomes indistinguishable from a capitalist economy. But there is more to this than meets the eye. In economic policy, both Yugoslavia and Hungary are more revisionist than the Soviet Union, but China is less hostile towards them. It seems that the term revisionism is used to cover the general decadence of a socialist state which has abandoned the original ideas of socialism, sought stability in dictatorial police control, and pursued expansionist or 'social imperialist' policies abroad.

If this is what Mao Tse-tung was seeking to avert through launching the Cultural Revolution in 1966, it is possible for people committed to western ideas of government to have more understanding of that event than seemed possible at the time. People in Britain are generally repelled by any form of political personality cult, but historical tradition in China has made such a cult less alien to popular ways of thought than it would have been in a western democracy.

The cult is now much less emphasised than it was a few years ago. If it was an implement in the pursuit of the goals of the Cultural Revolution, it is worth asking what those goals were and to what extent they were achieved. The Red Guards undoubtedly cut deeply into any tendencies towards bureaucracy and arrogance which were making themselves felt on the part of Communist Party cadres and other administrators. This helped in the formation of a type of administrator almost unknown in the communist countries of eastern Europe, where officialdom has become synonymous with bureaucracy. The ideal Chinese cadre lives plainly, takes part in manual labour, seeks no material advantage for himself or his family, and listens patiently to criticisms from below and above. According to one's view of human nature, one may or may not believe that any political system can create a large number of such people; but it is hard to quarrel with the ideal. On the other hand, the methods of 'class struggle', enforced self-criticism in public, devotion to a single line of thought and other aspects of the Chinese system are not acceptable to western ideas of individual rights. It is futile to pretend that Chinese society is not greatly different from western societies, or that they pursue the same ideals.

At present it seems that China has mainly benefited from the Cultural Revolution. Bureaucracy is minimal by the standards of communist countries, and local administrators seem prepared to take quite a lot of initiative in seeking answers to their economic and social problems. The idea of 'mobilising the masses' to cope with these problems is not an empty slogan. The Cultural Revolution was used to lay particular stress on this idea, but it has all along been an important method in the establishment of socialism. The elimination of such deeply-ingrained Chinese habits as gambling and polygamy, and the solving of river-control problems which had caused regular disasters for thousands of years, were not brought about without tremendous mass participation.

In viewing all communist countries, the western mind is troubled by the suppression of vocal opposition to the policies of the leadership. Certainly it is unheard-of for a foreigner in China today to meet anyone who openly opposes the leadership's policies. On the other hand, the official press constantly discusses the existence of opposition tendencies and the continuation of political struggle in Chinese society. This seems to refer more to a 'battle for hearts and minds' than to individual people who put themselves in a position of avowed opposition. There is a degree of abstraction in Chinese political writing which confuses people who are not accustomed to it.

The Cultural Revolution and its aftermath have also involved elements of personal power struggle among the leaders, and at lower levels as well. The plots which are said to have been fomented against Mao Tse-tung are ascribed by Chinese officials to the late Lin Piao, former Minister of Defence, who is said to have been killed in the crash of a British-made Trident aircraft in Outer Mongolia while, it is said, he was trying to escape to the Soviet Union after an attempted *coup*.

This event seems all but incomprehensible to people outside China. How, they ask, could Mao Tse-tung have put so much faith in Lin Piao, even proclaimed him officially as his successor, if Mao was considered so wise and if Lin's real intentions were so bad? The Chinese would probably reply that there is no foretelling the harm a person can do if his political thinking goes astray. In fact there is nothing more inherently astonishing about the fall of Lin Piao than about the disgrace of Liu Shao-chi. Both incidents serve to demonstrate the strong element of unpredictability in the politics of communist countries, which is a result of the relative lack of information about relationships among the leaders.

With Mao Tse-tung aged eighty and not in good health, the day-to-day administration of China's affairs of state is carried out by Premier Chou En-lai, a highly intelligent and fantastically hardworking veteran of the earliest days of the Chinese Communist Party and the Long March. Under the overall mantle of Mao's prestige and authority, Chou has seen to the restoration of order in the economy since the Cultural Revolution, the assumption by China of her place in the community of nations, and the progressive normalisation of relations with the United States. While exercising day-to-day authority in the most important matters, Chou continues to defer to Mao as the source of correct political guidance. With investigation still in progress concerning the persons responsible for the plots and excesses during and after the Cultural Revolution, it is not at all clear what order of succession there is for leadership posts in the future.

Whatever figures succeed Mao Tse-tung and Chou En-lai as the leaders of China, they are certain to seek to continue the progress achieved since 1949 in developing the economy. Mao Tse-tung's policy is that industry is the leading factor, agriculture is the base, and grain is the key. In other words, China must make herself self-sufficient in food supplies, expand industrial and export crops, and raise her industrial production to ever-higher levels of output and technology.

Rough estimates say that about four-fifths of China's population still lives in rural areas, though some proportion of it must be engaged in rural industries and not directly in agricultural production. The life of the rural population is organised by the People's Communes. When the communes were originally organised in the late 1950s, they were decried in the outside world as inhuman factory-farms which would destroy family life and turn the peasants into ant-like serfs. The communes have gone through numerous twists and turns in their development since 1958, but in their modern form they are a far cry from the predictions which were made about them by their detractors. Today's commune is normally an administrative unit covering several dozen farming villages, in which the families are largely those which lived there before 1949, and many traditional ways of life are still followed. The big differences between then and now are that the land has been distributed so that there are no private landlords any more; income in cash and kind is distributed to able-bodied commune members according to their labour; most children are receiving at least primary school education; health services have been introduced in areas where they were almost unknown before; and, most important of all, famine has been eliminated even in years of disastrous weather conditions.

Communes look after every aspect of non-industrial production: rice, wheat, maize, sorghum, millet, sweet potatoes, vegetables, fruit, cotton, silkworms, soya beans, tea, fish, meat, poultry – even pearl cultivation and hand-sewn embroidery are among their sources of income. Incomes vary quite widely from one part of the country to another, according to the richness of the land. Each commune is divided into several brigades, large administrative sub-units under which are the work-teams, generally corresponding to the old villages. Many decisions on investment, such as the purchase of a small tractor or a boat, are made at the level of the team through consultation among its members. A certain proportion of the team's production is paid to the state as tax; most of the rest is sold to the state in accordance with a plan decided in advance through consultation, and at a fixed price; the remainder can either be sold to the state at a higher price or kept in storage against bad crop years.

Each family has the use of a small amount of private land – the maximum is probably about one twenty-fifth of an acre – on which to grow vegetables or tobacco and raise pigs and poultry. Any production from the private plots not consumed by the peasants themselves may be sold off, but at relatively low prices.

The brigades and the commune itself operate the larger joint enterprises, for instance metal-working and mechanical workshops, sawmills or tea-processing plants. With the income derived, they can provide social facilities such as schools and clinics, or make fresh investments for the good of the commune as a whole, for instance in roads. Commune members are paid according to a system of work points for labour input, and these are calculated by an accountant, in consultation, it is said, with all the peasants of the team. Consultation is clearly an important aspect of the system, for without a great degree of unanimity among the peasants themselves, it would be impossible to satisfy individual people that they were receiving the correct number of work points.

With grain regarded as the key to agricultural production, an annual increase in the grain harvest (including sweet potatoes) is important if the country is to keep pace with population increase and to raise its living standards. Grain is still rationed throughout the country, though the ration is quite adequate and is flexible according to the amount of physical work a person has to do. Land cultivation in China is mostly intensive, concentrating on obtaining high yields of rice, wheat, etc., from small fields, through high inputs of manual labour and natural fertiliser. Most important of all is the question of water control. Much of China could double its grain yields if water were available in the right amounts at the right time. This is a problem which cannot be solved quickly, since the peasants on the spot have to be mobilised to take the decision to dig irrigation channels or wells, or finance the installation of pumps. However, the big water control schemes organised by the central government, for instance on the Yellow River, have been of great assistance, and over a period of decades the general problem of water supply is fairly certain to be solved.

The other priorities in agriculture are to obtain greater supplies of chemical fertiliser, both through imports and through the domestic industry, which is to a large extent decentralised into small plants supplying the needs of relatively small areas; and to finance higher levels of mechanisation through the gradual growth in farm output.

Small tractors, pumps and machinery for processing crops are the most important types of equipment required. The peasants also have to be educated further in the use of pesticides and high-yielding seed-strains. China's agricultural problems will not be solved for a long time, but she seems to be making steady progress, and this is the main thing.

Life on the communes is not an idyll. Cash incomes are low, and housing is primitive by the standards of north-west Europe or the United States. But rural China is no poorer than many parts of the Mediterranean area, and certainly much less poor than the below-subsistence economies of some other parts of Asia. There are many thousands of communes in the more fertile parts of China where life would appear to be a quite pleasant routine of diversified farming, handicrafts and small industries. The mass of China's peasants today enjoy a higher standard of living and greater personal freedom than at any time in recorded history. And according to what information one can gather, they have a considerable say in the decisions which are made concerning the development of their land and their communities.

As China progresses economically, more and more of her people will come to live in the cities – one of which, Shanghai, is believed to be the biggest in the world. In China, as in other countries, city life has its attractions and its drawbacks. Work in industry offers people the chance to learn a skilled trade and earn a higher salary, perhaps enter the administrative apparatus. Cash earnings are higher than on the communes, but this is partly balanced out by the fact that the peasants receive a large part of their income in kind. The shops in the cities are better stocked, and by comparison with the Soviet Union the Chinese consumer is well and rather cheaply supplied with most everyday necessities.

Exceptions are electrical household goods, which are in rather short supply, partly because of their relatively high production cost and partly because of the national power shortage. Clothing is also a lagging sector: cotton cloth is strictly rationed, and although nearly everyone is warmly dressed against the winter, clothes often seem worn and shabby. The most likely answer to this problem will be a large synthetic fibre industry.

The Chinese eat rather well, both in the cities and on the communes. Their daily diet is somewhat starchy, but not excessively so, and very many people seem able to eat the most luxurious dishes, such as Peking duck, at quite low prices, when they wish to celebrate a special occasion or simply blow a little cash. China is still the only country in the world which can rival France in variety and excellence of cuisine.

Housing needs much improvement. Since Chinese cities have traditionally been built of brick and stone, the fabric of the buildings has worn well, and the state has not been forced to mount massive rehousing programmes. The result is that China is lagging in new housing construction and installation of modern drainage in private homes. On the other hand, Chinese traditions of personal cleanliness and frugality in housekeeping mean that even the most ramshackle buildings are prevented from appearing as slums.

The state's limitations on individual freedom of movement and choice of work do not seem to arouse as much resentment in China, where they are linked to national economic priorities, as they would in a European country. The party and the state in practice have the power to direct people to places of work, but there is a limited freedom of choice within this framework, and importance is attached to consulting the opinion of a person's work-mates and neighbours in such questions. When the factories need more workers, communes are asked to decide which of their young people to send. And young graduates are frequently required to go and settle on the communes, so that the peasants may have the benefit of their skills. Not all young people have taken kindly to this system.

China's cultural life is gradually acquiring more of the diversification it enjoyed before the Cultural Revolution, when almost every performance or work of art was supposed to have a strong political content. Most classics of Chinese literature still cannot be bought in the bookshops, but officials insist that anyone who wants to study them can do so privately through libraries or other community institutions. Some classical Chinese is being taught in middle schools. More traditional arts and crafts are being produced without political themes. The leading cultural forms in China are the revolutionary opera and ballet, which incorporate many of the skills of traditional Chinese drama, but which are limited in their subject matter. However, variety acts and straight comedy have returned to the stage and television, though still with a strong political content.

Education was set back physically by the Cultural Revolution, since universities and colleges were closed for some four years and school teaching was disrupted by the activities of the Red Guards. Now order is being restored again, but the authorities insist that Chinese education is on a new pattern, giving more emphasis to politics, practice, productive labour and social work. However, the actual teaching in class seems quite conventional: China does not have the financial resources to mount sophisticated modern experiments with advanced teaching aids and methods. There are still some remote areas where it is questionable whether children even receive formal primary school education, though

237

the leadership's determination to progress further on this front is beyond doubt. Very few young people now enter university directly from school. Most are expected to work or to serve in the armed forces for at least a couple of years before being nominated for this privilege.

China is something of a technological paradox, since she has succeeded in making hydrogen bombs and launching an earth satellite, while most of the work on her farms is still done by hand and the general level of automation in industry is not high. Despite her emphasis on self-reliance, she is showing increasing interest in cutting corners by importing advanced technology from the West, and an important question for the 1970s is to what extent she will be able to expand her exports in order to pay for these increased imports. She continues to oppose the idea of accepting government-to-government aid or credits.

Traditional Chinese medicine has attracted great publicity in recent years, and although it is still somewhat controversial in the West, there is little doubt that herbal remedies and acupuncture have useful applications alongside western medicine. In the rural areas of China in particular they provide cheap substitutes for modern drugs, and for certain ailments they may be as effective, or even more so. However, there has been a tendency in the outside world to exaggerate the possibilities of acupuncture, and the Chinese themselves continue to practise and to carry out research in western medicine.

In the social sphere, the extent of crime in China is not clear to an outside observer. It is obvious that it has been phenomenally reduced since pre-1949 days. However, it would be naïve to imagine that it has ceased to exist. Since China's legal code was drawn up in the years before the Cultural Revolution, it presumably reflects what the leaders now consider to have been the revisionist tendencies which affected all social spheres in that period. So it is likely that at some stage new laws will be drawn up and published, reflecting the social order established by the Cultural Revolution. In the meantime, Chinese officials are reticent about this problem, emphasising that every attempt is made to cope with criminals by social pressure and persuasion rather than by punishment. Drug addiction, the scourge of the old China, really does seem to have been eliminated.

Religion plays no significant part in the life of the Chinese people on the mainland today, although Islam and Buddhism still have some hold among the minority races of western China. The Chinese themselves have traditionally been vague in their religious beliefs, straying between Buddhism, Taoism, ancestor worship, Christianity and a muddled set of superstitions and legends concerning the supernatural. Token sacrifices to the ancestors are believed still to be made by some of the older

238

peasants, and many people probably retain a vague belief in some form of personal survival after death. But the elimination of religion seems to have been accepted by the Chinese with much more ease than it has been in the socialist countries of eastern Europe, where it still has a strong hold.

China smiles at most of the rest of the world today in a manner which seems astonishing after the shrill self-righteousness which people considered typical of her during the Cultural Revolution. In particular she is anxious to improve her relations with the United States and western Europe. The possibilities include increased trade and cultural exchange, and political co-operation to contain what China regards as the threat of Soviet expansionism. At the same time, she retains her doctrinaire position that the United States is also a super-power and an oppressor of small nations. Her desire to retain friendship and influence with all the nations of the third world is not affected by her new attitude towards the West. But now the West is able to see it as a legitimate concern of China's, rather than as a series of subversive acts aimed at the isolation and defeat of western governments.

Peking is particularly favourable to the expansion of the European Economic Community, and its conversion into a tightly knit political and even strategic unit. In the meantime, she believes that American forces in western Europe are a safeguard against Soviet expansion. However, she continues to oppose the arms control measures being attempted by the United States and the Soviet Union, for she regards them as a means whereby the super-powers seek to retain a monopoly of nuclear weapons to lord it over others. Thus she continues with her own programme of nuclear tests.

The future of China's relations with the rest of the world depends on the future policies and personalities of her leaders. Since virtually nothing is known about the likely order of succession in the leadership, it is impossible to foresee Chinese international relations for more than a few years ahead. What is clear, however, is that the West now has an undreamed-of opportunity to establish close and harmonious relations with China in almost every sphere. The closer the relations that are established, the less likely it will be that any future Chinese leaders will turn their backs on them and revert to policies of hostility towards the West. The more both sides are committed, the more solid the relationship will be.

The West can learn from its own mistakes in the century and a half up to 1949, and from the subsequent mistakes made by the Soviet Union, that in dealing with the Chinese it is essential to show a proper respect for their culture and institutions. They are a proud though not an arrogant people, and when they are offended they may not show it until the wound is too deep to heal. Nor does it do any good to regard the Chinese as paragons, or to be sycophantic towards them. In general, they appreciate seriousness and good manners, though they are nowadays unceremonious. They neither understand nor appreciate flippancy in serious matters, although some of them, who have had longer experience of foreigners, are able to go along with such attitudes without taking offence. Humour does not easily cross cultural frontiers, and it should always be remembered that Chinese laughter frequently signifies embarrassment or sheer incomprehension. This does not mean that the Chinese are without a sense of humour – only that it is different from ours.

Chinese studies have been greatly neglected in the West, however brilliant and extensive the works of western scholars have been in the spheres of art, literature, history and archaeology. The Chinese language is still taught in only a tiny number of western schools, and in a minority of universities. Yet it is the language of about a quarter of the world's population. It is unquestionably a difficult language, yet it is by no means beyond the powers of a European person of average intelligence to learn it reasonably well with only a year or two's more study than it takes to learn a language more closely related to one's own. The Chinese themselves can help to encourage more teaching of their language in the West by sending teachers abroad to work, and letting more foreigners visit their country for longer periods.

Britain's past relations with China have played a vital role in the opening up of the country to contact with the West. This role is not one in which the British have always appeared in a flattering light. Drug addiction, military invasion and commercial exploitation are among the evils which China has suffered at the hands of past generations of Britons; from Britain she has gained much in terms of technology and industrial progress, as well as the know-how of commercial practice. Chinese political theory recognises that Marxism sprang in part from the early writings of the British economists of the late eighteenth and early nineteenth centuries. During the long years when the United States tried to isolate China, Britain gave diplomatic recognition to the People's Republic and managed to maintain a working relationship with regard to Hong Kong.

China pins much faith in the European Economic Community as a factor leading to the development of a more rational world. In ancient times, China and Rome were the two great centres of world civilisation. Since then, China and Europe have been eclipsed by the rise of American and Russian power. Both the Chinese and the Europeans have reason to be apprehensive of a world in which the United States and the Soviet Union divide countries up into spheres of influence and impose their own cultures on others, though the recent improvement of relations between the United States and China will have done much to assuage these fears.

The Chinese do not want to see themselves and the Europeans added to the list of super-powers. Rather they seek a world in which the concept of super-power will become meaningless and all nations can develop themselves peacefully. Even if one regards this concept as utopian, it is hard to quarrel with its principles.

Books for further reading

Balazs, E. *Chinese Civilization and Bureaucracy*, Yale University Press, New Haven and London, 1967

Barnett, A. Doak *Cadres, Bureaucracy and Political Power in Communist China*, Columbia University Press, New York, 1967

Birch, C. and Keene, D. (eds.) *Anthology of Chinese Literature*, Penguin, Harmondsworth, 1967

Buchanan, K. *The Transformation of the Chinese Earth*, G. Bell, London, 1970

Carrington Goodrich, L. *A Short History of the Chinese People*, Harper & Row, New York, 1959

Ch'en, J. *Mao and the Chinese Revolution*, Oxford University Press, London, 1968

Chubb, O. E. *20th Century China*, Columbia University Press, New York, 1965

Collis, M. *Foreign Mud (being an account of the Opium Imbroglio at Canton and the Anglo-Chinese War)*, Faber & Faber, London, 1964

Dawson, R. *Imperial China*, Hutchinson, London, 1972

Dawson, R. *The Legacy of China*, Clarendon Press, Oxford, 1964

Dawson, R. *The Chinese Chameleon: an analysis of European conceptions of Chinese civilisation*, Oxford University Press, London, 1967

Elvin, M. *The Pattern of the Chinese Past*, Eyre Methuen, London, 1973

Fairbank, J. K. (ed.) *The Chinese World Order: Traditional China's Foreign Relations*, Harvard University Press, Cambridge, Mass., 1970

Feuerwerker, A. *China's Early Industrialization*, Harvard University Press, Cambridge, Mass., 1958

Fitzgerald, C. P. *The Birth of Communist China*, Penguin, Harmondsworth, 1964

Fitzgerald, C. P. *China: A Short Cultural History*, Barrie & Jenkins, London, 1962

Fitzgerald, C. P. *The Southern Expansion of the Chinese People*, Barrie & Jenkins, London, 1972

Freedman, M. *Family and Kinship in Chinese Society*, Stanford University Press, Stanford, 1970

Gernet, J. *Ancient China, from the Beginnings to the Empire*, Faber & Faber, London, 1968

Jenner, W. J. F. and Yang, G. (eds.) *Modern Chinese Stories*, Oxford University Press, London, 1970

Kratochvil, P. *The Chinese Language Today*, Hutchinson, London, 1968

Kung-Ghuan Hsiao *Rural China: Imperial Control in the Nineteenth Century*, University of Washington Press, Seattle and London, 1967

Kwang-chih Chang *The Archaeology of Ancient China*, Yale University Press, London and New Haven, 1968

Lattimore, O. *Studies in Frontier History*, Mouton & Co, The Hague, 1962

Levenson, J. R. *Confucian China and its Modern Fate*, Routledge & Kegan Paul, London, 1958

Loewe, M. *Imperial China*, George Allen & Unwin, London, 1966

Loewe, M. *Everyday Life in Early Imperial China*, B. T. Batsford, London, 1968

Nivison, D. S. and Wright, A. F. (eds.) *Confucianism in Action*, Stanford University Press, Stanford, 1959

Purcell, V. *The Boxer Uprising: A Background Study*, Cambridge University Press, Cambridge, 1963

Reischauer, E. O. and Fairbank, J. K. *East Asia: the Great Tradition*, Houghton Mifflin Co., Boston, 1960

Schram, S. *Mao Tse-tung*, Penguin, Harmondsworth, 1972

Schurmann, F. *Ideology and Organization in Communist China*, University of California Press, Berkeley, Calif., 1969

Schurmann, F. and Schell, O. *Republican China*, Penguin, Harmondsworth, 1967

Shabad, T. *China's Changing Map: National and Regional Development, 1949–71*, Methuen & Co., London, 1972

Sickman, L. and Soper, A. *The Art and Architecture of China*, Penguin, Harmondsworth, 1971

Snow, E. *Red Star over China*, Penguin, Harmondsworth, 1972

Snow, E. *Red China Today*, Penguin, Harmondsworth, 1972

Ssu Teng and Fairbank, J. K. *China's Response to the West*, Atheneum, New York, 1970

Terrill, R. *800,000,000: The Real China*, Heinemann, London, 1972

Walker, K. R. *Planning in Chinese Agriculture: Socilization and the Private Sector, 1956–1962*, Frank Cass & Co, London, 1965

Wright, A. F. (ed.) *The Confucian Persuasion*, Stanford University Press, Stanford, 1960

Wright, M. C. *The Last Stand of Chinese Conservatism*, Stanford University Press, Stanford, 1957

Yang, C. K. *Chinese Communist Society: The Family and the Village*, The M.I.T. Press, Cambridge, Mass., 1966

Index

Lu Ting-yi, 221
Lung Men, 41–2

Macao, 230
Macartney, Lord, 141, 142, 144, 150
Manchu Ch'ing dynasty, 33, 136,
  137–46, 149
Manchukuo, 186, 192
Manchuria, 183, 191, 198
Mao Tse-tung, 64, 69, 74, 78, 89, 93, 95,
  100–1, 186, 188, 189, 196; favourite
  book, 61; *Little Red Book*, 89;
  formation of Communist Party,
  183; Long March, 189–90;
  Chungking negotiations, 198–9;
  proclamation of People's
  Republic, 200; transition to socialist
  state, 203; democratic coalition,
  204; economic objectives, 205;
  relations with Soviet Union, 209;
  visit to Moscow, 213;
  collectivisation, 211–12; Great
  Leap Forward, 216; criticism of,
  217; Cultural Revolution, 218,
  221–5, 226–7, 233; Socialist
  Education Campaign, 218–19;
  differences with Party leadership,
  220–1; Lin Piao plot, 225–6;
  personality cult, 232
Maoris, 103
Marco Polo, 129–30, 132
Maritime Customs Service, 161
Maritime expeditions, Ming, 133, 134,
  135
Marriage Law reform, 208
Marshall, General, 199
Medicine, 238
Mencius, 55
Meng Hao-jan, 53
Middle Ages, 40, 41
Minerals, 76–7
Ming dynasty, 132–7; porcelain, 45
Ming Huang: *see* Hsuan Tsung
Ming Precious Ships, 133
Mo Ti, 25
Mohammedanism, 30–1

Mohism, 25
Mongol conquest, 57
Mongol: *see* Yüan dynasty
Monkey, 60
Morality and ethics, 23, 24
'Most-favoured nation', 155
Munday, Peter, 65–6

Nanchao, 126, 129, 130
Nanking: Chiang Kai-shek
  government, 184–7
Nanking, Treaty of (1842), 155
Nanking arsenal, 163
Napier, Lord, 152
National People's Congress, 212, 216,
  221
National Revolutionary Army, 184
Nationalist Party, 179, 183; alliance
  with communists, 183; anti-
  communist policy, 184–5; Nanking
  government, 186–7; changes in
  policy, 187–8; campaigns against
  communists, 189; united front
  against Japan, 192, 194; decline,
  196; civil war, 199; withdrawal to
  Taiwan, 200
Natural disasters (1959–60), 215
Natural environment, 63–4
Nestorians, 31, 32, 122, 123
New Culture Movement, 181–2
New Democratic Revolution, 182
New Democratic Youth League,
  208
New Fourth Army, 196, 197
Nien Rebellion, 157
Nixon, President, 226
Northern Expedition, 184, 186, 190–1
Northern Sung, 128
Nuclear Test Ban Treaty (1963), 217
Nuclear weapons: first test, 221

Oil: offshore resources, 65; reserves,
  76; Teaching complex, 91–2
Old Democratic Revolution, 182
On Coalition Government, 203
On New Democracy, 203

250

United States – *continued*
  Revolution, 225; improvement in
  relations, 239

Versailles Treaty, 182
Vietnam, 126, 130, 131, 139, 167, 168;
  war, 218, 225

Waley, Arthur, 53, 60
'Walking on two legs', 86
Wan Li, 135, 141
Wang An-shih, 127–8
Wang Ching-wei, 195
Wang Mang, 115, 116
War lords, 184; demobilisation of
  armies, 186–7
Warring States, 110
Washington Conference (1921–2),
  190
Water resources, 68–71
Waterways, 90
Weather, 71–4
Wedemeyer, General, 197
Wei dynasty, 117, 119
Weihaiwei lease, 171
Western influences, 147–8
Whampoa Military Academy, 183,
  190

White Lotus Rebellion (1796–1804),
  149
Wu, Emperor, 114
Wu, Empress, 120–1, 122
Wu-fan movement, 209
Wu Han, 221
Wu San-kuei, 137
Wu Wei, 24
'Wu' wizards, 27
Wuhan: national government, 184–5

Yalta Conference, 198, 199
Yamen: *see* Tsungli-Yamen
Yang Kuei Fei, 53, 123
Yao Wen-yuan, 221
Yen Li-pen, 43
Yin and Yang doctrine, 22
Young Communist League, 208
Young Pioneers, 208
Youth League, 225
Yüan dynasty, 129–31
Yuan Shih-k'ai, 169, 170, 172, 174,
  175, 176, 177, 178–9, 180, 181
Yun Kang caves, 42
Yung Cheng, 139, 143
Yung Lo, 133, 134, 135

Zambia, 226

Other Fromm Paperbacks:

FLAUBERT & TURGENEV:
A Friendship in Letters
edited and translated by
Barbara Beaumont

SECRETS OF MARIE ANTOINETTE:
A Correspondence
edited by Olivier Bernier

KALLOCAIN: *A Novel*
by Karin Boye

TALLEYRAND: *A Biography*
by Duff Cooper

AMERICAN NOTES: *A Journey*
by Charles Dickens

BEFORE THE DELUGE: *A Portrait
of Berlin in the 1920's*
by Otto Friedrich

THE END OF THE WORLD:
A History
by Otto Friedrich

J. ROBERT OPPENHEIMER:
Shatterer of Worlds
by Peter Goodchild

THE ENTHUSIAST: *A Life
of Thornton Wilder*
by Gilbert A. Harrison

INDIAN SUMMER: *A Novel*
by William Dean Howells

A CRACK IN THE WALL:
Growing Up Under Hitler
by Horst Krüger

EDITH WHARTON: *A Biography*
by R. W. B. Lewis

THE CONQUEST OF MOROCCO
by Douglas Porch

THE CONQUEST OF THE SAHARA
by Douglas Porch

HENRY VIII: *The Politics of Tyranny*
by Jasper Ridley

INTIMATE STRANGERS:
The Culture of Celebrity
by Richard Schickel

BONE GAMES: *One Man's Search
for the Ultimate Athletic High*
by Rob Schultheis

KENNETH CLARK: *A Biography*
by Meryle Secrest

ALEXANDER OF RUSSIA:
Napoleon's Conqueror
by Henri Troyat